VOLUME 485                                      MAY 1986

# THE ANNALS

*of* The American Academy *of* Political
*and* Social Science

RICHARD D. LAMBERT, *Editor*
ALAN W. HESTON, *Associate Editor*

# FROM FOREIGN WORKERS TO SETTLERS? TRANSNATIONAL MIGRATION AND THE EMERGENCE OF NEW MINORITIES

*Special Editors of this Volume*

MARTIN O. HEISLER

*Department of Government and Politics*
*University of Maryland*
*College Park*

BARBARA SCHMITTER HEISLER

*Department of Sociology*
*Cleveland State University*
*Ohio*

Ⓢ SAGE PUBLICATIONS  Beverly Hills  Newbury Park  London  New Delhi

# THE ANNALS

© 1986 *by* The American Academy *of* Political *and* Social Science

ERICA GINSBURG, *Assistant Editor*

*Editorial Office:* 3937 Chestnut Street, Philadelphia, Pennsylvania 19104.

*For information about membership\* (individuals only) and subscriptions (institutions), address:*

SAGE PUBLICATIONS, INC.
275 South Beverly Drive
Beverly Hills, CA 90212 USA

*From India and South Asia,*
*write to:*
SAGE PUBLICATIONS INDIA Pvt. Ltd.
P.O. Box 4215
New Delhi 110 048
INDIA

*From the UK, Europe, the Middle*
*East and Africa, write to:*
SAGE PUBLICATIONS LTD
28 Banner Street
London EC1Y 8QE
ENGLAND

*SAGE Production Editor:* JACQUELINE SYROP
\* *Please note that members of The Academy receive THE ANNALS with their membership.*

Library of Congress Catalog Card Number 85-072101
International Standard Serial Number ISSN 0002-7162
International Standard Book Number ISBN 0-8039-2541-7 (Vol. 485, 1986 paper)
International Standard Book Number ISBN 0-8039-2540-9 (Vol. 485, 1986 cloth)
Manufactured in the United States of America. First printing, May 1986.

The articles appearing in THE ANNALS are indexed in *Book Review Index; Public Affairs Information Service Bulletin; Social Sciences Index; Monthly Periodical Index; Current Contents; Behavioral, Social Management Sciences;* and *Combined Retrospective Index Sets.* They are also abstracted and indexed in *ABC Pol Sci, Historical Abstracts, Human Resources Abstracts, Social Sciences Citation Index, United States Political Science Documents, Social Work Research & Abstracts, Peace Research Reviews, Sage Urban Studies Abstracts, International Political Science Abstracts, America: History and Life,* and/or *Family Resources Database.*

Information about membership rates, institutional subscriptions, and back issue prices may be found on the facing page.

**Advertising.** Current rates and specifications may be obtained by writing to THE ANNALS Advertising and Promotion Manager at the Beverly Hills office (address above).

**Claims.** Claims for undelivered copies must be made no later than three months following month of publication. The publisher will supply missing copies when losses have been sustained in transit and when the reserve stock will permit.

**Change of Address.** Six weeks' advance notice must be given when notifying of change of address to insure proper identification. Please specify name of journal. Send change of address to: THE ANNALS, c/o Sage Publications, Inc., 275 South Beverly Drive, Beverly Hills, CA 90212.

# The American Academy of Political and Social Science

3937 Chestnut Street                    Philadelphia, Pennsylvania 19104

---

**Origin and Purpose.** The Academy was organized December 14, 1889, to promote the progress of political and social science, especially through publications and meetings. The Academy does not take sides in controverted questions, but seeks to gather and present reliable information to assist the public in forming an intelligent and accurate judgment.

**Meetings.** The Academy holds an annual meeting in the spring extending over two days.

**Publications.** THE ANNALS is the bimonthly publication of The Academy. Each issue contains articles on some prominent social or political problem, written at the invitation of the editors. Also, monographs are published from time to time, numbers of which are distributed to pertinent professional organizations. These volumes constitute important reference works on the topics with which they deal, and they are extensively cited by authorities through-out the United States and abroad. The papers presented at the meetings of The Academy are included in THE ANNALS.

**Membership.** Each member of The Academy receives THE ANNALS and may attend the meetings of The Academy. Membership is open only to individuals. Annual dues: $26.00 for the regular paperbound edition (clothbound, $39.00). Add $9.00 per year for membership outside the U.S.A. Members may also purchase single issues of THE ANNALS for $6.95 each (clothbound, $10.00).

**Subscriptions.** THE ANNALS (ISSN 0002-7162) is published six times annually—in January, March, May, July, September, and November. Institutions may subscribe to THE ANNALS at the annual rate: $50.00 (clothbound, $66.00). Add $9.00 per year for subscriptions outside the U.S.A. Institutional rates for single issues: $10.00 each (clothbound, $15.00).

Second class postage paid at Philadelphia, Pennsylvania, and at additional mailing offices.

Single issues of THE ANNALS may be obtained by individuals who are not members of The Academy for $7.95 each (clothbound, $15.00). Single issues of THE ANNALS have proven to be excellent supplementary texts for classroom use. Direct inquiries regarding adoptions to THE ANNALS c/o Sage Publications (address below).

All correspondence concerning membership in The Academy, dues renewals, inquiries about membership status, and/or purchase of single issues of THE ANNALS should be sent to THE ANNALS c/o Sage Publications, Inc., 275 South Beverly Drive, Beverly Hills, CA 90212. *Please note that orders under $20 must be prepaid.* Sage affiliates in London and India will assist institutional subscribers abroad with regard to orders, claims, and inquiries for both subscriptions and single issues.

# THE ANNALS

## *of* The American Academy *of* Political *and* Social Science

**RICHARD D. LAMBERT,** *Editor*
**ALAN W. HESTON,** *Associate Editor*

_____ FORTHCOMING _____


### REGULATING CAMPAIGN FINANCE
Special Editors: Lloyd N. Cutler, Louis R. Cohen, and Roger M. Witten
Volume 486                                                July 1986


### IMMIGRATION AND AMERICAN PUBLIC POLICY
Special Editor: Rita J. Simon
Volume 487                                                September 1986


### REVITALIZING THE INDUSTRIAL CITY
Special Editors: Ralph R. Widner and Marvin E. Wolfgang
Volume 488                                                November 1986

_____

See page 3 for information on Academy membership and
purchase of single volumes of **The Annals.**

# CONTENTS

# BOOK DEPARTMENT CONTENTS

# PREFACE

There are a number of public policy issues that are so durable that *The Annals* returns to them again and again. During the nearly century-long publication of our journal, the volumes we publish on a particular subject have become a kind of mini-series. Taken collectively, they often provide an interesting longitudinal look at the nature of a persistent public policy problem, or at least our perceptions of it. This volume on the movement of guest workers into the developed economies takes its place within such a mini-series, one dealing repeatedly with one or another aspect of ethnic relationships around the world.

Most volumes in this series have been directed inward, probing the United States' problems in dealing with its own ethnic and racial diversity. In the early years of our journal, *The Annals* was concerned with the flow of immigration into the United States. For several decades after the 1920s, increasingly restrictive immigration laws and the Great Depression slowed down the immigrant flow, and ethnic relations in the United States received relatively little attention. In the decades after World War II, America's attention was absorbed by its intractable problems of race relations, and they seemed to march to a drummer all their own.

Our concern with ethnic relations in the United States has come alive again as a result of the recent surge of legal and illegal immigrants, and the reemerging salience of ethnicity as a matter of personal identity. As part of the expression of these concerns, in March 1981 we published the volume *America as a Multicultural Society,* and in the volume *Immigration and American Public Policy,* to be published in September 1986, we will deal more directly with immigration again.

The current volume of *The Annals* is part of an important substream in our continuing concerns with ethnic relations: problems of conflict and integration among ethnic communities around the world. The September 1977 volume, *Ethnic Conflict in the World Today,* provided a general analytic survey of different patterns of structures and problems of management of intra-country ethnic affairs. Our July 1980 volume, *Reflections on the Holocaust,* considered that ultimate pathology in ethnic relations. In May 1983 we examined refugee movements in *The Global Refugee Problem.* And in the current volume we turn to the transformation in ethnic relations that is accompanying the influx of largely unskilled workers from less developed countries into the highly industrialized societies of the world.

Since many of these volumes—all of the recent ones—have appeared during my tenure as editor of *The Annals* it might be useful for me to highlight some of the interesting contrasts and similarities between the American and the European situation as they have appeared in this literature. First of all, a quarter of a century of major transnational population movements—whether economically motivated as in the case of the European guest workers or the famine migrants of Africa, politically motivated in the case of the refugees, or both in the case of Hispanic migration to the United States—has given a new saliency to inter-ethnic relations in very many countries of the world. Even if international migration were to stop today, and even if the myth of return migration were to become a reality, the changes introduced in the receiving societies would be immense and durable. If they knew at the beginning of the process what they know now, I suspect that very few would have encouraged the massive importation of foreign workers.

A second impression derived from an examination of our mini-series is that the conceptualization of ethnic relations that guided most of our earlier discussion— that is, that improvement in ethnic relations is largely a matter of combating a majority's discrimination against a helpless minority—has had to be extensively modified as we come to grips with the obvious social costs of moving from an ethnically homogenous to a truly multicultural society. In the industrialized world, only the Japanese have seemed to escape this problem. Moreover, the number of sending countries in transnational migration has increased, and as immigrant minorities have come into competition with indigenous minorities, problems of embittered relationships between ethnic minorities—for example, between East and West Indians in Britain, between blacks and Hispanics in Miami or New York—have emerged. Minority-versus-minority conflicts have been added to the traditional majority-versus-minority conflicts, and they are likely to get more, not less, frequent.

Again, looking at our mini-series over the years, it would appear that a curious reversal is under way. Some of the structure of ethnic relationships and some of the persistent issues that plagued American society for many decades are now appearing in full form in Europe, and some that were uniquely characteristic of those societies are now appearing in the United States. For instance, in earlier years ethnic minorities in Europe tended to be concentrated in their own home territories and as a consequence ethnic conflict tended to take on the character of regional conflict. In the United States, on the other hand, while ethnic and racial minorities often resided in enclaved areas within the major cities, those cities themselves were dispersed, and ethnic groups had no geographically distinct homeland. This pattern of geographically dispersed ethnic minorities is changing with the concentration of the Hispanic migration in the southeast and the southwest United States, so that we have both territorially concentrated and dispersed ethnic minorities. In this respect, the European and American patterns seem to be coalescing.

In a similar fashion, the classic way that societies deal with people with a very different cultural tradition is to place them at the bottom of the social hierarchy. This is especially likely to happen if the function of the migration is to fill the occupations at the bottom of the ladder that are too onerous for indigenous workers to undertake gladly, as is the case with guest workers, immigrants, the slave trade, and the like. In both Europe and the United States, the open question is whether these groups will harden and become a permanent, ethnically distinct underclass that remains indigestible in and hostile to the society at large.

All of our recent volumes on ethnic relations, both those dealing with the United States and those dealing with Europe, focus a great deal of attention on the relationship of governments to their ethnic minorities. In particular, they are concerned with the representation of minorities in government—electoral strength, party participation, allocation of administrative posts, consociation-type power sharing; and with the use of the power of the state to control minorities—the embattled immigration service at our borders, governments trying to disentangle political refugees from economic migrants, police suppression of riots in the industrial slums of Britain. This volume, however, raises two other issues of government-ethnic relations that were not so fully addressed in earlier volumes. First, many of the articles discuss the strains on the welfare state introduced by the seemingly uncontrollable expansion of an ethnically distinct welfare class, strains that raise very general questions about the income-redistributive role of government and its ability to provide a safety net when one of the seams has split. Second, a number of articles comment on the continued strength of the contacts of individual migrants with their countries of origin and, even more surprisingly, the continued strength of the collective ties nurtured formally and informally by the governments of those countries. While the first of these issues is as pressing in the United States as it is in Europe, the second, as yet, has no exact parallel.

The Academy is quite pleased to add this volume to its mini-series and trusts that our readers will be as enlightened by it as we were.

RICHARD D. LAMBERT
*Editor*

ANNALS, *AAPSS,* **485,** May 1986

# Transnational Migration and the
# Modern Democratic State: Familiar Problems
# in New Form or a New Problem?

*By* BARBARA SCHMITTER HEISLER and MARTIN O. HEISLER

ABSTRACT: Migration to Western Europe in the past 20 to 25 years differs substantially in form and consequences from earlier large-scale population movements across national boundaries. The importation of temporary foreign workers on a modest scale—to meet labor shortages in arduous, low-status occupations—rapidly yielded massive political, economic, cultural, and international problems for the countries of in-migration. The temporary sojourn of mostly single males hired for specific jobs has been transmuted into the semi-settled presence of more than 15 million persons, most of whom are culturally very distinct from the host populations and are now dependents of the original migrants. Their protracted presence is explained in part by the economic and political attractiveness of the liberal welfare states, in part by the more limited opportunities in the countries of origin, and in part by the latter countries' policies. The host societies are strained by the new and substantial imported cultural diversity and the emergence of a socioeconomic and political underclass. The political ethos of the host countries and formal agreements with the sending countries preclude involuntary repatriation, and the myth of return associated with the semi-settled condition of the migrants militates against their assimilation. No ready solutions are apparent.

*Barbara Schmitter Heisler is assistant professor of sociology at Cleveland State University. She has published several articles on the subject of this issue of* The Annals *and, more recently, has worked on the policy and social-institutional responses to such manifestations of economic hard times as threats to home ownership.*

*Martin O. Heisler is a member of the government and politics faculty of the University of Maryland. His publications on social policy, ethnic relations, and international relations, reflect his principal interest in a comparative, theoretical approach to policy studies and transformations of the state.*

THE consolidation of the welfare state and the large-scale in-migration of culturally markedly different populations have been among the most important developments in Western industrialized democracies in the last 20 to 25 years.[1] And, arguably, the most important challenge confronting the less developed societies from which the migrants come is pursuing economic viability while striving to manage the dislocating and frequently destabilizing social and political dynamics of modernization. This issue of *The Annals* stems from the overarching hypothesis that these three sets of forces are fundamentally and comprehensively linked and from its corollary, that only a thorough grasp of the relationships between them will yield perspectives appropriate for understanding the nature and implications of the large-scale foreign presence in Western societies.

This is merely a working conclusion, an engine for intellectual speculation. It is as yet untested, and it is still difficult to articulate with specificity and precision. But, in the face of serious political, economic, and social problems for the countries of immigration and emigration and for the migrants themselves, the established theoretical approaches from economics, sociology, and political science seem too narrow and inappropriate for a thorough understanding of the multiple dynamics of the most important contemporary manifestations of migration. Thus, new departures seem warranted. They can be based on insights drawn from the multitude of empirical studies dealing with one or a few of the major cases in the settings of interest here, and those insights need to be viewed and organized through more eclectic, interdisciplinary perspectives than have generally been used.

FROM OLD OPTICS
TOWARD A NEW *PROBLÉMATIQUE*

We now know that those who set the processes of migration in motion—for the most part in the early and mid 1960s, with the decision to import foreign workers on a temporary basis—foresaw neither the eventual magnitude of such migration nor the ramifications of their policies. At the outset, such policies appeared to be modest in scope and, more important, controllable and reversible.

The optics of neither policymakers nor the scholarly specialities that have as their purview one or another aspect of the subject area—for instance, sociological studies of migration, labor market economics, or considerations of laws and regulations regarding immigration—permitted a glimpse of what lay beyond a relatively short period of 10 or 15 years. The long-term, progressively more structured and seemingly increasingly intractable consequences for the countries sending and receiving migrants, and the tens of millions of migrants themselves, crystallized with astonishing rapidity, on the time scale of major societal transformations.[2]

1. This volume focuses primarily on cross-national migration from less developed areas to the industrialized democracies of Western Europe. It touches, secondarily and in a fragmentary fashion, on the United States as well. Migration is, of course, an important phenomenon in many other parts of the world, most notably in South Asia, Southwest Asia, the Middle East, West Africa, southern Africa, and Central America. But several qualities of the receiving states in Western Europe make important policy-related, practical, and theoretical dimensions of the problem distinctive. Thus, the scope of this undertaking is restricted in order to increase its analytic and explanatory cogency.

2. There are approximately 15 million foreign workers, dependents, and other legally resident aliens in the Western European host societies at

Most of the unforeseen developments that are the elements of the multifaceted new *problématique* are treated in the articles that follow. Salient among these are:

— the continuation of immigration, even after the governments of the European countries of destination stopped admitting additional foreign workers in 1973-74;

— a shift in the composition of the immigration population from predominantly single or unaccompanied male workers to families—frequently extended families—among whom working-age men are now often a minority;

— the difficulty—for practical purposes, the near impossibility—of repatriating most of the migrants;

— the development of extensive international and transnational organizational networks that link migrants to their home countries, leading to a sustained myth of return and therefore to a sense of

---

present. In addition, 10 to 20 percent of that number are present as illegal or irregular-status immigrants. Because so many classes of temporary and permanent immigrants exist for the United States and because the number of aliens is in constant flux, due to periodic exit and return, change in status, and naturalization, no precise figures are available for the United States. At any given time, however, well over 10 million foreigners with resident alien or temporary work or student visas or with refugee status are present. Conservative estimates place the number of illegal immigrants in 1985 above 5 million, though the actual number is likely to be substantially higher. On this last point, see Milton D. Morris, *Immigration—the Beleaguered Bureaucracy* (Washington, DC: Brookings Institution, 1985), pp. 51-52. Thus, more than 30 million foreigners—legal immigrants, refugees, and illegal aliens—are present in the industrialized Western democracies that are treated as host societies in this volume.

temporariness and a concomitant resistance to integration into the host societies;

— a variety of direct and indirect effects on social, political, and economic manageability in both the host countries and the countries of origin; and

— complex, only partially understood psychological and social impacts on migrants and their children— the second generation, born or raised in alien, often inhospitable environments—who are truly at home neither in the receiving countries nor in the societies of their provenance.

THE OPTIC OF SOCIOLOGY

Two generations ago, Robert Park, an eminent sociologist of the Chicago school, averred that migration and its consequences constituted "one of the decisive forces in history." The sociological orientation toward migration, of which Park's work was an important exemplar, reflected the expectations not only of scholars but of policymakers and the publics of the receiving countries as well. It posited a multistage process of adaptation by immigrants to their new societies, ideally moving through ethnically differentiated groups, or enclaves, of immigrants toward acculturation and assimilation.

This perspective may have been appropriate for understanding many important manifestations of migration in the past, and it may still provide a useful perspective for examining most immigration in some host societies and some immigration in many such societies. But it is largely inappropriate for treating the recent waves of migration to the welfare states of northern and western Europe—and perhaps to the United States. Only some of the major differences between the empirical referents for the traditional sociological theories and the phenomena on which this volume focuses can be noted here, but even those demonstrate the need for developing new orientations to the subject.

First, policymakers and publics in the host societies and in most of the countries of emigration expected temporary—albeit, in some cases, long or open-ended—sojourns by migrants. With rare exceptions, the goal of ultimate assimilation was neither contemplated nor deemed desirable. Except in limited ways and degrees in Sweden until the late 1960s and in France until the early 1970s, the receiving countries did not envision accepting permanent settlers; in terms of their policies or intentions, they were not countries of immigration.

Second, the avowed policies of the sending countries have opposed the assimilation of migrants in the receiving states, and the extensive organizational links the sending countries established to their citizens were designed in large part to retain loyalties based on their citizens' national identification. These goals have been served well enough to impede assimilation in most cases. Again, the flow of foreign workers into the industrialized receiving countries of northern and western Europe was conditioned by an expectation that the workers would eventually return to their homelands.

A third differentiating factor that militates against the progress toward assimilation follows from a shift in the general geographic patterns in cross-national migrations. As the French geographer Alfred Sauvy has noted, earlier waves of migration were largely transatlantic, while those of the post-World War II period are essentially hemispheric.[3] There is a consequent facility of movement in this age of relatively easy and inexpensive travel, not only from the country of emigration to the land of destination, but back and forth, often leading to one or more trips each year. Travel and all modes of modern communication, coupled with the establishment of the networks of organizations linking migrants with governmental, political, and religious institutions in their home countries—discussed in depth by Barbara Heisler in her article—have reinforced the myth of return as well as resistance to assimilation for both migrants and their hosts.[4]

Finally, given their initial expectations and the myriad problems of accommodating large numbers of culturally very different immigrants in the malaise that has characterized most Western European economies since 1974-75, the populations of the host societies have been at least unreceptive and often markedly hostile to the extended alien presence. To be sure, there are notable excep-

3. Albert Sauvy, "Le reversement d'immigration séculaire," *Population*, 17(1):51-59 (1962).

4. Most of the large immigrant populations in Great Britain are exceptions in this regard, as well as in several other respects. Most have come from former colonies or Commonwealth states in the West Indies and South Asia and they show greater inclination to stay. The legal status of former British subjects differs in many important respects from that of migrants on the Continent and larger proportions apply for citizenship. See B. Guy Peters and Patricia Davis, "Migration to the United Kingdom and the Emergence of a New Politics," this issue of *The Annals* of the American Academy of Political and Social Science. Finally, although some ties to homelands exist and return visits are not uncommon, neither the comprehensive networks of institutionalized links nor the facility of travel are as great for these migrants as for most of their Continental counterparts.

tions to this generalization, but they are only that. In the constricted social, economic, and geographic spaces of European receiving states in the late twentieth century, such absence of receptivity is a greater impediment to integration and assimilation than was, for instance, anti-immigrant sentiment in a socially, economically, and geographically much more open America at the beginning of this century. Such hostility and the increasing tendency to politicize the protracted presence of immigrants are counterpoints in most of the articles in this volume. They are particularly vivid in the studies presented by James Hollifield and by B. Guy Peters and Patricia K. Davis of the experiences of Germany, France, and Britain, the societies with the largest numbers of immigrants.

Some sociological orientations to the problem area may be as relevant today as others were in Robert Park's day, as Robert Bach's article illustrates. Our point is that the great differences in the facts of migration for the host and sending countries and for the migrants lead to assumptions, models, and explanations that differ substantially from those of the traditional sociological approaches.

One source of such differences is the vastly increased importance of the state in the late twentieth century. We shall consider this element, which is crucial in practical and theoretical terms, after brief glances through the lenses of economics and political science. We shall suggest that the state serves as a useful prism for seeing the relationships of the three forces we noted in our opening paragraph. It is a perspective used explicitly in the articles by Gary Freeman and Martin Heisler.

THE OPTIC OF ECONOMICS

Whereas the traditional sociological perspective concentrates on the cultural and social characteristics of immigrants and receiving countries, most models from economics essentially disregard or play down such factors in transnational migration. Simply—but we hope not crudely—put, classical and neoclassical economic theories begin with differentials in wage rates between industrialized and less developed countries and suggest that rational, maximizing individuals will tend to gravitate toward the higher wages found in the former, migrating until the wage rates in the countries of origin and destination have been equalized.[5]

An important family of economic models departs from such conventional reasoning. It revolves around segmented or dual-labor-market theories. These focus on institutional barriers—principally socioeconomic rather than political—in the labor markets of the countries of immigration. They are depicted as structurally divided or segmented into primary and secondary markets, with markedly different working conditions and opportunities for security and advancement.

Primary labor markets offer such opportunities and tend, for social as well

5. Most economists probably recognize that, in their language, transnational migration is a lumpy good. To move great distances, with attendant transportation and relocation costs; to distance oneself from family, friends, and familiar cultural and often linguistic surroundings, or—perhaps more costly, especially in social and psychosocial terms—to move one's family; and to endure uncertainty· and possibly an unfriendly, even hostile, social environment entail considerations of vast costs and, necessarily, expectations of commensurate benefits. Such decisions are not easy and they are not likely to be made at the margin. Nonetheless, it follows from conventional economic reasoning that as travel becomes easier and cheaper, and especially if a sufficient number of co-nationals have preceded to the target society to provide a social and cultural landing platform, wage-maximizing migration will occur across great geographic and cultural distances.

as economic reasons, to be reserved for native workers, some settled immigrants, and refugees—these last because presumably their opportunities to return to the countries of their provenance are sharply limited. Secondary labor markets are peopled by indigenous housewives, students, and others whose attachment to their work roles may be seen as tenuous or at least not career directed. They tend to lack job security and attractive wage rates—they may hold minimum-wage jobs—and they have substantially lower rates of unionization. Migrants tend to be channeled into secondary labor markets because they presumably share some of the characteristics of housewives and students.

Michael Piore, whose work has been seminal in this as well as related theoretical approaches to migration from the discipline of economics, discusses and assesses the comparative utilities and limitations of the dual-labor-market orientation in his article. In an article focusing on the United States, Robert Bach, a sociologist, makes contact with these as well as other economic perspectives.

It should suffice to note that while the dual-labor-market approach is useful, in part because it integrates many important social and cultural elements in an elegant and parsimonious framework, it—like the conventional sociological perspective—tends to ignore the purposive actions of such major classes of political actors as the governments of sending and receiving countries, labor unions, and employers' organizations. Such actors also seek to maximize their collective advantages through migration-related policies. But their incentives, especially the states' incentives, are political as well as economic. Thus approaches that fail to integrate such actors and their concerns on their own terms are not likely to yield complete under-

standing. We need to turn to more explicitly political perspectives.

## THE PERSPECTIVE OF POLITICAL SCIENCE AND POLICY STUDIES

As Gary Freeman reminds us, all states make important distinctions between citizens and noncitizens. The responsibilities of governments for protecting and advancing the interests of the former constitute vital parts of the compact that defines the political society, and the latter are excluded as a matter of course from many of these tacit or explicit agreements. The collective interests of the society for which a particular government acts tend to be important points of reference for policies of immigration and emigration. Put somewhat more cynically, the political fortunes of policymakers are affected by how well they are perceived by their citizens to advance the citizens' interests through migration-related policies.

At the outset of the waves of migration that are of interest here, the receiving states' governments sought to enhance their economies' prospects for growth by importing foreign workers. They formulated and attempted to implement policies acceptable to employers and workers in their countries. Once the migrants were in place, these governments endeavored to manage their presence in ways that were responsive to their voters' expectations. Likewise, the governments of most of the sending countries have followed policies that can be characterized as blends of *raison d'état* and political expediency.

The initial policies of the receiving countries and the bilateral treaties between them and the countries of emigration led to narrow and relatively simple labor-related agreements. The decisions to recruit foreign labor followed from employers' perceptions of insufficiency in the numbers of native workers available for particular jobs, mostly in manufacturing, construction, agriculture, and mining. As we have already noted, in the early post-World War II period the receiving countries proceeded on the assumption that such workers were temporary and could be repatriated if job-market requirements or general economic conditions changed.

Available evidence suggests that, for the most part, the governments of the countries from which foreign workers came shared such assumptions. As Rosemarie Rogers and Mark Miller point out, few if any provisions were made in these early labor agreements for the long-term stay of migrants or for their political and social status in the host societies. Nor, for that matter, did the host governments prepare their publics or undertake efforts to legitimize policies for the extended presence of large numbers of foreigners—since such developments were not envisioned.[6] It is in large part from these roots that the host societies' present problems arise. Rogers, Freeman, and Martin Heisler in particular address these consequences in their articles.

When the intellectual requirements and potentials of conventional political science and policy studies are considered, the limitations of these disciplines for problems of the sort we are considering quickly become apparent. In summary terms, such problems blur distinctions generally deemed crucial for both political and legal manageability, lead to conflicting interaction effects among policies; and, especially in the receiving states, they bring into focus serious value conflicts that mar the political order. They also present the student of politics and policy with a multitude of complex international and transnational dimensions—factors outside the purview of national governments. In addition, to confound comparative policy analysis even more, there are great variations and flux in the formal or legal circumstances of migrants in and from different countries.[7]

Many of these problems arise from or are greatly exacerbated by one of the central elements of the new *problématique* with which we are concerned: the open-ended, semi-settled position of large majorities of the migrant populations in most of the host societies.

6. Only France contemplated courting permanent settlers, for demographic reasons explicated by Mark Miller, "Policy Ad-hocracy: The Paucity of Coordinated Perspectives and Policies," this issue of *The Annals*. But the country sought such immigrants from what were perceived to be culturally compatible populations—essentially those from Italy, Spain, and Portugal. Immigration policies did not include recruitment of future citizens from North Africa or other non-European, non-Catholic regions.

7. Thus, for instance, since membership in the European Community provides a different status for workers in particular and nationals in general than that accorded citizens of nonmember states, the accession of several major sending states carries—and, for states that are now prospective members, will carry in the near future—profound implications. Spain and Portugal will accede to membership in 1986 and Turkey, another important sending state, may accede shortly. Some receiving states, such as Sweden and Switzerland, are not members of the European Community. Several countries—most importantly, Algeria, Morocco, and Yugoslavia—from which large numbers of migrants come are neither members nor prospective members. These elements of complexity are addressed in Rosemarie Rogers, "The Transnational Nexus of Migration," this issue of *The Annals*. Finally, the special historical relationships between Great Britain and the countries from which most of its immigrants come entail different legal provisions for migration and a variety of different statuses for immigrants. See Peters and Davis, "Migration to the United Kingdom."

Indeed, if the circumstances of the migrants' residence were more certain, even the most difficult problems would be intellectually manageable through conventional approaches and much less intractable in practical, policy terms.

The inadequacy of our intellectual and policy tools for dealing with these circumstances becomes even more evident as we contemplate the relationships between the three elements of the new *problématique*. We conclude this introduction with a brief adumbration of those elements and some of the salient links between them.

### MIGRATION IN THE NEXUS OF WELFARE STATES AND SENDING COUNTRIES

The roles played by the state through public policies are crucial in modern democratic welfare states. Freeman's analysis of the dynamic relationships between migration and the political economy of the welfare state draws attention vividly to (1) the structural characteristics of such states that create the need for importing foreign workers from less developed societies; (2) the social services, public and private support agencies, and comparatively greater opportunities that hold migrants in receiving states even in the face of adverse economic conditions, high unemployment, cultural stress, and social discrimination; and (3) the high political and social costs, as well as the more obvious public financial costs, to the host countries that accompany the protracted stay of migrants.

An egalitarian ethos and governmental sensitivity to—and political accountability for—social and economic problems characterize mature welfare states.[8]

Once such development is consolidated over time, its values permeate and define the legitimacy of political practices in democratic regimes. Such values and practices circumscribe the freedom of legitimate action of policymakers, and altering or violating their essential provisions for political exigencies or ad hoc reasons becomes difficult or impossible.

The quasi-permanent presence of large numbers of foreigners poses serious problems for governments and citizens. The norms that define the democratic welfare state would be violated by the gross exclusion of migrants from the political, economic, and social benefits and privileges of such a society. But their inclusion would redefine the division of burdens and rights of those who struggled—together with, as well as against, their fellow citizens—to construct the collective bargains represented by the welfare state. If legitimate changes are to be made in those bargains, they must come through the societally sanctioned means. The inclusion of large numbers of culturally essentially alien migrants, particularly in view of the prevalence of the myth of return among them as well as among the host population, is seen by many as a significant alteration of the bargains and compromises entailed by the welfare state.

Yet, excluding large groups of residents—even sojourners and perhaps even illegal immigrants—is inconsistent with the ethos and political and social values that distinguish democratic welfare states from other types of regimes. This exclusion is the source of much of the tension for the indigenous popula-

8. Most students of the welfare state deem the United States to be less than a mature one, and one in which the programs and policies and the egalitarian ethos associated with European manifestations are both less extensive and less thoroughly consolidated. This is an important reason for treating the European and American settings of migration separately for some purposes.

tions and their governments. The populations of all of the receiving countries attach great importance to participatory democracy, but only in three countries do migrants have qualified voting rights, and then only on the local level. They are eligible to benefit from many of the social and financial programs associated with welfare states; as Freeman points out, however, they are coming to resemble a welfare class of the sort that welfare recipients are often deemed to constitute in the United States, a less than mature welfare state. Among citizens, distributive and redistributive policies do not distinguish, much less stigmatize, beneficiaries, since most people are perceived to benefit from, as well as pay for, some programs. It is thus considered to be wrong—a violation of welfare state norms—by large segments of the populations of host societies to deny social and economic rights to migrants. Extending such rights to them, however, is deemed wrong by many segments on a variety of grounds, including cost, nonparticipation in the basic political processes and responsibilities—for instance, military service—that constitute the citizens' side of the exchange of obligations with the state, or simply alienness and the absence of demonstrated loyalty.

Parenthetically, even if migrants could readily become citizens—a difficult proposition in most receiving states—many or most would choose not to do so. The myth of return is strong; most of the sending countries would be loath to have migrants give up their citizenship.

The modern state defines status and interposes itself between economic, cultural, and other types of private actors, almost as a matter of course. As William Safran's analysis of Islamic migration to Western Europe shows, the ethos of such modern states provides a plenitude of structure, quite formal at times, for social relationships, while in other settings only informal and far-from-extensive social structures might have existed. An important part of that ethos is a pervasive pluralism that now legitimates group-based claims and governmental responses to them; most immigrants in most of the host societies—not only those Safran treats directly—are able to avail themselves of such governmental intermediation. The tensions noted earlier are thus both fueled and harnessed.

*A note on
sending countries*

Safran touches on—and Rosemarie Rogers, Barbara Heisler, and Sabri Sayari develop more extensively in their contributions—the myriad roles of the sending countries in influencing not only host-country policies but the migrant experience in general. Such policies constitute purposive intervention. They serve many important functions for the sending countries. These include the ostensive purposes of protecting the interests of their citizens abroad and stimulating the inflow of cash remittances from foreign workers into their economies. They also extend to such other, often unacknowledged goals as deflecting young people from national labor markets and political arenas often overloaded by movement into the more modern sectors of the economy, society, and polity and discouraging them from leaving remote towns and villages for cities in numbers too great to be absorbed smoothly. Ignoring such goals poses threats to domestic stability.

These considerations are concomitants of rising expectations and modernization in societies struggling to cope with the challenges of development. The emigration and prolonged stay abroad of those with sufficient resources and initiative to migrate in the first place often serve as safety valves for the regimes of sending countries unable to absorb and accommodate the expectations of such people for jobs, improved living and social conditions, and perhaps political change.[9]

As Rogers notes, these and other elements of the sending countries' policy perspectives help to shape the relationships between migrants and host societies in ways and to degrees not found in earlier instances of large-scale migration. They call for different analytic sensibilities from those carried by more traditional approaches to migration.

## A SUMMARY AND A PREVIEW

All of these considerations and much of the rest of this *Annals* volume point up one of the most important differences between, on the one hand, the current foreign populations in Western Europe and, perhaps less clearly, those in the United States, and on the other hand, earlier waves of cross-national migration. With regard to the former, the crucial question is whether the migrants are settlers or sojourners. Most of those who entered the receiving countries as foreign workers have clearly stayed longer and have established themselves on more lasting terms than their hosts initially anticipated. But pressures from their home countries and the populations and governments of their hosts, as well as perhaps their own inclinations,

militate against settling for most migrants. The proportion of migrants moving toward citizenship in their host societies is very small, with the exception of those in Great Britain; for the reasons adumbrated previously and developed by Rosemarie Rogers, this is not likely to change appreciably in the foreseeable future.

The new realities, various aspects and ramifications of which are explored in the articles by Gary Freeman, Martin Heisler, and several others, suggest a development unprecedented on a large scale. Host and sending countries and migrants themselves need to accommodate to the protracted presence, not readily controllable by governments but not necessarily leading to settlement, much less to assimilation along the lines of historical assumptions.

The articles that compose this volume explore transnational migration to democratic welfare states on three levels. The articles by Michael Piore and Rosemarie Rogers provide overviews of the development of the theoretical and analytic perspectives preeminent in the study of the subject and of the evolving empirical and policy universes, respectively.

The largest group of articles consists of presentations and analyses of most of the salient thematic dimensions of the problem area. An illustrative study, by Mark Miller, traces the present policy difficulties of some of the most important receiving states to the ad hoc, uncoordinated policy approaches used since the earliest stages of the post-World War II migration wave and to the faulty assumptions on which early policies were based. While Rogers's account of more systematic and comprehensive policy approaches in recent years suggests some learning on the part of govern-

9. While in some of the literature on labor migration the job-market-related or economic safety-valve aspect is noted, here we wish to call attention to the similar social and political functions that migration may serve for the sending countries.

ments, Miller's characterization of "policy ad-hocracy" for the issue area as a whole remains essentially appropriate. Gary Freeman considers the tensions between the relatively recently closed systems that characterize European welfare states and the permeability of their geographic and systemic boundaries—a permeability exposed by the migration phenomenon. His article captures the essence of the problem from the host societies' perspective.

William Safran's article treats one important facet of that perspective: the position of Muslim immigrants in fundamentally Christian and secular societies and the responses of those societies and their governments to the Islamic presence. He ventures appropriate policy responses to a particular form of the challenge facing the receiving countries.

Sabri Sayari's article provides our only look in depth at the policy perspectives of a major sending country, Turkey. While no one country can be considered typical of the countries of emigration, the insights found in his article are invaluable for appreciating the vantage points of sending states and the policy challenges they face in the migration nexus.

Barbara Heisler focuses on one of the most critical but least explored structural manifestions of that nexus: the organizations that link migrants to their homelands. In retrospect, it was to be expected that the extended presence of large numbers of migrants in Western Europe would generate institutionalized ties between them and the sending countries, for a variety of reasons and in many forms. Most such organizations are premised on eventual return and therefore reinforce the myth of return. But the fact that such links are organized, sometimes quite elaborately, is also an indication that the migrants' sojourns are seen as extended.

Three articles focus on particular receiving states. James Hollifield provides a comparative view of France and the Federal Republic of Germany, the two European countries with the largest numbers of migrants. His analysis is much more than a case study. It permits the derivation of theoretically useful insights into what is common to all receiving states and what is specific to particular settings. Robert Bach, as already noted, treats the American case, which is empirically different from most European settings. Interesting structural similarities as well as differences between receiving countries emerge from his analysis. B. Guy Peters and Patricia K. Davis give an account of the British case, which also differs in some important respects from the continental European. Since immigrants to Britain are both more inclined and better situated in terms of their legal status to settle, Peters and Davis concentrate on some of the salient problems in integration and assimilation encountered by culturally and racially distinctive populations.

The concluding article, by Martin Heisler, attempts a general assessment of the problems arising from quasi settlement. The constraints on governments in the receiving states and the exigencies to which sending countries must respond are treated in the context of prolonged, but not definitive, settlement. The problems of adjustment for all three classes of actors—receiving and sending countries and migrants—cannot be solved. All concerned must become inured to an open-endedness that is uncomfortable for all.

ANNALS, *AAPSS*, **485**, May 1986

# The Shifting Grounds
# for Immigration

By MICHAEL J. PIORE

ABSTRACT: This article is addressed to the theory of the international migration of workers to low-wage sectors of developed industrial economies from underdeveloped regions. Its starting point is the framework of analysis originally put forward in *Birds of Passage,* a framework built around the notion of circular migration through the secondary sector of a dual labor market. It then discusses how that theory might be amended in light of recent developments in migration patterns to encompass enclave economies, immigrant entrepreneurship, and the settlement process.

*Michael J. Piore is a professor of economics at the Massachusetts Institute of Technology. He specializes in labor economics and industrial relations. The bulk of his work has focused on the structure of labor markets, particularly those for low-income and minority groups. His most recent book, coauthored with Charles Sabel, is* The Second Industrial Divide *(1984).*

THIS article provides some components of a conceptual framework for the analysis of changes in the size and composition of immigration and its impact on industrial economies. Its starting point is *Birds of Passage* and the conceptual apparatus developed there, which grew out of the attempt to understand the large flow of workers between underdeveloped and developed areas in North America and Western Europe that was apparent throughout much of the 1960s and the 1970s, as well as, in the United States at least, in the late nineteenth and early twentieth century.[1] After summarizing the principal features of that framework, the article then goes on to discuss how it might be modified in the light of the major shifts affecting immigration in the last ten years. I take these to be: (1) the increasing role of so-called refugees in the gross flows; (2) the growing numbers of people involved in the immigration process and the increasing length of time over which that process is being played out; and (3) possible changes in the economic structures, particularly the job structures.

TEMPORARY MIGRATION
AND SECONDARY JOBS

The central argument of *Birds of Passage* is that large-scale migration between developed and underdeveloped regions has to be understood in terms of the structure of job opportunities in developed areas and the peculiar motivation of migrant workers relative to the motivation of workers born and raised in the area in which they work. The understanding of the job structure was based upon the dual-labor-market hy-

pothesis. The hypothesis is that, for a variety of reasons we do not fully understand, developed industrial economies generate two distinct types of jobs. One of these sets of jobs, found in what is termed in this hypothesis the secondary sector, is characterized, relative to the other set of jobs, by low wages, menial social status, and considerable employment instability or, at least, uncertainty. National workers, because they are interested in long-term career prospects and normally expect a job to support their families and define their social position, shun such work. It is accepted, if it is accepted by national workers at all, only by those—such as students, retired workers, housewives, peasant workers, farm owners, among others—whose labor force commitment is marginal and who have other defining social roles. These people are frequently pulled away from industrial work by their other commitments, so that their labor force commitment is more commensurate with the instability of secondary jobs. Moreover, they tend to view their earnings as supplementary to those of other family members or designed basically to complement or facilitate their primary social activity. Housewives work for appliances, students work for tuition, peasants work to finance additional land purchases, and so forth. When such marginal native workers are limited in number or tied down geographically by their primary commitments, the society has a problem filling secondary jobs. Migrants are one solution to this problem.

Migrants are a solution because they typically view their migration as temporary. Their notion is to come to the developed area for a short period of time, earn and save as much money as possible, and then return home to use their savings to facilitate some activity in their place of origin. Often such

1. Michael J. Piore, *Birds of Passage: Migrant Labor and Industrial Societies* (New York: Cambridge University Press, 1979).

migrants are themselves peasants and what they are seeking are funds with which to purchase additional land, livestock, or farm equipment. But sometimes they are planning to open a small commercial enterprise or some kind of manufacturing facility. In any case, because they view their stay as temporary, they are undeterred by the lack of career prospects in the secondary labor market or by the short-run instability of the employment. Since they are only working temporarily and in any case derive their social status from their roles in their home community, they are also untouched be the menial, even demeaning, character of the work. They frequently come from areas where wages, and the general price level, are so low relative to those of the immigrant-receiving industrial country that the work seems much better paying than it does to national workers. But even when the wage differential is small, the way in which they live in the industrial area and their peculiar motivation for coming enable them to save a great deal more of their earnings than they would be able to do at home. For all of these reasons, the very jobs that are repugnant to primary national workers are acceptable, even attractive, to migrants; that acceptance is viewed in *Birds of Passage* as the engine of the migration process.

The difficulty with temporary migrants as a solution to the problem of filling secondary jobs is that they do not remain temporary. While many, maybe even most, actually return home, a significant number end up staying longer than originally intended. They then tend to bring their families from home or to form new families, and as a result many of their children grow up in the country of destination. Even if the original migrants eventually do return, the children tend to be attached to the destination.

They view that place as their permanent home and are thus essentially national workers, with the same aspirations toward stable jobs that provide for the support of a family and confer status and dignity on those who hold them. As these children mature, therefore, they come into competition with national workers for primary employment opportunities while at the same time re-creating a vacuum in the secondary sector. Finally, when a significant portion of a given migrant stream begins to settle in this way, it tends to create opportunities for more permanent migrants moving from the country of origin and planning to remain on a long-term basis with relatives at the destination. This afterwave of the first migrant stream also tends to compete with national workers for primary jobs.

This view of the migration process tended to minimize the problems that it posed for the developed country. It stressed the advantages both for the migrants themselves and to the place of origin, especially relative to other ways of managing a dual labor market. It pointed public policy away from efforts to curtail the migration process altogether and toward ways of managing the process and controlling the size of the secondary sector toward which it was targeted. It stressed in particular policies and procedures for facilitating the return of the migrants, for smoothing the upward mobility of their children who stayed, and for limiting the size of the secondary sector through minimum wages and other forms of labor legislation.

## MORE CONVENTIONAL
## ECONOMIC THEORIES

This view of the migration process may be contrasted with the view conventional in economics.[2] The latter is one in which migration is driven by an income differential between industrial areas and less developed countries or regions. People are assumed to be motivated almost entirely by income and as a result move toward industrial areas 'where the income is higher. The movement lowers the supply of labor in the area of origin, driving up wages there, and increases the supply of labor at the destination, forcing down its wages. Eventually, the wages in the two areas will equalize, bringing the migration to a halt. The basic model is, of course, modified to allow for costs such as transportation, job search, and the like. These costs are treated as an investment that the individual makes in order to obtain the higher income at the destination, and they must be deducted from the income there in order to determine the net returns from migration. When they are taken into account, wages in the two areas may not completely equalize, but since such costs are small, the wages will still be close. Models like these lie behind predictions that the population growth rates in Latin America will lead to a flood of immigrants. The notion is that the growth in population will swell the labor force, driving down wages and increasing the size of the income differential; as the income differential increases, the flow of migrants will rise.

As an explanation of the patterns of immigration that we actually observe, this model clearly does not work. In the American case, for example, it fails to explain the chief paradox of historical migration patterns: the American labor market drew first on distant European

2. For an example of this approach, see Michael J. Greenwood, "Research on Internal Migration in the United States: A Survey," *Journal of Economic Literature,* 13(2):397-433 (1975).

countries for labor and only lately has tapped domestic labor reserves in the rural South and those of its close neighbors in Latin America and the Caribbean, despite the fact that transportation costs for the latter were clearly less than for the former and the cultural and linguistic differences that would seem to determine other costs of migration were also less extreme. Patterns of recent migration into Europe cannot be explained by the income differential either.

That the economic model survives at all under these circumstances is explainable by the fact that one can almost always find some plausible imperfection—cost—in the form of information, transportation, or the like to introduce into the model to get the desired effect. The problem is that these costs tend to be introduced in an ad hoc fashion. The explanations that are generated may or may not be valid but they are not coming out of the economic model, and the latter—by being used to explain immigration in this way—is rendered tautological. The framework of *Birds of Passage* can be understood in these terms as an effort to add enough additional technological and sociological structure to the conventional model to make it once more a genuine theory. The result is nonetheless disturbing to most economists, because almost all actual migration processes to which the theory is applied are driven by the technological and sociological variable and not by cost differentials. I point that out merely to clarify the conceptual issues here. I happen to think that the process is actually driven by the technological and sociological variable.

The dual-labor-market model is sometimes characterized, especially by economists, as sociological, and hence it is useful to distinguish it from other sociological approaches. There are various explanations of migration that link the sociological characteristics of the workers at their place of origin to the roles they assume at the destination,[3] but generally the linkages are different for each ethnic group. For example, religion and the experience of oppression are used to explain Jewish success, family structure and the experience of oppression to explain the lack of black success, and so on. Most such theories, it should be added, are not designed to explain the migration process itself. Rather, they are addressed to the issue of assimilation or what is called, in the framework of *Birds of Passage*, settlement.

The dual-labor-market hypothesis attempts to identify a single set of factors common to all migrants and to relate those factors systematically to the economic structure of industrial and preindustrial societies. As a type of theory, it is thus closer to Marxism, although the structural factors that it makes responsible for movement are not those upon which classical Marxism focuses.

### ENCLAVE ECONOMY

Among structural theories that share this ambition, the major alternative in the migration literature to the dual-labor-market hypothesis is the notion of the enclave economy. The term "enclave economy" was coined by Alejandro Portes to explain the differences in the employment patterns of Mexican and Cu-

ban immigrants to the United States.[4] His argument is that the Mexican pattern conforms closely to the dual-labor-market hypothesis: circular migration through low-wage menial jobs attached to job hierarchies in which higher-level opportunities were held by American nationals. Jobs held by Mexicans were also located in enterprises owned and managed by native workers. The Cubans, however, succeeded in creating in Miami a whole economy composed of Cuban-owned enterprises. Even when Cuban immigrants were holding low-level jobs, they tended to work in enterprises in which there was an integrated job hierarchy. They were able to work their way up from bottom-level jobs and, often, eventually became managers and entrepreneurs in their own right. In this way, immigrants were able to obtain stable jobs and advancement in the first generation. First-generation immigrants still remained cut off from the mainstream of American society—remaining in the enclave economy, so to speak—but the integration of their children involved only lateral transfer out of the enclave and into positions of similar social status in the mainstream. In contrast, Mexican children had not only to move out of the ethnic community to integrate, but they also had to move across social and labor market barriers at the same time.

The Cuban economy in Miami is unique in the American, postwar immi-

3. See, for example, Nathan Glazer, ed., *Ethnicity* (Cambridge, MA: Harvard University Press, 1975); see esp. Orlando Patterson, "Context and Choice in Ethnic Allegiance: A Theoretical Framework and Caribbean Case Study," in ibid.; see also Nathan Glazer and Daniel P. Moynihan, *Beyond the Melting Pot* (Cambridge, MA: MIT Press, 1963).

4. Alejandro Portes, "Modes of Structural Incorporation and Present Theories of Immigration," in *Global Trends in Migration*, ed. Mary M. Kritz, Charles B. Keely, and Silvano M. Tomasi (Staten Island, NY: Center for Migration Studies Press, 1981), pp. 179-298; Kenneth L. Wilson and Alejandro Portes, "Ethnic Enclaves: A Comparison of the Cuban and Black Economies in Miami," *American Journal of Sociology*, 88(2):295-319 (1980). See also Ivan Light, "Immigrant and Ethnic Enterprise in North America," *Ethnic and Racial Studies*, 7(2):195-216 (Apr. 1984).

grant experience; indeed, it is difficult to find a comparable historical example. But a number of immigrant groups have managed to gain control over a significant segment of a regional industry so that social mobility of the kind envisaged in the enclave hypothesis is possible. Jews and Italians established such footholds in the New York City garment industry; the Irish and Italians have held similar positions in the construction industry in a number of cities. The Irish position in local government should have worked to similar effect. Most recently, Asian immigrants have advanced in a similar way.[5]

Tom Bailey and Roger Waldinger have attempted to explore modified versions of the enclave hypothesis in contemporary New York—Bailey in the restaurant industry[6] and Waldinger in the garment industry.[7] In both industries there is substantial immigrant entrepreneurship. The findings are complex. Entrepreneurship does not lead automatically to an enclave economy as Portes uses the term. Immigrant employers, like employers in general, often prefer to mix different ethnic groups, reserving higher-level positions for their own family and avoiding the paternalistic obligations that the employment of their compatriots seems to entail. But there are ethnic enclaves in these New York industries—particularly among the Chinese,

less so among Hispanic groups. Thus it seems meaningful to speak of the dual labor market and the enclave labor market as two distinct economic patterns associated with immigration. Once these two patterns are established, one is led to ask a series of analytical questions about when one or the other might prevail.

With regard to this distinction I find existing research too limited, and not sufficiently focused, to provide meaningful answers to this type of question, but it does suggest several observations. First, enclave economies appear to require immigrant entrepreneurship and, hence, bring to the fore the question of why some immigrant groups engage in significant entrepreneurial activities and others do not. Second, entrepreneurship is not sufficient to establish such activities for at least two reasons. One of these is that, as we have just seen, some immigrant employers do not like to employ members of their own ethnic group. The other is that many small business activities do not provide many supplementary employment opportunities. Almost every immigrant community seems to provide minimal business opportunities for its own members—ethnic food stores, travel and moving agencies involved in the immigration process itself, legal and medical services—but none of these are big employers. For the latter, the immigrant entrepreneurs have to gain a foothold in the larger market, as the examples of garment, construction, and government services suggest.

The two patterns of dualism and enclavism and the observations about the latter, limited though they are, are growing in significance because they appear to shed some light on the principal changes presently occurring in the immigrant process, namely, the shift toward settlement among the older immigrants

5. Light, "Immigrant and Ethnic Enterprise in North America."

6. Roger Waldinger, "Ethnic Enterprise and Industrial Change: A Case Study of the New York City Garment Industry" (Ph.D. diss., Harvard University, 1983); idem, "Immigrant Enterprise in the New York Garment Industry," *Social Problems,* 32(1):60-71 (Oct. 1984).

7. Thomas Bailey, "Labor Market Competition and Economic Mobility in Low-Wage Employment: A Case Study of Immigrants in the Restaurant Industry" (Ph.D. diss., Massachusetts Institute of Technology, 1983).

and toward refugees as a principal source of new immigration.

## REFUGEES

The major difference between refugees and other migrants is that refugees appear to see their immigration from the very start as permanent. They may entertain dreams of returning to their home and engage in extensive political activity designed to permit them to do this, but they seem to see their economic future as dependent upon the ability to establish a secure position and advance within the economy of the destination. They are not, moreover, in a position simply to leave and return home when economic conditions turn bad at the destination, as are temporary migrants.

One of the results of this distinction is that where there are the two types of migrants moving into a single, and limited, set of employment opportunities, the refugees are likely to displace the temporary migrants. Because the temporaries have an overwhelmingly economic motivation, they do not remain unless it is profitable to do so. Undocumented migrants in the United States frequently say that there is no point in staying unless they can hold down two jobs, and very few are willing to wait around if they cannot find any jobs at all.

Refugees, on the other hand, have no place to go, and hence they are likely to be more persistent in getting and keeping whatever jobs are available. It is true that because they are permanent, they may be more concerned about the social character of their jobs than temporary migrants are, but unlike national workers, they generally have few economic alternatives. This is so in part because they often lack access to transfer payments and other social services. But the exclusive emphasis on governmental aid in policy debates on this subject seems to me to miss the major point. Most aid in an established community comes from other members of the community, especially close family members, and governmental aid is—historically, at least—better seen as an institutional expression of community rather than an artificial intrusion upon private affairs. If the aid enables people to refuse secondary jobs and hold out for higher stakes and better jobs, it is because job characteristics reflect upon the family and larger community of which the worker is a part. Refugee families are not in a position to protect their status in this way. Sometimes they manage to preserve status structures from their communities of origin as a substitute for status that is unavailable in the place of refuge, but that does not prevent—in fact, it may even facilitate—their acceptance of low-status, low-wage jobs.

This is particularly important in the United States at the moment. It implies that widely expressed fears that the refugees will be added to a labor force already overbloated with undocumented migrants are unfounded. To the extent that the refugees have been flowing into the secondary sector of a dual labor market, they have probably displaced temporary migrants and cut back the undocumented migration flow, albeit maybe not on a one-for-one basis.

The other likelihood is that the refugees are more apt to form economic enclaves. The enclaves will affect not only the process of integration and social mobility but possibly the total number of available economic opportunities.

## THE SETTLEMENT OF
## TEMPORARY MIGRANT STREAMS

The other factor making the enclave hypothesis increasingly significant is the settlement of previously temporary streams of migrants. The new migration began in Europe in the early 1960s and in the United States in the latter half of that decade. It has now been going on in a number of places for over 20 years. Even if most of the migrants went home eventually, the period of time and the numbers involved imply a substantial residue of settled people, and direct observation suggests that there are indeed stable communities that are being joined by new, permanent settlers from families that initially remained behind. This has become the central problem of migration policy in Europe, where, because the migration in the 1960s and 1970s was designed to be temporary, it has come as something of a shock.

We seem to know very little about the capacity of such initially temporary migrant streams to develop enclave-type structures. Perhaps, if a careful investigation were possible, it would prove that only refugees actually do so, although the prevalence of such structures among the Italians, Portuguese, and Greeks in the United States and northern Europe as well as the Jews and Irish among the nineteenth-century immigrants to the United States implies that this is not the case.

## JOB STRUCTURES

The other half of the framework of analysis originally developed in *Birds of Passage* centered on the job structure. Two types of developments in this aspect of the problem in recent years are affecting the migration process. First, the actual employment structure—certainly in Europe and possibly in the United States as well—appears to have become less conducive to international migration in the last decade. This devel-

opment is readily understood in terms of the original framework. Second, the forces guiding that structure appear to be in the process of change. This does not necessarily imply that the particular hypotheses about the job structure upon which the original analysis rested were wrong, but it does suggest that they are likely to become increasingly irrelevant. One must then ask what the new forces imply for the evolution of the migration process.

### The evolution of actual employment

In Western Europe, the principal trends have been a stagnation in the overall level of employment, a precipitous rise in the level of unemployment, and a shift in the composition of employment opportunities away from manufacturing toward services and within manufacturing out of heavy, so-called smokestack industries. There has also been a vociferous demand on the part of European employers for more flexibility in employment commitments and an attempt to make greater use of part-time and temporary workers.

U.S. employment levels have varied more radically over the business cycle than those of Western Europe, but there has been, in marked contrast to Europe, a large increase in the number of jobs. Overall levels of unemployment have also increased in the past decade but relatively less than in Europe. The structure of employment opportunities has changed as well. The shift in the structure has paralleled that of Europe. There have been relative declines in smokestack industries and in manufacturing as a whole; relative increases in services, although because aggregate employment expanded, the structural shift involved a much larger absolute expansion of the service section; a smaller decline in heavy industry; and a slight expansion in overall manufacturing employment. In the United States, traditional light industry, such as shoes, garments, and textiles, also exhibited declining employment between 1981 and 1985, although unlike other employment changes, this seemed to be less a trend than a reflection of the temporary overvaluation of the dollar.

The net effect of these changes was probably a decline in the demand for migrants relative to national workers. This decline is clearly evident in Western Europe, where it can be documented statistically. In Europe, in fact, there has been a net outflow of migrants in most recent years. Since those who returned home were probably the least attached to the country of destination, the effect was to make the migrant population a more permanent and more settled one. This was in addition to the effects of refugees and of the mere passage of time on settlement. Data are not available to document these effects in the United States, since such a large portion of the transient migrants is clandestine, but the changing composition of employment opportunities may not have reduced the level of migration or contributed significantly to settlement because the absolute level of employment did not decrease.

Most of these changes in the composition of employment are readily understandable within the framework of the dual-labor-market hypothesis. The secondary sector, into which the migrants are recruited, exists in this hypothesis in large part because the jobs held by nationals in the primary sector are secured by institutional arrangements from the flux and uncertainty of a capitalist economy. The flux and uncertainty themselves continue, however, and lead the employers to create a secondary sector that can absorb them. It is not surprising, therefore, that when the instability and uncertainty that the secondary sector was designed to handle materialized with a vengence in the late 1970s and early 1980s, it should hit migrant employment hardest and the migrants should respond by going—or being sent—home. That the most temporary should leave first, and the residual migrant population should become increasingly stable, also follows from the theory. If in the United States migration has fallen off less than in Europe, it is because U.S. employment levels, after declining in 1981 and 1982, recovered and then went on to expand whereas in Europe they did not recover.

The increasing reliance on national workers in the secondary sector can be understood in similar terms. If uncertainty and instability remain once the temporary migrants have been sent home, employers must obviously look for other sources of labor to absorb them. The future of temporary migration may, however, come to depend upon whether employers can find the flexibility they are still looking for at home in other labor force groups. In Europe, the focus at the moment is on changes in the institutional structures securing employment that would let employers use nationals more flexibly, that is, more as they treated migrants in the past. Managers do not seem to doubt that they will be able to find national workers who are willing to be used in this way if they can obtain the legal reforms that such use would require.

These legal barriers do not exist in the United States, and employers have relied heavily on the postwar baby boom, which bloated the youth age cohort, and on women to provide a flexible national labor force. The baby-boom cohorts are, however, becoming adult and the female labor force may be approaching the limit in terms of both its size and its willingness to accept part-time and/or unstable work. The focus in public policy is then likely to shift—indeed, it has already begun to do so—to the retired work force and those aspects of pensions and social security that determine whether retirees need, and can easily take, postretirement jobs. A political impasse on this question would force greater reliance upon migrants if the dual-labor-market structure persists. Other developments, however, suggest that the underlying structure of the labor market may be shifting as well.

## The end of mass production

The dual-labor-market structure emerged in a world that had two critical characteristics. First, the technology was dominated by mass production, and the labor market institutions were structured by that technical form. Second, production was oriented largely toward domestic demand.

The dominance of mass production led to the division of the economy into a technologically progressive core, which focused on mass production, and a subordinate, relatively backward periphery. In the core, efficiency was achieved through the progressive division of the productive process into increasingly narrow, highly defined tasks and through the development of specialized resources specifically tailored to the peculiarities of the particular operation to which they were assigned. These specialized resources consisted first of narrowly trained workers—called, in the United States, semiskilled and called

simply, in Europe, specialized—and then of dedicated pieces of capital equipment. The job structure of the core was composed of the semiskilled workers on the one hand and of managers and engineers who designed, directed, and coordinated the otherwise isolated and independent work stations, on the other.

Mass production was efficient, however, only for markets that were large enough to support the extensive division of labor and stable enough to keep the specialized resources fully employed. Hence, it was surrounded by a more flexible periphery that produced products with inherently small markets such as luxury goods, specialized equipment for mass production, and new products. This peripheral sector also met the unstable portion of the demand for mass-produced goods. The periphery typically used much more general resources: tools or multipurpose equipment and a job structure that relied on broad craftsmen supplemented wherever possible by unskilled workers doing simple tasks to economize the time and talent of the highly trained.

In Europe, some of the immigrant employment was found in the most rudimentary and monotonous jobs in the mass-production core. But more often in Europe and typically in the United States, the immigrants took the unskilled jobs in the periphery, and the highly skilled professional managerial and craft jobs in both sectors were reserved for natives. In some of the oldest peripheral industries that never developed true mass production—construction, high-fashion garments, restaurants—immigrants took over highskilled jobs as well, apparently because they brought the high skills with them.

The argument of *Birds of Passage* implies that technological progress through the division of labor is somehow basic or natural and the resultant job structure is thus a permanent and inevitable characteristic of industrial society. But recent industrial history suggests this presumption is wrong. Over the last decade, the technological dynamic has shifted away from mass production.[8] New technologies seem now to favor small-batch production characteristic of what used to be the periphery of the economy. The computer is emblematic of this technological trend. In manufacturing, for example, economies of production once possible only through the physical dedication of the equipment to a particular make and model of a specific product can now be obtained through the software attached to general machinery; the design, and even the basic product under production, can be altered by changing the software without touching the equipment itself. Other technologies work in the same direction. The laser is a completely general cutting tool. Photocopying reduces economies of scale in printing; bioengineering has a like effect in the production of organic products. As a result of such developments, small firms, producing in batches, have come into their own technologically and no longer operate solely as an adjunct of mass production.

At the same time, the economy as a whole, and producers in the periphery in particular, have become much less dependent upon the domestic market. Because they produce in small batches, firms can often find a niche for their product in the international market, whatever the state of domestic demand. For an economy composed increasingly of small-scale producers, economic opportunities are thus much less scarce.

8. Michael J. Piore and Charles F. Sabel, *The Second Industrial Divide: Possibilities for Prosperity* (New York: Basic Books, 1984).

These developments would tend by and large to create a favorable environment for permanent migration. Small-scale batch production lends itself to entrepreneurial activity and enclave economies, as is suggested by the role of immigrant entrepreneurs in the industries that exemplify this type of structure. The ethnic community also appears to provide a good vehicle for the development of craft skills and for the creation and maintenance of the industrial infrastructure that the small firms composing such a community seem to require. The internationalization of markets suggests that these new enclaves could absorb demand that would otherwise go to other countries; the enclaves could thereby develop without taking jobs away from nationals, even indirectly. Thus, fortuitously, the structure of the economy seems to be moving in the very same direction as the structure of immigration. Things seem to be working out very neatly.

Too neatly, perhaps, in at least one respect. The kicker here is the technology. The older technologies of industries like garments and construction were virtually stagnant. Their nature had not really changed in 100 years and that is one of the reasons why immigrants were capable of moving into even the skilled jobs. The current dynamism of small-scale production derives from the latest technologies, primarily computers but also such developments as photo printing, laser cutting, and biotechnologies. Developments in computer technology suggest that their innate sophistication need not block access by the relatively unschooled, but whether the developments that are promoting the growth of the types of jobs previously dominated by immigrants are really accessible to them remains to be seen.

ANNALS, *AAPSS*, **485**, May 1986

# The Transnational
# Nexus of Migration

*By* ROSEMARIE ROGERS

ABSTRACT: The large-scale post-World War II labor migrations from the Mediterranean countries and North Africa to northern and western Europe have resulted in the presence of millions of foreigners and their families in the host countries. This article discusses the ambiguous situation of many of these migrants, who are not fully settled in the countries in which they live, but are nevertheless likely to remain there in the near future or indeed for good. The article also inquires into the ways in which the political, cultural, and economic relations between the migrants' countries of origin and their countries of residence have been affected by these migrations, and into the bilateral and multilateral arrangements that regulate these processes of migration and settling.

*Rosemarie Rogers holds a Ph.D. in political science from the Massachusetts Institute of Technology. She is a professor and the academic dean at The Fletcher School of Law and Diplomacy at Tufts University. Her recent research has dealt with the effects of European labor migrations and with immigration and refugee policy in Europe and in the Western Hemisphere. She has most recently published an edited volume,* Guests Come to Stay: The Effects of European Labor Migration on Sending and Receiving Countries *(1985).*

MANY important chapters that compose the story of the post-World War II migrations from the Mediterranean littoral to northern and western continental Europe have already been written.[1] They tell of employers' initiatives in these movements, of host and home countries' reactive, incremental policies toward the recruitment of foreign labor, of expectations by all concerned that there would be a constant turnover among this work force, of initially grudging policies of family reunification, and—despite all of this—of a pattern of longer and longer stays on the part of some of the migrants.

In the early 1970s the host countries began to reevaluate these movements because it was becoming clear that their impacts went far beyond the economic benefits. The presence of the new migrants was creating substantial demands on these societies' infrastructures and was changing their ethnic composition. The sending countries, too, were beginning to perceive costs: loss of skilled workers, separated families. But, except for Switzerland and Sweden, which acted earlier, the turning point did not occur until 1973-74, when the host countries unilaterally chose to halt the recruitment of foreign labor, explaining their

decisions primarily by the economic recession.

At the same time as entries of new foreign workers ceased, there was, however, a realization that the large numbers of foreigners living in the host countries could not be sent home en masse because the labor of many of them was still needed, because some had in any case acquired a protected status due to long residence, and because mass expulsions of workers, like those happening recently in Nigeria, would have been inconsistent with the ideologies of Western liberal democracies. It was also evident that many migrants would not soon return of their own accord, and therefore family reunification has continued to be permitted. The home countries have continued to benefit from migrants' remittances.

It is appropriate that the title of this Annals issue, From Foreign Workers to Settlers? be phrased as a question. Settling is a multifaceted process, which happens over time. The Mediterranean labor migrants in Europe today are more settled than they were ten or twenty years ago, as indicated by longer average length of stay of the different migrant populations and by more balanced sex ratios, declining activity rates, larger percentages of foreigners born in the host countries among all foreigners living there, greater frequency of intermarriage between migrants and natives of the host countries, and the number of migrant organizations and of mass media in the migrants' languages. Yet the migrants cannot be said to be fully settled in the host countries, with the exception of Sweden; their rights in several spheres of life do not match those of the native populations. They are in an anomalous position: working and paying taxes and bringing up their children in the new

1. See comparative works such as Stephen Castles and Godula Kosack, *Immigrant Workers and Class Structure in Western Europe* (London: Oxford University Press, 1973); Ronald E. Krane, ed., *International Labor Migration in Europe* (New York: Praeger, 1979); Mark J. Miller, *Foreign Workers in Western Europe: An Emerging Political Force* (New York: Praeger, 1981); Rosemarie Rogers, ed., *Guests Come to Stay: The Effects of European Labor Migration on Sending and Receiving Countries* (Boulder, CO: Westview Press, 1985); Tomas Hammar, ed., *European Immigration Policy: A Comparative Study* (New York: Cambridge University Press, 1985); and the many monographic works available in English and other languages.

country—without being fully secure and fully participant members of that country, and emotionally still strongly attached to the old country—without in most cases having the opportunity to effect a successful return.

This article will explore some of the most salient aspects of these migrants' still unsettled status in the host countries. It must be noted, however, that the parameters of the system are not fixed: a country's accession to the European Economic Community (EEC) has immediate implications for the status of its migrants who are already resident in an EEC country, and it will eventually open doors for new migration. The article will also inquire into some of the ways in which these migration flows have affected the political, cultural, and economic relations between the host and sending countries, and into the bilateral and multilateral arrangements that serve to regulate these processes of migration and settling. Because of the necessary brevity of the article, the findings presented are illustrative rather than comprehensive. They derive from a larger study in progress, which analyzes the changing migration policies in Europe and the migrations' effects on the relations between the countries involved.[2]

## THE CONTEXT

Table 1 offers data on the size of the migrant groups in five major European host countries, France, the Federal Republic of Germany, the Netherlands,

Sweden, and Switzerland.[3] France, Germany, and the Netherlands belong to the EEC. During the decades of heavy migration flows only one sending country, Italy, was an EEC member; however, many Italians migrated outside the European Community, to Switzerland, where in fact they constitute the largest migrant group. The European Community's southern enlargement, which began with the accession of Greece in 1981, has as yet not brought about any new migration flows, since free movement for Greeks must await the completion of a seven-year transition period. With one exception that is not relevant here, migration flows between the remaining EEC countries are relatively small and go in both directions, so that net flows are far smaller still.[4] The migrations with which this article is concerned were, until the southern enlargement, mainly outside the EEC or from non-EEC to EEC countries.[5] The European

2. This study, Migration Policies in Western Europe and the Mediterranean since 1955: Patterns, Sources, and Effects, is directed by Rosemarie Rogers, The Fletcher School of Law and Diplomacy, Tufts University, Medford, MA. It is funded by a grant from the Ford Foundation.

3. Other European countries that have received labor migrants from the Mediterranean are Austria, Denmark, and Luxembourg; and labor migrants have arrived in Belgium in large numbers. Much of the general discussion in this article applies to these countries as well. Great Britain, which rivals France and Germany in the size of its migrant population, is a different case; few of its migrants hail from the Mediterranean region or Finland, the latter being relevant for Sweden.

4. The exception is migration from Ireland to the United Kingdom, two countries that joined the European Community in 1973. For disaggregated data on stocks of EEC migrants in the member countries in the 1970s, see Eurostat, *Demographic Statistics 1981* (Brussels: Statistical Office of the European Communities, 1983), Country Tables 12.

5. Some European host countries experienced inflows of Mediterranean workers earlier than others: for example, Switzerland, as compared with Germany, which throughout the 1950s received large numbers of German refugees from Eastern Europe, and with Austria, which experienced little need for foreign labor until the mid-1960s. Certain sending countries were places of recruitment earlier than others, either because of geographical prox-

Community has had little impact on its member countries with respect to their migration policies toward nonmember countries. Sweden's most substantial migration is from Finland, with which it shares membership in the Common Nordic Labour Market. Sweden is unique in that the number of naturalized Swedish citizens approximately equals that of the foreign resident population.

In addition to the migration flows already mentioned, the host countries in Table 1 have also received migrants from their former colonies—in the case of France and the Netherlands—as well as refugees invited for resettlement, and, especially in the last decade, asylum seekers.

Policymakers in the host countries are keenly aware of their neighbors' policies and of any new policy initiatives, and host-country policies have indeed converged over the last decade. However, except for policies applicable within the EEC, one cannot speak of policy coordination between either the host or the sending countries.

### CONTINUING OBSTACLES TO SETTLING

There are four points at which the process of labor migration can be regu-

lated by a receiving country: entry of workers; entry of family members; admission of family members to the work force; and return.[6] Until 1973-74 all major European host countries, with the exception of Switzerland and Sweden, were very liberal in admitting foreign workers in response to employer demands. Sweden decided in 1968 on a restrictive policy concerning the recruitment of Mediterranean labor, while the Finns enjoy free movement to Sweden. Switzerland, in 1970, initiated its stabilization policy, which has sharply restricted the number of new migrants admitted every year. Interestingly, these two countries—unlike France, Germany, and the Netherlands—have not found it necessary to continue to experiment with restrictive policies at the three other points of regulation, even though they have widely divergent policies in most other respects—conditions for permanent residence and naturalization, migrants' political rights, education, and so forth—and even though they differ indeed in basic philosophy. Sweden now sees itself as an immigration country and Switzerland insists that it is not. Germany has created a greater number of obstacles to a smooth settling process than any of the other countries.

In all five host countries, obstacles to family reunification—uniting spouses and minor children with migrant spouses—were progressively removed during the 1960s, until the waiting periods, if any, were generally no longer than a year. Entries of family members have indeed occurred on an extensive

imity to the host countries, such as the proximity of Italy to Switzerland, or because of particular historical relationships, such as that between Algeria and France. Exits from certain sending countries—Portugal, Yugoslavia—were not always generally permitted. In interviews in the host countries, government officials and managers in the enterprises employing foreign workers spontaneously categorize migrant groups according to different degrees of their integration. For example, the French consider the Algerians, Moroccans, and black Africans as the least integrated among their migrants; the Germans put the Turkish population in their country into this category; and the Dutch, the Moroccans and Turks.

6. These categories are adapted from Georges P. Tapinos, "European Migration Patterns: Economic Linkages and Policy Experiences," in Mary M. Kritz, ed., *U.S. Immigration and Refugee Policy: Global and Domestic Issues* (Lexington, MA: Lexington Books, 1983), p. 64.

TABLE 1
FOREIGNERS RESIDING IN SELECTED EUROPEAN HOST COUNTRIES
BY COUNTRY OF CITIZENSHIP, 1983 (in thousands)

| Country of Citizenship | France* | Federal Republic of Germany | Netherlands | Sweden | Switzerland |
|---|---|---|---|---|---|
| European Economic Community (EEC) countries | | | | | |
| Italy | 333.7 | 565.0 | 20.9 | 4.2 | 404.8 |
| Greece | 7.9 | 292.3 | 4.0 | 11.8 | 9.0 |
| Portugal | 764.9 | 99.5 | 7.8 | 1.6 | 19.7 |
| Spain | 321.4 | 166.0 | 21.6 | 3.2 | 104.2 |
| Other EEC countries | 150.0 | 307.5 | 119.5 | 52.9 | 163.7 |
| Finland | 1.0 | 9.9 | 0.6 | 150.6 | 1.4 |
| Algeria | 795.9 | 5.1 | 0.6 | 0.5 | 1.9 |
| Morocco | 431.1 | 44.2 | 106.4 | 1.3 | 1.3 |
| Tunisia | 189.4 | 25.3 | 2.8 | 0.9 | 1.9 |
| Turkey | 123.5 | 1,555.3 | 155.3 | 20.9 | 48.5 |
| Yugoslavia | 64.4 | 612.8 | 12.7 | 38.3 | 58.9 |
| Not specified | 496.9 | 852.0 | 100.2 | 110.9 | 110.3 |
| Total | 3,680.1 | 4,534.9 | 552.4 | 397.1 | 925.6 |
| As percentage of total population | (6.8) | (7.4) | (3.8) | (4.8) | (14.4) |

SOURCES: Institut national de la statistique et des études économiques, *Recensement général de la population de 1982: Les étrangers,* Série boulier, RP 82/5, Migrations et sociétés, no. 6 (Paris: Documentation française, n.d.) pp. 56-57; idem, *Recensement général de la population de 1982: Principaux résultats* (Paris: Documentation francaise, 1984), p. 90; Organization for Economic Cooperation and Development, *SOPEMI 1984,* mimeographed report (Paris: Organization for Economic Cooperation and Development, 1985), p. 78. Reprinted by permission.
*The data for France are from census results for 1982.

scale since the recruitment stopped. However, Germany has recently sought to influence the volume of in-migration by manipulating family reunification rules. The age up to which foreign children are permitted to join their parents was lowered from 18 to 16 years after a prolonged discussion in which an upper age limit of only 6 years had been seriously considered—a discussion that can only have served to send a message to the migrants that their settling, while tolerated, is hardly welcomed.

As second-generation migrants have begun to marry, often finding their spouses in their home countries, they are encountering obstacles to establishing their new families in the host countries. In the Netherlands, a law prohibiting young migrants from bringing their spouses unless their wages are at or above the legal minimum can cause a wait of several years, since employers are not required to pay minimum wages to workers under 23 years old. In Germany, a second-generation migrant must have lived in the country for at least eight years and must have been married for at least one year—two *Länder* require three years—before he or she can be joined by a foreign spouse.

Some host countries have considered the admission of migrants' family members to the work force, once they were admitted to residence in the country, as automatic, whereas other countries have insisted on lengthy waiting periods. Keeping young people unoccupied for several years is, of course, a recipe for social problems: the numerous changes in German policy reflect on the one hand a continued restrictive stance, but, on the other, a discomfort with such policies.[7] Today, newly arrived spouses of first-generation migrants in Germany must still wait four years before they may seek work, and the children must wait two years, although there are waivers for those who have received some education or training in Germany. France, too, has experimented with restrictive policies in this area.

Finally, France, the Netherlands, and Germany have experimented with incentive schemes aimed at inducing migrants and their families to return to their home countries. Proposals for programs involving a cash bonus as an incentive to return were rejected by the Dutch and German governments in the 1970s, but France did institute such a program in 1977. It was later terminated because of the questionable legality of the procedure by which it had been established, but its success had been small in any case. It appears to have functioned as a reintegration scheme for migrants who were already planning to return, rather than as a return-incentive scheme. A Dutch training and aid scheme aimed at employment generation in certain sending countries by returning migrants was terminated in 1984, partly because it had been very costly.[8]

New return programs have been tested in the 1980s, or are currently in existence, in all three countries. Some of them consist of several components. Some are aimed exclusively at unemployed workers or at workers who are about to lose their jobs. The programs or their components include cash incentives; the repayment of social security contributions in lump sums, as if they were deposited savings; payment, to workers above a certain age, of unemployment benefits at home rather than in the host country; repayments of deposits into voluntary savings schemes—for example, home-construction funds—normally operative only in a host country; and, again, aid offered to migrants for employment creation in the home countries.

Most of these schemes were or are advertised as available for only a certain period of time, a fact that undoubtedly adds pressure on the migrants to utilize them. Some observers maintain that any official discussion of returns or offers of return help—however strong the stress on a program's voluntary nature—contributes to making the migrants feel less secure about their position in the host countries.

7. See the various *Stichtagsregelungen,* as summarized in Ursula Mehrländer, "Second-Generation Migrants in the Federal Republic of Germany," in *Guests Come to Stay,* ed. Rogers, p. 176.

8. See Rosemarie Rogers, "Incentives to Return: Patterns of Policies and Migrants' Responses," in *Global Trends in Migration: Theory and Research on International Population Movements,* ed. Mary M. Kritz, Charles B. Keely, and Silvano M. Tomasi (Staten Island, NY: Center for Migration Studies, 1981), pp. 338-64.

## THE MIGRANTS' INSECURE STATUS

Depending on the length of time that they have spent in the host countries, the migrants have a more or less protected residence status. Sweden offers permanent residence after one year, Switzerland after five or ten, depending on the migrants' origin. The policies of France and the Netherlands are closer to Sweden's, France having radically simplified in 1984 its formerly highly complex system of three types of work and three types of residence permits. Germany still has three types of residence status; a migrant may apply for the most protected status after a minimum stay in the country of eight years.[9]

In all host countries except Sweden, migrants who do not enjoy fully protected status can be asked to leave—that is, applications for extension of their residence permits can be refused—if they are unemployed and have received the unemployment benefits to which they were entitled; they need not be granted social welfare benefits indefinitely. Data on existing practice are not publicly available, but officials assert in inter-

views that the numbers of migrants who are forced to leave because of unemployment are negligible.

There are four other types of limitations, which apply to the status of all or of certain types of migrants. First, all host countries are free to expel migrants who come into serious conflicts with their laws. Tragic cases have been reported of second-generation migrants thus expelled who had lived in a host country all their lives and were then forced to go to a country in which they had no immediate family and were really foreigners.

Second, problems arise for migrants whose status in a host country is derived from that of a spouse or a parent. This status applies—in Germany—to a wife who becomes divorced from her husband and must appeal to humanitarian considerations in order to be able to stay on. It also applies—generally—to minor children who must return to their so-called home countries when their parents decide to return. There are abundant examples of older children who did not succeed in becoming integrated into their parents' home countries, not primarily for economic reasons but because they had been socialized differently. There are examples of high-level bureaucrats making exceptions and readmitting such children to the host countries, even several years after their departure. Such decisions, however, cannot make up for the human suffering involved and they are entirely dependent on an official's goodwill.

Third, one type of problem is experienced by all first-generation migrants today: they lack the option of returning to their countries of origin on a trial basis and then returning once again to the host country if their attempted reintegration into the home country has failed. This is true even in as liberal a country as

---

9. In Switzerland the acquisition of permanent resident status is automatic after the required number of years, and by now more than three-quarters of all foreigners living in the country year-round—that is, excluding seasonal workers—have acquired this status. In Germany, in contrast, the migrant is merely permitted to apply, and the official in charge bases his or her decision on, among other factors, the migrant's degree of acculturation. By 1984 only 142,894 foreigners in Germany had been granted the most secure residence status, *Aufenthaltsberechtigung*. See Federal Republic of Germany, Deutscher Bundestag, "Antwort der Bundesregierung auf die Grosse Anfrage," Drucksache 10/2071, 10. Wahlperiode, 3 Oct. 1984, p. 9. German social work agencies are now making a concerted effort to encourage the large numbers of eligible migrants to apply for this status.

Sweden, although it appears that there it is relatively easy for migrants to get around the legal obstacles, and there is probably a considerable number of foreigners who maintain their official residence in Sweden while attempting to reestablish themselves in their home countries.

Finally, certain sending countries keep a hold on their emigrants, at least on the males, through requirements to perform military service at home, even if these citizens have become established abroad and returning for military service would mean a loss of their jobs. Once they have passed a certain age, such individuals are no longer free to return home for family visits or vacations; they have become exiles. Turkey is perhaps the most extreme case among those here considered,[10] but Greece and Italy have made similar demands as well.

Thus, we are dealing with foreign populations that remain between two countries, unsettled not only because they experience conflicting feelings of loyalty or a nostalgia for home, but also because they suffer from diminished rights in the receiving countries and, in certain instances, from unreasonable demands made upon them by their countries of origin. Nothing has yet been said about migrants' political rights in the host countries, which are also limited. Individuals—including some prominent host-country politicians—who are impatient with criticisms of migrants' limited rights, have suggested that migrants with long-term residence should simply fish or cut bait—either stay and change their citizenship, or return.

## BECOMING A CITIZEN OF THE HOST COUNTRY

Why have more migrants not become citizens of the host countries by now? In Sweden, where migrants are invited to become citizens after only three years of residence, about 5 percent of the foreign population has become naturalized every year in recent years, and there are today about as many naturalized Swedish citizens as foreigners in the country. Among those who do not choose to take this step are some whose residence will indeed be temporary, especially young migrants from Finland, but others who are staying on for ever-longer periods also maintain their original citizenship, out of a strong sentimental attachment to their home country.

Naturalizations in Switzerland in recent years have amounted to about 1 percent of the number of foreigners living in the country, and in Germany they have been around the 0.5 percent mark and even lower. The French and Dutch percentages have been somewhat higher than the Swiss, but still far from the Swedish.[11] France and the Netherlands, however, have recently introduced important changes in their laws with respect to the second generation, for whom the application of the *jus soli* is now an option. A host country's policies are thus a second, significant determinant of the frequency of naturalizations.

Simply put, certain countries—for example Sweden or the United States—see the conferral of citizenship upon a migrant as a means to facilitate his or her integration into the society, whereas others see it as the culmination of an integration and acculturation process.

10. In 1985 it was possible for Turkish migrants to pay a relatively high sum of money—DM 14,750—in exchange for being exempted from military service.

11. See the Organization for Economic Cooperation and Development's yearly *SOPEMI* reports (Paris, Organization for Economic Cooperation and Development).

In Switzerland, many cantons charge considerable fees for the process, in addition to confronting the migrant with strict national and local residence requirements and the burden of proof that he or she has become integrated into the community. In Germany, an official makes a judgment as to "whether the requested naturalization is in the state's interest," and the official "examines, in particular, whether the applicant's naturalization is desirable according to general political, economic, and cultural considerations."[12]

In addition to the desires of the migrants themselves, and to the host countries' policies, a third set of factors influencing the frequencies of naturalization comprises pressures or explicit obstacles originating in the cultures or legal structures of the home countries. Migrants, at least from certain Muslim countries, feel that it is extremely disloyal—almost an act of treason—to give up their citizenship for that of the host country. Some who have done so have kept it a secret from their countrymen. Certain countries—Turkey is an example—have a system of releasing their citizens from citizenship. Host countries respect this convention and will not naturalize a migrant if no release has been obtained; when the home country holds up the release, the migrant remains truly in between—sometimes for years.

12. Further, "naturalization is not intended as an instrument for facilitating integration, but rather, it should come at the end of a successful process of integration." Federal Republic of Germany, Der Bundesminister des Innern, "Aufzeichnung zur Ausländerpolitik und zum Ausländerrecht in der Bundesrepublik Deutschland," mimeographed report, no. 7 1-937 020/15, Oct. 1984, p. 31.

It is too simplistic, then, to see as a simple decision the migrants' choice between joining the host country's polity—that is, becoming citizens—and not. More would like to join, but not at the cost of saying no to another country that they also love, and in the case of many of them the choice is not really theirs.

## MIGRANTS' POLITICAL RIGHTS

Many in the host countries have been concerned about the anomaly of large foreign populations living within the borders of a country that is for them the place of long-term or permanent residence, the place where they work and pay taxes and bring up their children, but where they are excluded from the political process because they are not citizens. It is true that in all host countries migrants have been offered a voice in consultative bodies at local political levels and frequently also at higher ones. The fact that participation in such groups has tended to be low has given rise to two opposite types of arguments: either that this low participation shows a lack of interest in the political process and that the migrants have, therefore, forfeited any claims to other forms of political involvement, or that, on the contrary, it is rational for anyone to abstain when he or she has no real power and that migrants may well be eager to participate in elections when they know that their votes will be counted.

Besides facilitating and encouraging naturalizations, there are two other means of creating opportunities for migrants' participation in host country politics: making double citizenship more easily accessible and granting voting rights to foreign residents. There seems currently to be little discussion of the former option. The second option, offering voting rights to foreigners, is a radical choice for all host countries. It is least controversial—though still opposed by many—when communal elections are involved, and it is generally perceived as inappropriate at the national level, where foreign policy is made and serious conflicts might therefore arise. However, the intermediate levels are similarly problematic in some countries—for example, in France and the Netherlands—since officeholders at these levels participate in turn in the selection of certain delegates to the national legislatures.

Foreigners do vote today in political elections in three European countries. Their rights are broadest in Sweden, where they vote and may stand for election at the local and provincial levels. These rights were conferred upon them in 1976 through a change in Swedish electoral law.[13] In the Netherlands a change in the country's constitution in 1983 created the right of foreigners to participate in local elections, after a number of communities had adopted laws to this effect several years earlier. Finally, foreigners have traditionally participated in local elections in two Swiss cantons, which, however, are not cantons with a heavy foreign concentration. Today the introduction of such rights is widely discussed in other parts of Switzerland and in Germany and France, and their extension to the national level has been proposed in Sweden. The outcome of these discussions is by no means certain, but it is clear that any changes are unlikely to come quickly.

13. Prognoses of apathy have been proved wrong with respect to migrants' participation in the Swedish elections. See Tomas Hammar, "Citizenship, Aliens' Political Rights, and Politicians' Concern for Migrants: The Case of Sweden," in *Guests Come to Stay,* ed. Rogers, pp. 85-107.

Thus many migrants will continue to live with one foot in each of two countries. Migrant associations in the host countries hardly ever embrace migrants from more than one country of origin; when the associations are of a political nature, home-country politics usually represent an important concern. Some migrants use elections in their country of origin as an occasion to return for a holiday. Italian migrants are offered subsidized travel to return home to vote in national elections. A system of voting by absentee ballot, recently instituted by Spain for its citizens abroad, has not functioned well so far.

Some migrant associations receive funding from the home countries and may be used by the regimes to spy on their citizens. An internal report of a German ministry estimates that about 3.5 percent of foreigners in Germany who are more than 16 years old are members of extremist groups. Occasionally a particular group acts as the mouthpiece for a political party that is banned in the home country. Some groups organize protest marches to criticize conditions at home. A few have been involved in violent clashes with their countrymen at the opposite end of the political or ideological spectrum and have engaged in other illegal activities as well. Some have expressed criticism of the host country, whether for its support of unpopular policies in the migrants' home country or for other matters. Citizens of the host country have sometimes shown solidarity with such groups and participated in demonstrations organized by them.

Another example of the many linkages between the sending and receiving countries is the fact that a domestic political issue in a migrant-sending country can almost simultaneously become an item of discussion for the lawmakers in the receiving country. News about human rights violations in Turkey, for example, has traveled quickly to Germany through the migrants' associations and has been brought before the German Parliament by the Greens. Of course, one does not need migrants as transmission belts in order for human rights violations in one country to become matters of interest in another—recall, for example, U.S. policy during the Carter administration—but in Europe today there are many cases in which the presence of migrants is clearly the major reason for such attention.

### OFFICIAL AGREEMENTS
### AND CONTACTS

The history of the European labor migrations and the changing relationships between the home and host countries are mirrored in the nature of the agreements concluded between the different countries over the last three decades. The agreements of the 1950s and 1960s deal with relatively narrow concerns: the recruitment of workers, work contracts, travel to the host country, and sometimes housing. They were necessarily followed by further agreements concerning such matters as payment of health and accident benefits, retirement benefits, and so forth. As more and more migrants brought their families, and as some families' stays in the host countries grew longer and longer, new issues arose that called for cooperation or at least for some form of understanding between host and sending countries: the schooling of the migrants' children, and the nurturing of the migrants' cultural life in the host countries. Finally, there are some agreements from the 1970s and 1980s that deal with aid to the

sending countries either as a consequence of the presence of migrants in the host country or in some way connected with return migration. Delays by the sending countries in the implementation of some of these latter agreements, and the unilateral nature of the host countries' explicit return-incentive programs, are indications of the serious concern about large-scale returns on the part of the sending countries.

The recruitment of labor migrants was handled differently in the different host countries. For example, in Switzerland the process of recruitment itself was left to employers, while in Germany the state became involved in the recruitment process. Recruitment offices were established by the German government, in cooperation with home-country governments, in the capitals and in some of the provincial cities of the recruitment countries. With the exception of an office in Rome—which has remained open upon the specific request of the Italian government—the German recruitment offices were gradually closed after the recruitment stop of 1973. However, these offices had fulfilled not only the narrow function of facilitating recruitment, but they had been useful channels for a variety of communications on migration issues between the host and sending countries. Senior officials in the German Federal Labor Office today regret the loss of these channels, although certain alternative channels are, of course, available.

The recruitment agreements themselves have generally been allowed to expire. Even though those without expiration dates have not necessarily been revoked, they are de facto inoperative. Sweden has revoked all its agreements with the exception of that with Yugoslavia, which the Yugoslavs have insisted on keeping in force; however, there is no difference between Yugoslavia and other former recruitment countries with respect either to opportunities for further recruitment or to the treatment of migrants currently resident in Sweden.

There exist, of course, manifold contacts, at different governmental levels, between host and sending countries. Some of them are specific to countries involved in labor migrations, while others are the routine contacts between any pair of countries, but are affected by the existence of the migrant populations. The emigration countries' embassies and consulates have special responsibilities of attending to the needs of their citizens in the host countries and, to a greater or lesser degree, of monitoring these citizens' activities. There are contacts between labor ministries and between labor offices in pairs of countries. Sweden and Finland, members of the Common Nordic Labour Market, go as far as exchanging their labor office personnel. Social work organizations in the host countries—some of them officially government sponsored and others voluntary and in receipt of government support for their work—periodically send delegations to the sending countries or hold meetings there to increase their personnel's sensitivity to the migrants' cultures and particular needs. The volume and content of contacts between host and sending countries' trade unions are strongly influenced by the political situations of the sending countries at any given time.

In a few cases the old recruitment agreements have been explicitly substituted for by new agreements. An example is the 1977 "Agreement between the French Government and the Portuguese Government concerning the immigration and the situation of, and social assis-

tance to, Portuguese workers and their families in France,"[14] which replaced the orginal agreement of 1963. Lack of space does not permit a systematic comparison of the two documents, nor a comparison of the new Portuguese agreement with recent agreements between France and other emigration countries, but it is worth making two observations about the results of such comparisons and listing at least some of the topics covered by the 1977 document.

Far from the narrow emphasis on the recruitment process and the migrant's position as a worker in the new country, which was typical of the earlier agreement with Portugal, the new document deals in considerable detail with every step in a migrant's move, pays particular attention to all aspects of his or her life in the host country, and is permeated by an emphasis on the two countries' mutual responsibility in the implementation of its provisions. As compared with recent French agreements with other countries, it is far more specific concerning ways of facilitating the migrant's life in the host country, and it offers to Portuguese migrants specific advantages that are not universally available to migrants in France, for example, the application of Portuguese law concerning age of majority—21 years for females—in the admission of the migrants' children to the country; the possibility of Portuguese migrants' parents being included in family reunification; and a provision for Portuguese migrant workers to move into self-employment in trade and commerce.[15]

14. Ministère du Travail, Decree no. 77-496, *Journal officiel,* 17 May 1977. Most recently, EEC legislation has, of course, become applicable to the relationship between the two countries.

15. The following is a list of the major topics covered in the new French-Portuguese agreement:

The issues most frequently addressed today in the contacts between host and sending countries concern the migrants' cultural life, including the education and occupational training of the second and third generations, and various questions relating to return. It is not surprising that some of the cultural issues should be difficult and delicate, given the migrants' location in two cultures, the close connection that exists between culture and politics, the greater political freedom enjoyed by migrants in the host countries than in certain sending countries, and the wide spectrum of political views in some of the migrant populations.

Different approaches have been used in different host countries, and indeed in different parts of the same host country, to the teaching of migrants' native languages and cultures. The options range

---

recruitment, including transport, equal treatment with respect to work, social security, and the like; in-principle renewal of work permits even in the event of unemployment or long illness; facilitation of reentry after a migrant's return home for military service; family reunification, including family members' access to the labor market; transfers of migrants' savings to Portugal; the need to stem illegal entries and work; housing; information for migrants about their rights in France; use of bilingual personnel in administrative, social, and medical services; health education, including family planning; concern about migrants' mental health; accident prevention; treatment of Portuguese migrants in prisons; help to migrants and their families in adapting to French society and work, including teaching them the French language; joint decisions concerning occupational training for would-be returnees at the opportune time; cultural links with the home country, which are covered in great detail; Portuguese programs on French radio and television; literacy education in both languages; the education of migrant children, including special classes, normal classes, and Portuguese teachers; a mixed Portuguese-French commission to meet periodically to implement the agreement; and meetings of experts.

from national schools, on the one hand, to the study of native languages and cultures as a strictly extracurricular activity, on the other. Intermediate solutions include transition classes in the native languages, which students attend until they are ready to join the mainstream— with, however, the danger of extending these classes for too long—and the teaching of the migrants' languages and cultures as separate subjects in the regular curriculum.

Home countries have sought to influence the education of their citizens in various ways, and conflicts have arisen particularly in cases in which teachers and teaching materials were supplied by home countries the regimes of which embraced ideologies in conflict with those of the receiving countries. However, conflicts can arise also between migrants and the educational systems in the host countries, for a variety of cultural reasons. Dutch officials report, for example, that certain Muslim families have come into conflict with Dutch law by taking their daughters out of school when they reached puberty because only coeducational schools were available to them.

In recent years the circle has been completed, as the migrations have begun to affect, in turn, aspects of formal and informal education in the home countries. Second-generation migrants who return must now be integrated into the home-country schools. Selected Greek and Turkish schools have begun, on a modest level, to use German as the medium of instruction—the reverse of the transition classes established in the host countries. An experiment undertaken by Portuguese teachers working in rural Portugal for the Intergovernmental Committee on Migration is also of interest. In addition to teaching French language and culture to migrants' family members planning to leave France, they have recently added classes to acquaint nonmigrants with the ways of the country in which their relatives are settling and—using instruction in French cooking as a point of departure—to introduce these villagers to new practices of hygiene and nutrition.

Migrant groups' cultural activities in the host countries are not infrequently a source of controversy between the migrants and their home-country officials or between various migrant groups. Examples are radio and television broadcasts in the migrants' languages. The content of certain programs has elicited protestations from the home countries' ambassadors, but the host countries have upheld the migrants' freedom of speech. Concerts and poetry readings have also been used by migrants as vehicles of political protest.

A very difficult set of relationships between host and sending countries concerns matters involving return. Return-incentive schemes unilaterally devised by the host countries have met, predictably, with disapproval in the sending countries. Occasionally such disapproval has been explicitly expressed in the form of urgent advice to migrants not to utilize the benefits offered. Aid agreements that appeared to involve pressures or incentives for the return of migrants have often been left unimplemented through lack of response by home-country authorities. Among the examples are credits offered in the 1970s by Germany—and accepted in principle by Turkey—to further the Turkish workers' companies and related efforts, and offers in the 1980s by the Netherlands—and accepted in principle by Yugoslavia—to train Yugoslav workers in specific skills supposedly in short supply in

Yugoslavia. It is similarly revealing that before a large French firm was permitted to build subsidiaries in Spain and Portugal, it had to sign agreements promising that it would not employ return migrants in the new enterprises.

A question of considerable concern to the EEC today is Turkey's future relationship with the European Community. When an association treaty was signed in 1963, and an additional protocol was signed in 1970, policymakers in the host countries did not realize the extent of the pressure to migrate that was very quickly developing in Turkey, where there was a waiting list of over 1 million at the time of the recruitment stops. They also did not foresee the existence in Germany today of a community of over 1.5 million Turks, of whom almost one-half are under 20 years of age and whose rate of unemployment is the highest among all groups of foreigners in the country,[16] nor did they predict the repeated attempts in several host countries to stimulate returns. The association treaty has served to secure for Turkish migrants in Germany a somewhat more favorable status than is enjoyed by migrants from other non-EEC countries,[17] but as of November 1985 there was no expectation that free movement of labor between Turkey and the European Community would come about by December 1986, as intended by the association treaty. The question ulti-

16. In 1984 the rate of unemployment for Turks in Germany was 17.7 percent, as compared with an unemployment rate of 14.7 percent for all foreigners and 9.6 percent for the total population. Organization for Economic Cooperation and Development, *SOPEMI 1984* (1985), pp. 34–35.

17. Turkish migrants are granted a special work permit after four rather than five years of work, Turkish family members' waiting periods before entry into the labor market are somewhat shorter, and so forth.

mately comes down to whether Turkey will accept Germany's offers of quid pro quos—increased economic and military aid, and perhaps a further improvement in the status of Turkish citizens already in the country—for not insisting on a strict interpretation of the treaty, or whether Germany will in fact find itself in the position of breaking an official agreement.

The European countries have on their agendas today several other migration-related issues calling for international cooperation. It will suffice to mention two of them. The need to control illegal immigration, in all the countries here discussed,[18] comes into conflict with the value of open borders espoused by these countries, because of their tourist trade, among other reasons. Border controls are especially light in certain instances—for example, at the borders between the three Benelux countries. The traditional host countries stress that illegal immigration negatively influences the progress of integration of the legal migrants within their borders, and it is recognized that international cooperation is highly desirable, if not indeed essential, for the control of illegal movements.

A second issue calling for international cooperation, and one that has already spawned certain efforts in this respect, is the arrival in the European host countries of asylum seekers from ever farther

corners of the world. For example, France, Switzerland, Germany, and the Netherlands have recently experienced considerable inflows of asylum seekers from Sri Lanka. For some time these entries were being encouraged by the German Democratic Republic, which issued transit visas to supposed tourists arriving by air, even if they did not carry entry visas for their countries of destination. Now that an accommodation with the German Democratic Republic has been reached, inflows are nevertheless continuing through other paths. As authorities in the asylum countries are adjudicating the applicants' claims, a need for international cooperation has been recognized: there is a need to establish principles for dealing with applications from individuals who, before applying for asylum in one country, have spent considerable time in another asylum country; there is a need for mechanisms to detect cases of individuals' applying for asylum in two countries simultaneously; and—though this is seen as a more difficult problem—there is a need to establish identical criteria for the granting of asylum.

### COMMENTS AND CONCLUSIONS

The policies of foreign-worker employment of the 1960s have resulted in the settlement of millions of migrant families in the host countries by the 1980s. This settling process has not been a smooth one, nor is it complete, not only because of indecisions by some of the migrants—these are observed in classical immigration contexts as well—but because of ambiguities and limitations concerning the migrants' legal status.

Different host countries have responded differently to the profound

18. On illegal immigration to three Mediterranean sending countries, see S. Ricca, "Administering Migrant Workers in an Irregular Situation in Greece, Italy, and Spain," International Migration for Employment Working Paper no. 11E (Geneva: International Labour Office, 1984). For France, see an important report by a ministerial committee, Mission de liaison interministerielle pour la lutte contre les trafics de main-d'oeuvre, *Bilan de la lutte contre les trafics de main-d'oeuvre* (Paris: Documentation française, 1983).

changes that have occurred in their societies as a result of the migrations. Sweden has explicitly recognized its transformation from a relatively homogeneous society ethnically into a multiethnic one, not only as a result of the labor migrations from the Mediterranean, but also because of its liberal admission of refugees. Sweden also encourages a measure of multiculturalism. The Netherlands has incorporated a minorities policy that aims to support the incorporation into Dutch society of Mediterranean labor migrants and other immigrant groups, such as Moluccans and Surinamers, among others.

France and Germany have, in absolute numbers, the largest foreign populations. Policymakers in the two countries observe that certain nationalities are more difficult to integrate than others. The large cultural distance between them and the native populations is experienced by the migrants both directly and as reflected in the less friendly reception they receive from their hosts. Unilaterally formulated return-incentive schemes in both countries have been primarily aimed at these migrant groups, even though the incentives were advertised to all migrants, except where precluded by law or agreements, primarily EEC law. However, with respect to most other policies, France has been considerably more open to migrants than has Germany, as has most recently been evidenced by the two countries' differing policies toward citizenship and family reunification for the second generation.

Switzerland presents yet a different case. It is a country with a higher percentage of foreigners in its population than any of the other major host countries and with a far lower unemployment rate. It maintains a policy of continued admission of foreigners within a framework of stabilization—that is, a continued measured response to labor market demands—and strict rules concerning permanent residence and naturalization, and it has no need for experiments with obstacles to family members' entry into the labor market or with return incentives. A comparative study shows that the integration of foreign migrants into the host society, as indicated, for example, by occupational mobility and residential integration, is considerably further advanced in Switzerland than in Germany.[19]

Until this decade Italy was the only recruitment country that had a special position with respect to several host countries, due to its membership in the EEC; however, this special status was of relatively little significance as long as migration flows were high. Now three more southern European countries have joined the European Community, a development that has been of immediate benefit to their migrants in EEC countries and that will eventually allow free movement within the EEC for all their citizens. A further southern European expansion of the European Community is unlikely in the near future. The expansion that has occurred has now created two classes among the former recruitment countries. And, with the exception of Yugoslavia, whose migrants are being integrated relatively easily into the host societies, those sending countries that

19. Hans-Joachim Hoffmann-Nowotny and Karl-Otto Hondrich, eds., *Ausländer in der Bundesrepublik Deutschland und in der Schweiz* (Frankfurt: Campus Verlag, 1982). There remains, however, the important fact, which has been slighted in this article, that Switzerland has an additional, unintegrated foreign population: those seasonal migrants who spend the better part of a year in the country and who work in jobs that could as well be defined as permanent, rather than as seasonal.

have now come to be on the outs with respect to future migratory opportunities for their citizens are the same countries whose migrants are commonly perceived in the host countries as the most difficult to integrate.

The post-World War II labor migrations have created a myriad of connections between sending and receiving countries through the extended families that now span two or even more countries. In the sending countries, the migrations have raised the levels of awareness and information about the host countries and, through returning migrants, have increased the reservoir of speakers of host-country languages. These new language skills are being utilized in the tourist business. In general, there has been created in these countries a culture of migration. These developments at the level of individuals and families have necessarily been paralleled by an increase in the official links between the countries involved: a rapid expansion of the emigration countries' consular representation in the host countries; the increased utilization of existing institutional mechanisms at different governmental levels for contacts between pairs of countries, and the creation of new ones; a greater range of subjects discussed at such meetings; and increased attention paid by policymakers in one country to events in the other.

This article has attempted to illustrate and characterize some of the major facets of the transnational nexus of migration. It has used two foci: the migrants themselves and the official contacts between the countries. The vast monographic literature on the European labor migrations that is by now available has been almost exclusively devoted to the first subject; little attention has so far been paid to the international-relations aspects of the migrations, and a systematic, comprehensive analysis—quantitative as well as qualitative—of these phenomena is certainly still outstanding. Demographic analyses, assessments of the migrations' economic and social impacts, and descriptions of individual countries' migration policies are considerably more advanced than is our understanding of the migrations' impacts on various aspects of the political and economic relationships between the countries involved.

ANNALS, *AAPSS,* **485,** May 1986

# Migration and the Political Economy of the Welfare State

*By* GARY P. FREEMAN

ABSTRACT: National welfare states are compelled by their logic to be closed systems that seek to insulate themselves from external pressures and that restrict rights and benefits to members. They nonetheless fail to be perfectly bounded in a global economy marked by competition, interdependence, and extreme inequality. This article explores the consequences of transnational flows of labor both for the status of migrants who move to welfare states and for the viability of welfare states themselves. The consequences of migration for the fiscal and political stability of welfare states are discussed, and it is argued that migration has contributed to the Americanization of European welfare politics. It is concluded that the relatively free movement of labor across national frontiers exposes the tension between closed welfare states and open economies and that, ultimately, national welfare states cannot coexist with the free movement of labor.

*Gary P. Freeman is associate professor of government at the University of Texas, Austin. He graduated from Emory University in 1967 and received a doctorate in political science from the University of Wisconsin, Madison, in 1975. He is the author of* Immigrant Labor and Racial Conflict in Industrial Societies *(1979) and has published articles on the comparative politics of the welfare state in Europe and America. His research has been supported by grants from the National Endowment for the Humanities and the German Marshall Fund of the United States.*

NATIONAL welfare states are by their nature meant to be closed systems. The logic of the welfare state implies the existence of boundaries that distinguish those who are members of a community from those who are not. Yet the welfare state is necessarily at least partially open to its external environment. International trade, the mobility of capital, and especially the migration of labor continuously intrude on and challenge the endogenous nature of the welfare state. The development of the welfare state may be seen as a dialectic between the distributive logic of closure—mutual aid undertaken by members of a community according to socially defined conceptions of need—and the distributive logic of openness—treatment according to one's performance in the marketplace without regard to membership status or need.

### THE WELFARE STATE AS A CLOSED SYSTEM

The welfare state requires boundaries because it establishes a principle of distributive justice that departs from the distributive principles of the free market. The principle that—imperfectly—governs distribution in the welfare state is that of human need. It does not replace the market principle of distribution according to economic performance, but it significantly alters it by establishing a social minimum and broadening the sphere of collective consumption.[1] As Michael Walzer has observed, "The idea of distributive justice presupposes a bounded world within which distributions take place: a group of people committed to dividing, ex-

changing, and sharing social goods, first of all among themselves."[2]

The welfare state is a closed system because a community with shared social goods requires for its moral base some aspect of kinship or fellow feeling. The individuals who agree to share according to need have to experience a sense of solidarity that comes from common membership in some human community. But the concept of membership implies the existence of persons who are not members and who are, therefore, excluded from the process of sharing.

Historically, the welfare state developed hand in hand with the nation-state. Following Marshall, we may say that the eighteenth century saw the establishment of civil rights, the nineteenth century the establishment of political rights, and the twentieth century, social rights.[3] All of these rights emerged within the context of the particular national states that granted and protected them. Progress toward the recognition of basic human equality inside particular states has not been accompanied by similar developments within the international state system, which is marked by gross inequalities in power, wealth, and prestige between its component parts. Because of this it is possible for certain states to ensure a much wider and more generous array of rights, especially social rights, than others can afford. The enjoyment of these rights by the members of the most fortunate states—the protection of these privileges—requires that the less fortunate be excluded from their enjoyment. I do not mean to argue that the equality achieved inside the advanced welfare states is necessarily

1. Claus Offe, "Advanced Capitalism and the Welfare State," *Politics and Society*, 2:479-88 (1972).

2. Michael Walzer, *Spheres of Justice* (New York: Basic Books, 1983), p. 31.
3. T. H. Marshall, *Class, Citizenship, and Social Development* (New York: Doubleday, 1965).

based on or causes the backwardness and inequality in the rest of the world. All I want to suggest is that the preservation of the advantages of the welfare states entails limited access to their benefits.

The crucial political issue in a closed system is who is or is not a member. For most purposes, membership is synonymous with citizenship. Citizens are persons who live in a national territory by right and participate fully in its governance and mutual benefits. The law of citizenship always accords such rights to persons born in a country to parents who are citizens; sometimes it grants such rights to persons born in the country to foreign parents, or to children of nationals who are born abroad. Citizenship can also be acquired. It is in the specification of the circumstances under which citizenship—and thus full membership in the community—may be acquired by outsiders that all states confront the limits of their generosity and universalism.

All states control entry and exit and the distribution of citizenship. As Walzer puts it, "The restraint of entry serves to defend the liberty and welfare, the politics and culture of a group of people committed to one another and to their common life."[4] The welfare systems of national states recognize this fact. For all the universalism and generality that one finds in the language of the welfare state, there is usually an implicit acknowledgment that it applies only to citizens of that state. The Republican Constitution of 1793 in France, for example, proclaims that "public relief is a sacred debt. Society owes subsistence to citizens in misfortune." It is for citizens that the full range of rights, benefits, and

obligations is reserved, and only citizens can be assured of the continuing ability to claim benefits by right.

But the coincidence between citizenship and the right to welfare is not perfect. Within its boundaries the rhetoric of the welfare state is universal, but its practice is not. Even among citizens access to benefits is differentiated according to one's relationship to the labor force. Entitlements to pensions, jobless benefits, and medical insurance are linked to contributions paid on wages earned at work. Persons who are neither workers nor dependents of workers may be guaranteed protection as well, but it is almost always at a lower level and usually contingent on absence of means. The dual basis upon which benefits may be claimed has important consequences for migrant labor. It makes the exclusion of migrants from the protection of the welfare state difficult, but at the same time it fragments the beneficiary population into groups of citizens and noncitizens, workers and nonworkers.

Limitations on access to residence and citizenship are not the only manifestations of the closed character of welfare states. Becaue welfare states exist in an anarchic, dangerous, and competitive world of scarce resources, they must seek to encourage the flow of resources into their territory and discourage their loss. It is not an accident that state-sponsored social protection schemes first emerged in countries pursuing essentially mercantilist economic policies.[5] The same impulses that lay behind tariffs, subsidies, and other protectionist measures designed to preserve and enhance national wealth drive the effort to insulate national populations from the dis-

4. Walzer, *Spheres of Justice*, p. 39.

5. Gaston V. Rimlinger, *Welfare Policy and Industrialization in Europe, America, and Russia* (New York: John Wiley, 1971), pp. 14-18.

ruptions to their livelihoods caused by world business cycles. In this sense, the welfare state may be seen as the pursuit of protectionism by other means.

The welfare state, in summary, is inward looking. It seeks to take care of its own, and its ability to do so is premised on its ability to construct a kind of safe house in which to shelter its members from the outside world. Unfortunately, though the welfare state assumes boundedness, and requires it, it is in fact deeply implicated in the logic of the global political and economic order.

### THE WELFARE STATE
### IN OPEN ECONOMIES

National welfare states, whatever their internal principles, exist in a global political economy that is, on the one hand, increasingly interdependent and, on the other, divided into zones of sharply disparate conditions.[6] The national economies of the welfare states are structurally integrated into this larger system and engage in systematic exchanges with it. The openness of national economies poses enormous challenges to the viability and character of welfare states.

The key to understanding this problem lies in recognizing the wide inequality between benefits levels and socially determined living standards that exists among the welfare states themselves and between them and the outside world. These inequalities are themselves the source of some of the most serious problems emanating from the external environment. In any case, pressures from the international economy serve to disrupt

and threaten the privileges that the welfare states represent and that they want to protect. These may assume manifold forms.

All states are vulnerable in one way or the other to fluctuations in the level of economic activity in the global economy. Apart from the very largest economies, states can do little unilaterally to affect the international economic order. Instead, they are limited to efforts to adapt to it.[7] The extent to which this is possible is significantly determined by the degree to which the economy is dependent on international trade. The limited data available indicate a relatively positive impact of trade dependence on social spending in the advanced capitalist states.[8] Not only the proportion of an economy involved in trade, but the structure of trading relationships may have implications for the welfare state. Very extensive trade dependence may encourage the expansion of social spending, but between principal trading partners there is reason to believe that there will be pressures for benefit and spend-

6. Aristide R. Zolberg, "Contemporary Transnational Migrations in Historical Perspective: Patterns and Dilemmas," in *U.S. Immigration and Refugee Policy*, ed. Mary M. Kritz (Lexington, MA: Lexington Books, 1983), p. 36.

7. Stephen D. Krasner, "United States Commercial and Monetary Policy: Unravelling the Paradox of External Strength and Internal Weakness," in *Between Power and Plenty: Foreign Economic Policies of Advanced Industrial States*, ed. Peter J. Katzenstein (Madison: University of Wisconsin Press, 1979), p. 52; Assar Lindbeck, "Stabilization Policy in Open Economies with Endogenous Politicians," *American Economic Review*, 66:1-19 (1976).

8. David R. Cameron, "The Expansion of the Public Economy: A Comparative Analysis," *American Political Science Review*, 72:1243-61 (1978); Francis G. Castles and Robert D. McKinlay, "Public Welfare Provision, Scandinavia, and the Sheer Futility of the Sociological Approach to Politics," *British Journal of Political Science*, 9:157-71 (1979); Gary P. Freeman, "Social Security in One Country? Foreign Economic Policies and Domestic Social Programs" (Paper delivered at the Annual Meeting of the American Political Science Association, Chicago, 1983).

ing levels to converge in order to offset competitive advantages associated with differential labor costs.[9]

The freedom of capital to migrate across national borders may also place limits on the development of the welfare state since reformist efforts that are seen as excessive by capitalists may provoke capital flight to more congenial locales or temporary investment strikes until the government is brought to heel. Nor is it only the behavior of domestic capital that is pertinent. Foreign direct investment may be curtailed as well. Multinational commercial banks and international lending authorities often impose stringent conditions on governments that are perceived as too generous with the public treasure. All of the external constraints arising out of the international financial and credit markets may limit the possibilities of social democratic reforms in particular countries.

Each of the aspects of the global political economy that has been mentioned so far can be expected to have at least indirect effects on the welfare state. At the least they contribute to the general context within which welfare state policies are made. What is arguably the most important and directly relevant external economic factor from the point of view of the welfare state is foreign labor.

## LABOR MIGRATION AND THE SOCIAL WAGE

The migration of labor is a threat to the welfare state, but the very existence of inequality of benefits between states stimulates migration. The compensation workers receive for their labor is composed of two parts. The first is the direct money income and other fringe

benefits paid by the employer—the direct wage. The second is the range of benefits, protections, and rights workers receive indirectly from the state—the indirect wage. Countries differ significantly not only with respect to the level of real wages, but with respect to the level of the social wage and the proportion of the total wage that it contributes. The existence of a nationally differentiated social wage has crucial consequences for labor migration, consequences that are ultimately more lasting and profound than differences in real, direct wages.

Piore argues that "the critical factors governing the migration process are the social forces that differentiate the market for men from the market for shirts."[10] One of these social forces is the welfare state, an arrangement that asserts that human beings may not be treated as if they were commodities. Along with the high real, direct wages, the social wage is part of the package of compensation that exerts an attractive pull on workers in less prosperous societies, drawing them to the rich countries in anticipation of better lives.

But the welfare state does not simply attract migrants. The availability of its benefits to indigenous workers helps set in train the sequence of events that creates the demand of the receiving countries for migrant labor in the first place. The common claim that the advanced capitalist societies resorted to the importation of workers during the fifties and sixties because they were experiencing labor shortages ought to be greeted with a certain skepticism. The extent to which indigenous labor supplies are or are not adequate is at least

9. Freeman, "Social Security in One Country?"

10. Michael J. Piore, *Birds of Passage: Migrant Labor and Industrial Societies* (Cambridge: Cambridge University Press, 1979), p. 8.

partly politically determined. The ability of workers to organize to oppose capital-intensive modernization, production speedups, and shift work, and to avoid certain tasks altogether, contributes to employers' perceptions of labor scarcity. The availability of labor is a matter negotiated between capital and labor. The presence of such welfare state benefits as unemployment compensation, subsidized housing, and free medical care facilitates the refusal by national workers of certain tasks and their resistance to changes in the characteristics of the jobs they do accept. In the face of these problems, employers begin to look abroad.

Foreign labor is the only real alternative to the elimination of the privileges of the indigenous work force that depress the rate of accumulation. Employers are unable to take these privileges away form their employees, or in any case they find it easier to bring in new, more tractable workers. Indigenous workers, for their part, are unwilling to forfeit their privileged position and, therefore, engage in a tacit form of collusion with employers importing labor.

Thus the guest-worker system is born. Temporary labor is preferred by both employers and unions. Migration addresses the problems caused by welfare state constraints on the flexibility of the labor market only if the new workers are excluded from the exercise of welfare state rights. For a variety of reasons, permanent family immigration for settlement is much less profitable from the receiving country's perspective and more threatening to its citizen-workers than temporary migration. Permanent immigrants would either claim or hope to claim eventually all the rights of citizenship in the welfare state. Temporary migrants can be refused such rights to an important extent.

The importance of welfare benefits in the calculations of policymakers considering a guest-worker scheme cannot be overemphasized. Imagine a state with no social wage at all. The entire income of workers is earned from wages paid by their employers. If these wages are interrupted, the worker must fall back on private means. In such a laissez-faire state, employers would, if they could, import labor beyond the requirements of the labor market in order to relieve wage pressure, create a reserve army of the unemployed, and reduce the advantages that flow to organized workers in tight labor markets.[11] The state might acquiesce in such a policy until the idle workers created a threat to public order, but neither employers nor state policymakers would have any strictly economic motives for limiting immigration. From the employers' point of view, the more the merrier.

In a welfare state, however, the situation is very different. Unemployment simply transfers the burden of maintaining workers from employers to the state in the form of unemployment and other benefits. This is why states have always been ahead of employers in moving to limit entry and to create strictly regulated guest-worker programs that tie the right of residence to the possession of a job. Temporary migration appeals to state decision makers because it eases the burden of the welfare state budget. The principal allies of the state in changing a laissez-faire immigration policy into a guest-worker system are indigenous workers.

In the absence of legal restrictions on continued residence after one has lost one's job, migrants would have power-

11. On the dynamics of labor markets and the power of organized labor, the classic analysis is Michal Kalecki, "Political Aspects of Full Employment," *Political Quarterly,* 14:322-31 (1943).

ful incentives to stay on even if they were unemployed. Zolberg summarizes this dynamic in the following manner:

The collective good component of income helps explain why the tendency to move from poor to rich countries is somewhat independent of given labor market conjuncture in the place of destination, why the supply of foreign labor tends always to outrun the demand for it, why many who set out as migrants strive to become immigrants, and especially why, in the final analysis, all relatively advantaged countries must adopt restrictive immigration policies to protect their advantages.[12]

The truth of this claim is self-evident. Imagine, once again, a country with no welfare provisions at all. Migrants are attracted by jobs and higher real wages. As they become unemployed in large numbers during recessions, however, there would be severe economic pressures for them to go home. These would be reinforced by social and cultural factors. One might think that it would still be better for a Turkish worker to be unemployed in Germany than in Turkey. But from the point of view of the Turk it is not at all clear that this is the case. Without the welfare state, Germany would lose whatever charm it now holds for unemployed migrants. The difficult language, the strange and unfamiliar culture, the unpalatable diet, the discrimination, the separation from relatives and friends, and the absence of the simple means of subsistence that a largely agrarian society provides would drive the migrant back home. It is the welfare state, above all else, that keeps the migrant abroad in hard times.

The relationship between the welfare state in open economies and transnational labor flows is complex and contradictory. The welfare state constitutes a part

of the higher standard of living that attracts migrants. Its benefits contribute to the ability of workers to engineer the labor market shortages that are the immediate condition that both stimulates and justifies migration. The desire to preserve the advantages of the indigenous work force and to ease the pressure on the state budget lead labor and the state to support a guest-worker system of temporary migration. But the availability of the social wage helps turn temporary migrants into permanent immigrants.

### MIGRATION AND WELFARE STATE BUDGETS

It is easy to construct an argument demonstrating that migration has made a positive contribution to receiving countries in postwar Europe. Unfortunately, it is just as easy to build a case against immigration, particularly on grounds that the long-run costs outweigh the benefits. Much depends on the factors one chooses to include in the analysis.[13] This leads me to conclude that any cost-benefit approach to immigration at the most general level of analysis is not feasible. It is much more practical, however, to talk about the more direct and limited impact of migration on particular social and economic groups and sectors. My comments here will be limited to the effects of migration on the welfare states in Western Europe in the postwar period.

We can identify three distinct phases in the postwar migration, the exact dates varying from country to country. The first phase involved the bulk of

12. Zolberg, "Contemporary Transnational Migrations," p. 37.

13. Ibid., p. 47. Cf. E. J. Mishan, "Does Immigration Confer Economic Benefits on the Host Country?" in *Economic Issues in Immigration* (London: Institute of Economic Affairs, 1970), pp. 89-122.

primary migration by single young people for work. This came to an end around 1973 and 1974, coincidentally with the onset of world recession, as restrictions on labor migration were imposed by almost all the Western European countries. Phase two was marked by family reunification as those workers already abroad sought to bring in their dependents. In some cases total immigration rates declined hardly at all during this period and governments gradually whittled down the rights of reunification as a result. The third phase, just under way, is that of permanent settlement.[14] The impact of migration on the welfare state will be different in each stage of this process. I will discuss the net impact of migration in its temporary and family-reunification phases on (1) the financial stability of welfare state programs and (2) the political and ideological consensus that supports the welfare state.

There can be little doubt that in the phase of temporary migration the welfare state is a net beneficiary. The sociodemographic characteristics of a temporary migration for work, whether it is largely spontaneous, organized by employers, or strictly controlled by the state, will ensure that more is paid in taxes than is taken out in services. Temporary migrants are usually male, single, young, and relatively healthy. They arrive as adults, relieving the host country of the costs of raising them from birth to working age. As a whole they have a much higher activity rate and a lower dependency ratio than the indigenous population. They are much less likely to need or to utilize the various services of the welfare state than are native workers.[15]

The chief benefits that temporary migrants might seek out include (1) special reception and orientation programs on arrival; (2) housing built for them or access to subsidized social housing; (3) health services; (4) family allowances; and (5) unemployment benefits. All receiving countries have made some effort to provide a modicum of aid to arriving migrants, but there is no evidence that this has anywhere been a very costly operation. Much of the most useful work in this regard is done by voluntary agencies only partly funded by the state, and large numbers of migrants have routinely slipped through the net of reception programs by entering a country spontaneously or irregularly. Moreover, reception services are often paid for out of revenues derived from the migrants themselves, as will be discussed later.

Lack of adequate housing has perhaps been the single most persistent and controversial problem related to the issue of social services for migrants. The sprawling and shabby *bidonvilles* that spring up around centers of migrant employment are testimony to the fact that far from all migrants are settled in state-subsidized housing. The practice of building dormitory-style accommodations for single workers has never managed to cope with the majority of migrants; and, in any case, much of the cost of such housing is met by employers.[16] Access to the regular social hous-

Godula Kosack, *Immigrant Workers and Class Structure in Western Europe* (London: Oxford University Press, 1973), pp. 50-56; Albano Cordeiro, *Pourquoi l'immigration en France?* (Creteil: Office municipal des migrants, 1981), pp. 88-103.

16. Castles and Kosack, *Immigrant Workers,* pp. 240-317; *Le logement des migrants* (Paris: Société d'édition, 1973); Ray C. Rist, *Guestworkers in Germany: The Prospects for Pluralism* (New

14. Stephen Castles, *Here for Good: Western Europe's New Ethnic Minorities* (London: Pluto Press, 1984), pp. 11-15.

15. Ibid., pp. 96-125; Stephen Castles and

ing that serves the indigenous population has normally been severely restricted either by requiring migrants to queue up behind nationals already on the waiting lists or by imposing quotas on migrant concentrations in housing projects in order to avoid crossing what has been called the threshold of tolerance.[17] The common explanation that governments have used to excuse the inadequacy of migrant housing arrangements—that the migrants' desire to save makes them reluctant to purchase the decent accommodations that are available—is probably more accurate than critics have been willing to concede. The combination of all these factors would suggest that though migrants have surely exacerbated shortages in the low-income housing market, they have not generated large state expenditures on new housing.[18]

Migrants might well utilize health and hospital services at a rate equal to or greater than that of the indigenous population of the same age, because they tend to work in sectors of the economy associated with large numbers of accidents and work-related illnesses. Available evidence, though inadequate for a confident conclusion, indicates that at worst temporary migrants cost the health services about the same per capita as nationals.[19]

Family allowances are one program that potentially could be extremely beneficial even to temporary migrants. Average family size is much greater among migrants than among the host population. Bilateral agreements negotiated between host and sending countries have provided for the payment of family allowances, even if the dependents remain in the home country. Potentially, such an arrangement could constitute a huge drain on the resources of family allowance funds since migrants would pay contributions on relatively low incomes but derive benefits for relatively large families. This outcome is avoided, however, by reducing the payments to dependents abroad in some rough proportion to the differences in living standards between sending and receiving countries. This scheme has meant that family allowance programs have realized a sizable windfall from migration. A part, but only a part, of this windfall is devoted to other services for migrants.[20]

In a strict guest-worker system, unemployment benefits are no problem at all. Migrants who lose their jobs will find that their work permits will not be renewed when they expire. They will have strong incentives to find other jobs rather than draw jobless benefits. Moreover, in an authentic temporary migration, workers who have difficulty finding work simply go back home since the thing that took them abroad in the first place—the promise of a job—has disappeared.[21]

York: Praeger, 1978), pp. 149-58; Mark J. Miller and Philip L. Martin, *Administering Foreign-Worker Programs: Lessons from Europe* (Lexington, MA: Lexington Books, 1982), pp. 77-78.

17. Gary P. Freeman, *Immigrant Labor and Racial Conflict in Industrial Societies: The French and British Experience, 1945-1975* (Princeton, NJ: Princeton University Press, 1979), pp. 157-61; Francoise Briot and Gilles Verbunt, *Immigrés dans la crise* (Paris: Editions ouvrières, 1981), pp. 165-71.

18. Cordeiro, *Pourquoi l'immigration,* pp. 66-68.

19. Ibid., pp. 88-93; Castles and Kosack, *Immigrant Workers,* pp. 318-340.

20. Cordeiro, *Pourquoi l'immigration,* pp. 93-95; Jean-Pierre Garson and Georges Tapinos, *L'argent des immigres: Revenus, epargne et transferts de huit nationalités immigrées en France* (Paris: Presses universitaires de France, 1981), pp. 15-18; Freeman, *Immigrant Labor,* pp. 78-79, 170-71.

21. Gregory C. Schmid, "Foreign Workers and Labor Market Flexibility," *Journal of Common Market Studies,* 9:246-53 (1971); Castles, *Here for*

The single most expensive income maintenance item—pensions—surely enjoys a positive cash flow in this period. Migrants pay social security contributions but few become old enough to retire or work long enough to collect full benefits. If they go home to retire, they may fail to apply for benefits altogether; and if they die, their survivors are even less likely to bother.[22] In summary, so long as a migration is essentially temporary, the fiscal condition of welfare state programs will at the very least be undamaged and most likely be significantly improved.

The problem with the guest-worker system from the point of view of the host state is that it tends to break down. Potential migrants evade its regulatory apparatus and find employers willing to assist them. Unemployed migrants elect to stay on in the hope of future employment or to consume the services available to the unemployed. Some migrants become legal citizens; others become de facto permanent residents. As temporary migration turns into permanent settlement, the desire to be reunited with one's family becomes overwhelming. Family immigration changes the financial picture of the welfare state in significant ways. By reducing the differences between migrants and nationals, family immigration tends to eliminate the fiscal bonuses that temporary migration brought with it. Moreover, by dramatically changing the sociodemographic structure of the immigrant population, it probably contributes to the immigrant population's becoming or tending to become a net drain on many welfare state programs, such as those concern-

ing education, medical care, housing, family allowances, and unemployment.

This is a broad and, to the extent that it cannot be satisfactorily documented, outrageous generalization, but it stands to reason. Large numbers of low-income families with numerous dependents will be net consumers in the welfare state or the whole rationale and structure of the social services is badly askew.

There is, however, at least one crucial exception to this conclusion. The age structure of immigrants is such as to make the ratio of working to retired persons among them higher than that for the indigenous population.[23] This will make immigrants net contributors to state pension programs for the foreseeable future. To the degree that their children continue the practice of having large families, this benefit might last indefinitely. The worsening dependency ratio associated with societal aging is one of the principal sources of the long-range financial problems of state pension systems. Immigration is the most direct and efficient remedy available. Because pensions are such a large part of the financial crisis of the welfare state, the immigrants' effect on a society's dependency ratio is not a matter to be taken lightly.

### THE AMERICANIZATION OF EUROPEAN WELFARE POLITICS

The very inconclusiveness of attempts to assess the economic and fiscal effects of migration suggests that migration's political consequences might ultimately be more important. One is free to believe more or less what one wishes about the economic impact of migration because the facts are so much in dispute.

Good, pp. 143-49; Cordeiro, *Pourquoi l'immigration*, pp. 71-77.

22. Cordeiro, *Pourquoi l'immigration*, pp. 93-98.

23. Castles, *Here for Good*, pp. 96-125.

From the perspective of the politics of the welfare state, however, there can be no doubt that migration has been little short of a disaster. It has reduced the political clout of those social strata that have traditionally been the chief source of support for welfare state development, and it has contributed to the erosion of the political consensus on which the welfare state rests. It has led to the Americanization of European welfare politics.

The entry of large numbers of ethnically diverse, racially distinct workers to take socially inferior jobs has profoundly altered the European working class and has shifted the balance of welfare state politics. This process has many nuances and subtleties, but the most significant seem to be the following. Widespread migration has reduced the power of organized labor by dividing the working class into national and immigrant camps, by easing the tight labor market conditions that would have enhanced labor's strategic resources, and by provoking a resurgence of right-wing and nativist political movements.

One of the strongest generalizations that can be made about the origins and growth of the welfare state is that where trade unions and social democratic parties are strong, the welfare state has thrived.[24] Anything that reduces the political strength of social democratic forces will tend to undermine support for the welfare state. Migrant labor has tended to threaten welfare state support by breaking the unity of labor movements. Weak labor movements are generally found in those countries that are

ethnically heterogeneous.[25] The most notable example is, of course, the United States, where racial divisions have historically vitiated the efforts of the labor movement to push for social reform. By making racially diverse societies out of previously homogeneous ones, migration has complicated social and political cleavages.

The presence of large numbers of migrants helped ease relatively tight labor market conditions in the sixties and early seventies. Given the association between labor market conditions and the propensity and ability of labor to press its interests, this plausibly diminished social democratic pressure during the greatest expansionary period in modern times. When this era came to an end in 1974, the migrants absorbed a major share of the burden of unemployment, either by being exported or by losing their jobs in large numbers.[26] This is true even though the tendency of migrants to become permanent residents has reduced their role as a buffer against domestic unemployment. A little-noticed but potentially crucial consequence of the countercyclical role of migrants is that by making relatively high levels of unemployment tolerable, it has contributed to the establishment of a dangerous precedent: the smashing of the full-employment norm that has been in effect since the end of the war.

Michael Walzer observes that open borders have traditionally been accompanied by closed neighborhoods.[27] Post-

24. Michael Shalev, "The Social Democratic Model and Beyond: Two 'Generations' of Comparative Research on the Welfare State," in *The Welfare State, 1883-1983*, ed. Richard F. Tomasson (Greenwich, CT: JAI Press, 1983), pp. 315-52.

25. John Stephens, *The Transition from Capitalism to Socialism* (London: Macmillan, 1979), p. 111.

26. Schmid, "Foreign Workers and Labor Market Flexibility"; Castles, *Here for Good*, pp. 143-49; Cordeiro, *Pourquoi l'immigration*, pp. 71-77.

27. Walzer, *Spheres of Justice*, p. 38.

war migration in Europe has stimulated an outburst of reactionary, nativist, and sometimes neofascist political activity, as native workers organize to resist the invaders. Immigration and the race issue have given the political Right materials with which to appeal to voters and to bash the Left. In few instances have such extremist groups had much visible success, but they have profoundly affected the terms of political discourse in Europe. Enoch Powell fairly dominated British politics for a number of years; Schwarzenbach shaped the political agenda in Switzerland for a decade; Le Pen remains a visible and increasingly potent figure on the French scene.[28]

These movements have helped shift the ideological center of European politics to the right. The threat they represent has both pushed more traditional conservatives to move against immigration and made them seem all the more reasonable when they have done so. They have succeeded in identifying the Left with an unpopular and alien minority. The social democratic parties and trade unions, which, as I have argued, tacitly collaborated in the formation of immigrant minorities, are now caught in a pincers' movement: attacked from the right for coddling immigrants, they are also criticized from within their own ranks for being insufficiently stout in the defense of immigrant rights. The Left is in a no-win situation. The immigration crisis is a problem the Left did not need and cannot easily handle and it has greatly exacerbated the already serious dilemmas the Left faces.

Quite apart from the role of the labor movement, immigration has tended to

28. Freeman, *Immigrant Labor*, pp. 259-307; Zig Layton-Henry, *The Politics of Race in Britain* (London: George Allen & Unwin, 1984); Castles, *Here for Good*, pp. 190-212.

erode the more general normative consensus on which the welfare state is built. Welfare state benefits are now for the first time associated in the public mind with a visible and subordinate minority. This, more than any other factor, explains the rancorous and unpleasant conflict that has so long disfigured the politics of welfare in the United States. When the welfare state is seen as something for "them" paid for by "us," its days as a consensual solution to societal problems are numbered. The injection of race into European welfare politics has already produced a coarsening of public discussion and bodes ill for the future of the welfare state in a time of severe fiscal stress.

CONCLUSION

The welfare state asserts the distributive principle of mutual aid according to need against the distributive principle of the marketplace. In this sense, the welfare state represents an imperfect but important structural transformation of capitalism. Most critics of the welfare state have been preoccupied with the internal contradictions and limits of welfare state programs and rhetoric. These are, however, much less profound than the disjuncture between the logic of the welfare state's internal relations and that of its external relations.

The distributive logic of the welfare state extends only to members. Outside national borders, the dynamics of global economic competition proceed unabated. The sharp discontinuity between the internal and external logics of the welfare state is acutely exposed precisely at its national borders when outsiders seek admission. Foreign workers demonstrate the extent to which the distributive principle of mutual aid according to need is viable only so long as it is restricted to members. Migration illustrates both the logically closed character of the welfare state and the difficulty with which that closure is maintained.

ANNALS, *AAPSS*, 485, May 1986

# Policy Ad-Hocracy: The Paucity
# of Coordinated Perspectives and Policies

*By* MARK J. MILLER

ABSTRACT: Postwar Western European foreign-worker policies generally evolved in an ad hoc, piecemeal fashion and were characterized by a lack of long-term planning and coordination with emigrant-sending countries. In some instances official immigration policies were poorly implemented or unenforced, and therefore unofficial, de facto policies emerged. In other cases official assumptions concerning postwar labor migration persisted long after they had been shown to be inadequate, contributing to inconsistencies between declared and de facto policies. Policy ad-hocracy arose from the disjuncture between official and de facto policies, from an inability to foresee the outcomes of policy decisions and subsequently to harmonize public policies with the unplanned situations that developed, as well as from the poor adaptation of sovereign states to transnational policy processes. Immigration policy ad-hocracy resulted in largely unplanned settlement and persisting policy dilemma or malaise. Specific examples are examined in France, Switzerland, and the Federal Republic of Germany to illustrate the general patterns and to suggest some significant variations across national contexts.

*Mark J. Miller is an associate professor of political science at the University of Delaware and an assistant editor of the* International Migration Review. *He received undergraduate and graduate degrees from the University of Wisconsin, Madison. He is the author of* Foreign Workers in Western Europe: An Emerging Political Force *(1981); coauthor of* Administering Foreign Worker Programs: Lessons from Europe *(1982); and coeditor of* The Unavoidable Issue: U. S. Immigration Policy in the 1980s *(1983). Since 1983, Miller has served as the U.S. correspondent to the Continuous Reporting System on Migration, the Organization for Economic Cooperation and Development's committee of immigration experts.*

THE Western European immigration dilemma arises in part from factors outside the control of any single government. Global imbalances in population growth, job-creation capabilities, capital flows, and political stability have created migratory pressures that affect most industrial democracies. Nonetheless, Western Europe's dilemma is largely one of its own making. The European malaise over immigration is a legacy of deliberate decisions to recruit foreign labor. Foreign workers and their dependents are now frequently blamed for a variety of sociopolitical and economic ills. They have become scapegoats for postwar migration policies gone awry.

For reasons of parsimony, the scope of this article will be limited to the Federal Republic of Germany, France, and Switzerland. Together, these countries received well over half of Western Europe's total postwar labor migration. Comparison of the three countries involves important contextual variations, such as colonial relationships and membership in the European Community, the presence or absence of which have marked the evolution of foreign labor policies in individual states in different ways. The intent here is to illustrate patterns of problems in policy formation and implementation that led ultimately to fundamental policy incoherences and contradictions. These policy shortcomings are a much more appropriate focus for blame for the immigration malaise than are the immigrants themselves. Immigrants and indigenous Western Europeans alike have become victims of labor-recruitment policies flawed by unwarranted assumptions, inadequate coordination and implementation, and perhaps, too, by the myopia of employers' interests.

## THE HISTORICAL CONTEXT

Postwar labor migration began in a climate marked by the cataclysm of World War II and the lingering trauma of the Great Depression. All three countries had well-developed traditions of labor immigration.[1] Indeed, the use of foreign workers was a structural or permanent feature of Western European labor markets by the interwar period, if not earlier.[2]

France, in particular, massively recruited foreign labor in the interwar period.[3] Labor recruitment was organized by employers, but the government increasingly intervened. By 1931, the Ministry of Labor could publish a tome of international conventions signed by France relative to the immigration and treatment of foreign labor.[4]

Wartime population losses heightened long-standing French fears of demographic insufficiency. Several studies and commissions convinced the post-Liberation coalition government of the need for massive immigration. The noted demographer Alfred Sauvy suggested that France needed over 5 million immigrants to restore demographic equilibrium.[5] In 1945, the National Immigra-

1. Stephen Castles and Godula Kosack, *Immigrant Workers and Class Structure in Western Europe* (London: Oxford University Press, 1973), pp. 15-25.

2. See, for example, Raphael-Emmanuel Verhaeren, *Crise et migrations internationales*, CORDES monograph (Grenoble: Institut de recherche économique et de planification du développement, 1980), pp. 8, 16-23.

3. Gary S. Cross, *Immigrant Workers in Industrial France* (Philadelphia: Temple University Press, 1983).

4. Ministère du travail, *Recueil de conventions internationales relatives a l'immigration et au traitement de la main-d'oeuvre étrangère en France* (Paris: Imprimerie nationale, 1931).

5. Alfred Sauvy, "Evaluation des besoins de l'immigration française," *Population*, 1(1):95 (Jan.-Mar. 1946).

tion Office (ONI) was established and was granted a monopoly over immigration policies.

The French desire for immigration on demographic grounds contrasted with the German and Swiss situations. Neither the Swiss nor the West Germans could envisage permanent immigration. In all three countries, what Sauvy might have termed Malthusian preoccupations and vivid memories of the Great Depression created an atmosphere hostile to the introduction of foreign labor. These attitudes mitigated pro-immigration sentiment on demographic grounds in the French case.[6]

The term *Ueberfremdung*, connoting a malaise caused by too many aliens in Switzerland, had been coined before World War I. Swiss authorities regarded the labor shortages that became manifest in the immediate postwar period as strictly conjunctural.[7] In 1948, a bilateral labor treaty was signed with Italy, authorizing temporary admission for employment purposes on very restrictive permits.

In the western zones of post-World War II Germany enormous unemployment and the mistreatment of foreign labor under the Nazis simply ruled out consideration of immigration in the immediate postwar period. A large influx of Germans from the east continued until 1961. In 1955, the Federal Republic signed an accord with Italy, authorizing seasonal employment in agriculture and construction. Although the overall unemployment rate in the Federal Republic was 5.1 percent in 1955, the then

minister for economics, Ludwig Erhardt, feared that wage increases for agricultural workers in the early 1950s presaged general wage inflation. Erhardt agreed with German employers, over the objections of the German union representing farm worker interests,[8] that foreign labor was needed.

It is important to note that postwar labor recruitment was regulated from the outset by bilateral labor treaties. The League of Nations labor adjunct had proposed a convention concerning foreign labor in 1939, and its successor, the International Labor Organization, adopted Convention 97 and Recommendation 86 pertaining to migrant labor in 1949, encouraging regulation on the basis of bilateral accords.[9] Bilateral agreements guaranteeing equality of treatment and pay for foreign workers helped to placate trade union fears. The initial German and Swiss postwar labor agreements reflected the prevailing assumption that the foreign-labor phenomenon would be temporary and small scale. The legal status of the foreign workers themselves was short-term and revocable in the event of recession, something that was seen as inevitable.

France differed in that it also planned for permanent immigration on demographic grounds. The French clearly hoped to attract assimilable immigrants from nearby, predominantly Catholic societies. They planned for immigration from Italy and, to a lesser extent, from the Iberian peninsula, but ended up with

6. Louis Chevalier, "Bilan d'une immigration," *Population*, 5(1):131-33 (Jan.-Mar. 1950).

7. Denis Maillat, "L'immigration en Suisse. Evolution de la politique d'immigration et consequences economiques," in *Les travailleurs étrangers en Europe occidentale*, ed. Philippe Bernard (Paris: Mouton, 1976), pp. 105-10.

8. Knuth Dohse, *Ausländische Arbeiter und buergerlicher Staat* (Königstein/Ts.: Anton Hain, 1981), pp. 147-49.

9. J.H. Lasserre-Bigorry, "Réglementations internationales concernant les migrations clandestines," in *Les travailleurs étrangers et le droit international*, ed. Société française pour le droit international (Paris: Editions A. Pedone, 1979), p. 134.

large foreign population groups often considered unassimilable.[10]

Ambivalence over immigration goals and poor execution of plans and administrative structures conceived in the 1945-47 period fostered the development of ad hoc procedures that characterized French immigration policy until the 1970s. These procedures—in particular the routine legalization of migrants with technically irregular statuses—undercut official efforts to organize immigration and fostered uncontrolled entry and residence.

### THE FRANCO-ITALIAN IMMIGRATION ACCORDS OF 1947

The Communist minister of labor in the postwar French government, Ambroise Croizat, became a key governmental actor in the elaboration of policy principles and administrative procedures that were to guide postwar immigration policy.[11] In many respects policies enunciated in the 1945-47 period closely mirrored positions embraced by left-wing parties and unions during the 1930s.[12] The creation of ONI gave the government—rather than employers—control over labor recruitment. A tripartite ONI advisory commission was to ensure evenhanded application of policy. Foreign workers were to be guaranteed equality of pay and working conditions along with a host of legal and social protections. Labor recruitment was to be regulated on the basis of bilateral

accords, to protect the interests of all concerned parties.

The Franco-Italian immigration accord of 1947, which was preceded by a more limited 1946 agreement and which was somewhat revised in 1948, was to translate the plans, principles, and recommendations formulated in the post-Liberation period into practice.[13] On the basis of the law of 2 November 1945, which created ONI, employers were to recruit foreign labor only through ONI. In conjunction with labor officials, ONI was to ascertain whether employers' requests for foreign labor were justified; and it charged a fee for each foreign worker placed.[14] Employers were required to have adequate lodging available to receive foreign labor.

Signature of the 1946 and 1947 accords took place in the context of fairly extensive, illegal or irregular Italian migration into France.[15] Italian labor traditionally played an important role in construction and agriculture in southeastern France and in mining and heavy industry in eastern France. In 1946, the problem of illegal entry was regarded as sufficiently serious to warrant adoption of four governmental measures designed specifically to combat it, including *refoulement* ("expulsion"), a legalization procedure, and the imposition of sanctions against employers of irregular-status migrants.[16]

Implementation of the 1947 accord was frustrated by employers' resistance to a recruitment system that limited employers' hiring flexibility in order to safeguard against exploitation of for-

10. Georges Tapinos, *L'immigration etrangère en France, 1946-1973* (Paris: Presses universitaires de France, 1975), pp. 18-19.

11. Andre Vieuguet, *Français et immigrés* (Paris: Editions sociales, 1975), pp. 123-25.

12. Ibid., pp. 115-17; Leon Gani, *Syndicats et travailleurs étrangers* (Paris: Editions sociales, 1972), pp. 23-24.

13. See *Population,* 2(2):398-401 (Apr.-June 1947).

14. Gani, *Syndicats et travailleurs étrangers,* pp. 35-36.

15. Ibid., p. 40.

16. Chevalier, "Bilan d'une immigration," p. 134.

eign labor and adverse effects on French labor. Trade unions complained of employer "sabotage" of the 1947 accords through hiring of technically irregular-status migrants.[17] Employers complained that ONI recruitment procedures were cumbersome and insufficiently responsive to their needs.

Initially, French employers and their agents were not allowed to play an active role in the recruitment process. All recruitment was done by so-called anonymous requests that required an employer to pay a fee of Fr 6000 for a worker of unknown quality who might leave the job after a short period of time.[18] Apparently many Italian workers admitted for employment in specific occupations illegally took other jobs. This caused some social tension as did disputes between French and Italian workers in the construction industry.[19]

The 1948 revision of the accords gave employers and their agents a right to recruit in Italy and to make requests by name for specific individuals.[20] This seemed to improve the functioning of ONI, which Chevalier described as "broken in" by late 1948. But it also raised problems from the Italian perspective and from the standpoint of regulation, since it enabled French employers to pick and choose workers, whereas Italy had an interest in regulating who left. Like other countries of emigration, Italy wanted to facilitate emigration of the unemployed and the underem-

ployed. Requests by name tended to undermine control and to foster irregular migration. They were, according to Sauvy, "a half-opened door which can be opened further."[21]

Despite some apparent improvement in the functioning of ONI from the standpoint of employers by 1948, employers increasingly ignored ONI procedures.[22] Widespread illegal migration and the legalization procedure undercut attempts to regulate migration as stipulated by the accords. Many employers apparently preferred irregular-status workers and would retain them despite the availability of legal foreign workers. Illegal entry followed by legalization became a way to cut red tape from the point of view of employers. By 1950, serious consideration was given to calls to eliminate ONI.

Implementation of the treaties was further undermined as employers often interpreted regulations in either an excessively strict or a very loose sense.[23] For example, the guarantee of equal pay to alien workers in the construction industry could be honored in principle by paying alien workers the set minimum wage but violated in practice by denying to aliens the premiums and bonuses accorded French workers. Since bonuses comprise an important part of a French construction worker's overall compensation, employers could realize substantial savings through hiring foreign labor.

The inability of the French government to implement the 1946 and 1947 accords meant that many of the social and legal protections guaranteed for-

17. Gani, *Syndicats et travailleurs étrangers*, p. 37.

18. Alfred Sauvy, "Besoins et possibilités de l'immigration en France," part two, *Population* 5(3):423 (July-Sept. 1950).

19. Chevalier, "Bilan d'une immigration,"p. 139; Gani, *Syndicats et travailleurs étrangers*, p. 46.

20. Chevalier, "Bilan d'une immigration," p. 136.

21. Sauvy, "Besoins et possibilités de l'immigration en France," p. 423.

22. Ibid., p. 423.

23. Gani, *Syndicats et travailleurs étrangers*, pp. 37-38.

eign labor in principle were denied them in practice. Underneath the veneer of official policy that was enunciated in bilateral agreements and law arose an unofficial but tolerated policy of laissez-faire immigration. Between 1948 and 1981, 1.4 million, or 60 percent, of the 2.35 million legally admitted aliens in France—not including Algerians and sub-Saharan Africans—would receive their permits through post hoc legalization.[24]

The early shortcomings of postwar French immigration policy, as illustrated in the case of the Franco-Italian accord of 1947, had deleterious short-term and long-term consequences. The influx of Italian workers was followed by waves of foreign workers from other countries. In most cases, bilateral agreements also regulated their entry. But the pattern of poor policy implementation and of ad hoc solutions, first discernible in the experience with the Franco-Italian accords, persisted. In particular, legal provisions pertaining to conditions of foreign-worker entry and the housing of foreign workers were routinely ignored. French employers were able to hire foreign labor virtually at will.

Switzerland and the Federal Republic never legalized illegal workers, nor did they have problems of policy implementation to the degree experienced by the French. Immigration ad-hocracy in the German and Swiss cases stemmed mainly from the disjuncture between policies based on the promise of temporariness and the reality of de facto immigration or long-term settlement.

## THE 1964 ITALO-SWISS LABOR TREATY

The underlying similarity between the three countries' postwar immigration policies was apparent in their labor and residency permit systems. While quite different in terms of detail, each system ensured that alien workers were funneled into industries that needed foreign labor. Foreign-worker residency rights, except for European Community workers, were contingent upon employment. In the French case, so-called unassimilable foreign workers—Arabs and Africans, in particular—were largely assumed to be temporary workers who would return home one day.[25] In the German and Swiss cases, the fundamental assumption underlying postwar migration policies was that virtually all foreign workers would return home. West Germany, however, did foresee the prospect of limited immigration, following from its European Community membership.[26]

Employment and residency permits, which were combined in the Swiss case, essentially restricted the employment and residential mobility of foreign workers. Both kinds of permits were very restrictive initially and reflected official presumptions of foreign-worker temporariness. However, such permit systems came to be liberalized over time, thereby permitting foreign workers and their dependents to become de facto immigrants.

By 1960 there were about 500,000 alien workers living in Switzerland year round; in addition, there were approximately 200,000 seasonal workers, who were required to return home at the end

24. France, Ministry of Social Affairs and National Solidarity, "The Employment Market and Immigrants in an Irregular Situation: Lessons from the Recent Legalization Exercise in France," *International Migration Review,* 18(3):559 (Fall 1984).

25. Tapinos, *L'immigration étrangère en France,* pp. 18-19.

26. W. R. Boehning, *Studies in International Migration* (New York: St. Martin's Press, 1984), pp. 126-27.

of their contract period of less than a year. Excluding seasonal and frontier workers, aliens already comprised almost 10 percent of the total population in Switzerland. Alien labor clearly was structural rather than temporary in nature, but governmental policy "remained opposed to any idea of prolonged immigrant sojourn in Switzerland."[27] Swiss officials continued to believe that alien labor was a cyclical phenomenon that would ebb with inevitable recession.

The vast majority of alien workers in Switzerland at the time were Italians. Their condition, particularly that of seasonal workers, became an issue in Italo-Swiss relations when the Italian minister of labor and other Italian officials criticized Swiss treatment of foreign labor.[28] Official Italian perceptions of the lot of foreign workers in Switzerland were influenced by grievances articulated by organizations representing Italian emigrants in Switzerland, such as the Federation of Free Italian Colonies, founded during the 1930s.[29]

The souring of Italo-Swiss relations due to Italian unhappiness with the condition of Italian emigrant workers prompted renegotiation of the 1948 Italo-Swiss labor treaty. A new treaty was signed in 1964. It marked a turning point in Swiss policy and contained a number of important concessions from the Swiss point of view.[30] Entry for the dependents of Italian workers was facilitated. Employment and residency restrictions on long-term Italian migrants and their dependents were eased. The

rights of and protections for Italian seasonal workers were expanded.

Signature of the 1964 treaty sparked intense political reaction in Switzerland. The antialien National Action movement regarded the treaty as signaling the transformation of Switzerland into an immigration country. Repeal or nullification of the treaty became a rallying cry for the *Ueberfremdung* referendum movement. As late as 1977, an unsuccessful referendum drive was made to repeal the treaty.[31]

In 1972, a new Italo-Swiss labor accord was signed. This agreement further liberalized the status of resident Italian workers and their dependents and consecrated the Swiss immigration-stabilization policy begun in the early 1960s. Swiss stabilization policy involved two key components and presaged immigration policy changes in France, West Germany, and elsewhere in Europe in the 1973-74 period. Stabilization involved the progressive elimination of employment and residency restrictions on nonseasonal alien workers and their dependents in order to improve their status and integration into Swiss society, along with the sharp curtailment of the recruitment of new workers.

The Swiss immigration situation differed most sharply from that in other European immigrant-receiving states in terms of the proportion of seasonal workers. The Federal Republic did not require any foreign workers to repatriate in less than a year's time. France had seasonal workers, but they were a much smaller proportion of the total alien work force than in the Swiss case. In the latter there was, in 1964, approximately one seasonal worker for every two alien workers not required by law to repatri-

27. Maillat, "L'immigration en Suisse," p. 107.

28. *Le Monde,* 13 Nov. 1961.

29. See generally Ann Matasar, "Labor Transfer in Western Europe: The Problem of Italian Migrant Workers in Switzerland" (Ph.D. diss., Columbia University, 1968).

30. Ibid., pp. 198, 239, 302.

31. *New York Times,* 14 Mar. 1977.

ate, or, overall, 206,305 compared to 465,355, respectively.[32] The important proportion of seasonal workers allowed Swiss authorities to reduce the alien work force through administrative means, by progressively reducing the annual quotas of seasonal workers. Levels of seasonal-worker employment fell to 150,000 by 1969 and to a postwar low of 60,000 in 1976.[33] The seasonal-worker policy gave Swiss authorities greater flexibility than French and German authorities possessed.

Swiss flexibility concerning alien manpower came at a considerable cost in social democratic norms, however. The status of seasonal workers in Switzerland remains a source of controversy, although Swiss authorities eventually agreed to permit seasonal workers who returned year after year to qualify for nonseasonal, year-round status. Between 1968 and 1979 some 90,000 seasonal workers qualified for and received annual permits.[34]

THE 1970 BAVARIAN EFFORT
TO INDUCE REPATRIATION
ADMINISTRATIVELY

In the Federal Republic of Germany, relatively substantial foreign-worker repatriation during the 1967 recession seemed to validate the prevailing view that foreign-worker employment was rotational and temporary in nature. A three- or four-month limitation on eligibility for unemployment compensation and, in some instances, refusals to renew work and residency papers encouraged unemployed foreigners to return home.[35]

However, between 1968 and 1970, the number of employed aliens doubled to 1.9 million, and it rose to a high point of 2.6 million in 1973.[36]

The turning point in postwar German immigration came in 1970. A Bavarian administrative court ruled that a foreign worker's sojourn of more than five years was sufficient grounds "to deny further residency [authorization] as each longer residency [authorization] would tend toward settlement, which ordinarily runs counter to state interests because the Federal Republic of Germany is not an immigration country."[37] The Bavarian effort—as well as that of several other state governments—to enforce the rotation principle administratively was overruled at the federal level.[38] In 1972, the federal government stated, as a matter of policy, that "the limitation of the duration of stay of foreign employees will not be effected through [police] measures under the law relating to foreigners."[39] Simultaneously, it maintained that "given past experience, the federal government continues to proceed from the assumption that the overwhelming number of foreign employees will not stay permanently in the Federal Republic."[40]

In late 1973, in the face of growing sociopolitical problems, the West German government halted further recruitment of foreign labor. This action, coupled with a steady, voluntary repatri-

32. Maillat, "L'immigration en Suisse," p. 109.
33. *Information*, no. 10, p. 136 (Feb. 1980).
34. Boehning, *Studies in International Migration*, p. 132.
35. H. Reister, *Ausländerbeschäftigung und Ausländerpolitik in der Bundesrepublik Deutsch-*

*land,* Fachhochschule für Verwaltung und Rechtspflege, monograph no. 38 (Berlin: Fachhochschule für Verwaltung und Rechtspflege, 1983), p. 39.
36. Ibid., p. 42.
37. Ibid., p. 4.
38. Boehning, *Studies in International Migration*, p. 126.
39. Ibid., p. 126; see also Reister, *Ausländerbeschäftigung und Ausländerpolitik*, p. 55.
40. Boehning, *Studies in International Migration*, p. 127.

ation, slowed the growth rate of the foreign population, although family reunification continued to frustrate governmental hopes that the foreign population would decline naturally. According to Boehning, between 1974 and 1978, out of 6.37 million requests by other than European Community citizens for a new work permit or renewal of an existing one, only about 152,000, or 2.4 percent, of requests were refused.[41] Economic, political, and moral considerations prevented administrative implementation of the rotation principle. Some employers urged adoption of a seasonal-worker policy along Swiss lines in the wake of the halt of recruitment, but this option was rejected as unfeasible and unconscionable in a period of mounting unemployment.

SUSTAINING THE MYTH OF RETURN

The notion of a myth of return should be attributed to Rudolf Braun or perhaps Henri Le Masne.[42] As conceived by these authors, the notion referred to the disjuncture between the stated intent of most foreign workers to return home after a relatively brief sojourn in Western Europe and their prolonged stay in the host countries. Braun already noted in the mid-1960s that many foreign workers had unrealistic expectations concerning the length of their stay in Western Europe. Migrants' expectations concerning the likelihood and desirability of return dovetailed nicely with slogans like "Germany is not an immigration country."

Surveys of foreign workers' intentions accorded with official policies of both the sending and the receiving countries. Even when it had become obvious to all that alien sojourns in Western Europe were long term or open ended, many sending countries persisted in propagating the idea of the temporariness of emigration. Emigrants were told they had a duty to return and were warned of the dangers of assimilation. Return was presented as a desirable and realistic possibility.

Officially, the Algerian government always regarded labor emigration as a temporary phenomenon—a sequel of colonialism. Each of the labor agreements negotiated with France included a provision for return. But despite a vast number of annual comings and goings between France and Algeria, a large Algerian population continued to reside in France.

After the end of recruitment in 1973, French governments sought to encourage Algerian repatriation through a number of policies. Under the accords, returning Algerians were to receive training in skills that would help them to find work and to reintegrate into the Algerian economy and society. Due in part to shortfalls in funding, however, very few Algerian workers received such training or returned home as stipulated in the accords.[43] During the Giscard d'Estaing presidency, from 1974 to 1981, the government seemed at one point to be close to a decision not to renew hundreds of thousands of Algerian permits.[44] Instead, an *aide au retour* program—a program providing a cash incentive for repatriation—was instituted in 1977. It was specifically aimed at se-

41. Ibid.
42. Rudolf Braun, *Sozio-Kulturelle Probleme der Eingliederung italienischer Arbeitskräfte in der Schweiz* (Zurich: Eugen Rentsch, 1970); Henri Le Masne, "Les émigrés algériens et la perspective de retour," mémoire, Mar. 1974, Faculté de droit et science économiques, Algiers.

43. *Le Monde*, 24-25 June 1979.
44. Ibid.

curing the definitive repatriation of North Africans. However, only 3515 Algerians returned—3.7 percent of the total number of returnees under the program.[45] Contrary to its official policy, the Algerian government did not in fact encourage its nationals to return under the program. The cash incentive was largely—and correctly—perceived as inadequate for and prejudicial to Algerian nationals, especially in light of their contributions to the French social security sytem.

The Algerian government clearly welcomed the election of François Mitterrand and his Socialist Party in 1981. French left-wing parties and trade unions had vociferously criticized the *aide au retour* program. But a return program specifically for Algerians that had been provided for in the 1980 Franco-Algerian accords was continued by the new government.[46] Negotiations between France and Algeria since 1981 have made the return option more attractive to Algerian nationals in terms of financial and training incentives. However, relatively few Algerians return home under the program; nor does the Algerian government actively promote repatriation through the program. The two governments now agree that return should be a voluntary decision. In reality, in spite of official return policy, massive repatriation of Algerians would compound unemployment problems in Algeria, reduce the homeward flow of wage remittances, and perhaps foster sociopolitical instability.

Like other homeland governments, the Algerian government actively fosters the national allegiance and identity of its nationals abroad.[47] Such policies may contradict and counteract the host society's policies aimed at encouraging the foreign workers' integration. The Turkish reaction to one of the recommendations by the German Kuehn Commission to facilitate the acquisition of German citizenship suggests how a myth of return sustained by the homelands contributes to overall policy incoherence in societies that have massive de facto immigration but that are unable to accept that they have become countries of immigration.

Among its various recommendations—most of which were not adopted by the federal government—the Kuehn Commission suggested facilitating the granting of German citizenship to second-generation aliens.[48] Turkish authorities immediately protested the proposed easing of citizenship requirements and the German government eventually rejected the proposal. Turkish opposition to policies that encourage assimilation has become a constraint on German policymaking, and it serves to maintain the anomalous situation of millions of foreigners in the Federal Republic.

Like Algeria, Turkey has signed a number of agreements or accords intended to facilitate repatriation of its nationals from Western Europe. In general, these programs have had meager

45. Heinz Werner and Ingeborg König, *Ausländerbeschäftigung und Ausländerpolitik in einigen westeuropäischen Industriestaaten* (Nuremburg: Institut für Arbeitsmarkt und Berufsforschung, 1984), p. 49.

46. Catherine Wihtol de Wenden, "L'échange de lettres franco-algérien du 18 septembre 1980 et son évolution en 1981 et 1982: Réflexions sur une politique de concertation bilatérale" (Unpublished paper, CNRS, Paris), p. 5.

47. Mark J. Miller, *Foreign Workers in Western Europe: An Emerging Political Force* (New York: Praeger, 1981), pp. 30–42.

48. Reister, *Ausländerbeschäftigung und Auslanderpolitik,* pp. 62–63.

results.[49] In 1984, however, the West German government succeeded in inducing the repatriation of some 300,000 aliens, including at least 134,459 Turks.[50] The large number of Turkish returnees should not be taken as an indication of Turkish governmental cooperation in return policy.

German officials did inform the Turkish government of plans to offer a cash incentive for a return program. However, the program appears to have been more a unilateral German initiative than one based on consultation with Turkish authorities.[51] Turkish authorities would never close the door to returning migrants, but the return of so many Turks did not generate great enthusiasm in Ankara.

It appears that most of the Turks who opted to return under the program probably would have gone home anyway.[52] Several European experts agree that high unemployment among Turks, difficult economic conditions in general, and the hostile, antialien sociopolitical climate in the Federal Republic were probably more important contributors to the upsurge in Turkish repatriation than the financial inducements offered under the return program. There have been reports suggesting that some individuals' decisions to repatriate were made in a context of pressure to return home, rather than wholly voluntarily.

The repatriation program proved to be quite costly over the short run. In the long run, it may benefit the strained German social welfare system, since the returnees renounced all of their claims to retirement and other social welfare programs.[53]

Despite the large number of Turkish returnees in 1984, 1.5 million Turks remain in the Federal Republic. In light of Turkey's economic woes, it seems reasonable to suggest that the Turkish government would not welcome massive repatriation despite its official policy in favor of return.

Expectations of homeland government participation in return policies beyond agreement to accept resettlement of citizens who voluntarily return and cooperation in retraining and investment schemes, which thus far have met with meager results, lack credibility. Still, homeland sensitivities and stated long-term policy goals must be taken seriously, lest bilateral relations suffer. Ironically, the myth of return promoted by homelands feeds the myth of return sustained by anti-immigrant political forces.

## SUMMARY AND CONCLUSION

Save for France's long-term demographic concerns, postwar foreign labor policies in the three host countries considered here were not expected to lead to settlement or immigration. Yet, the Western European governments eventually found that they could not legally force most migrants to repatriate, even if they wanted to.

While Western Europe's postwar economic growth was facilitated by the presence of foreign workers, virtually no one seemed to have thought that the admission of foreign workers might lead to

49. Gianpier Rellini, "Les politiques de retour," in *Les travailleurs étrangers et le droit international,* ed. Societé française pour le droit international, p. 149.

50. *Sozialpolitische Umschau,* 3 Aug. 1984, p. 1.

51. This is the gist of an authoritative response to the author's verbal inquiries in 1983.

52. Observation made by André Lebon, Paris, Oct. 1984.

53. DGB press release, 2 Aug. 1985; *Week in Germany,* 25 Jan. 1985, p. 3.

settlement or indefinite sojourns. Foreign workers were expected to return home if an economic recession occurred. The work and residence restrictions initially placed on them were intended to ensure just that. But as European economies surged, labor shortages increased. What began as relatively inconsequential labor market adjustments spawned long-term and large-scale population movements. Neither public policies nor public perceptions and expectations adjusted to emerging realities appropriately.

Foreign workers were regarded as temporary, but most were funneled into permanent or long-term jobs. Even in the cases of French and Swiss seasonal workers, many jobs were actually of a permanent nature, thus contributing to a *faux saisonnier* phenomenon, whereby de facto permanent workers were admitted and readmitted as temporary workers.[54] With time, certain types of jobs in key industrial sectors came to be held almost exclusively by foreign workers. Foreign-worker employment in such industries as construction and auto assembly became so extensive that massive forced repatriation would have led to considerable economic dislocation. In France, for example, one of every three construction workers and one of every four auto assembly employees was an alien by the early 1970s.[55] The assumption of temporariness long masked the structural or permanent nature of foreign-worker employment.

Foreign workers have disproportionately borne the brunt of unemployment in Western Europe in recent years, yet they have become scapegoats for a host of problems. Movements like the National Front in France draw their strength from a deep-seated malaise linked to immigration; and governments seem to validate anti-immigrant theses by encouraging repatriation through cash inducements. Given the relatively meager results of such programs, the programs serve to renew the myth of temporariness. The myth enables host societies and homelands to avoid a painful political reckoning that would show that postwar labor migration policies have involved long-term costs, particularly of a sociopolitical nature, in addition to short-term economic benefits.

The myth of return nurtured by immigration policy ad-hocracy throughout the postwar period persists today and challenges the legitimacy of immigrant settlement. Anti-immigrant movements such as the National Front have renewed the myth of return and can be seen as a major political consequence of immigration policy ad-hocracy.

54. Mark Miller, "Seasonal Workers in France and Switzerland: Western Europe's Braceros" (Paper delivered at the Council for European Studies Convention, Washington, DC, 1981).

55. Mark Miller, "Industrial Policy and the Rights of Labor: The Case of Foreign Workers in the French Auto Assembly Industry," *Michigan Yearbook of International Law* (in press).

# Immigrant Settlement and the Structure of Emergent Immigrant Communities in Western Europe

*By* BARBARA SCHMITTER HEISLER

ABSTRACT: Throughout modern history the majority of immigrants have occupied inferior socioeconomic positions and have settled in segregated communities. The migrant workers who came to the advanced industrial countries in Western Europe have had similar experiences. A closer examination of the legal and political circumstances surrounding their unanticipated prolonged presence reveals significant differences between the Western European situation and that encountered elsewhere. The original contract labor system legally provided sending countries with the opportunity to establish networks of organizations and institutions in the countries of destination. Although the sending countries' networks may vary in specifics, each represents an important dimension of that national community and helps to maintain an ideology of return. This, in turn, represents an important force in defining the situation for all participants— host societies, sending countries, and immigrants. The argument that one cannot approach all aspects of the European experience using theoretical models that may be appropriate for other situations is illustrated by examples of sending-country organizations active in the Federal Republic of Germany.

*Barbara Schmitter Heisler received a Ph.D. in sociology from the University of Chicago in 1979. She was a postdoctoral fellow at Duke University and taught at the State University of New York, Buffalo, before joining the sociology faculty at Cleveland State University in 1982. Her research interests center on structural problems of advanced industrial societies, particularly immigration and industrial change. She has published several articles on immigration in Western Europe.*

T HIRTY-FIVE years after the first foreign workers arrived in Western Europe, the countries of destination—which include all the advanced industrial countries—confront sizable foreign populations, ranging from a high of 25 percent in tiny Luxembourg to a low of 2 percent in Norway, with averages around 8 or 9 percent in France, West Germany, and Belgium.[1] Although originally recruited to help solve the seemingly temporary labor shortages created by rapid economic growth in the post-World War II period, in the mid-1980s there can be little doubt that many—perhaps most—of the foreigners are not likely to return to their countries of origin in the foreseeable future. In short, the foreign workers, migrant workers, or guest workers of the 1950s and 1960s have become permanent or at least quasi-permanent settlers in the 1980s.[2]

This process of settlement has presented European host countries with many social and political problems they had not anticipated. The culturally distinct migrants from southern Europe, the European periphery—Turkey and North Africa—and former colonies elsewhere tend to occupy inferior socioeconomic positions and often confront prejudice, discrimination, and increasingly overt hostility from the populations and institutions of the host societies. Like immigrants elsewhere and in earlier periods,

they have been geographically concentrated in certain regions in the host countries and within these they have tended to settle in inner-city neighborhoods, many of which have come to resemble immigrant communities or ethnic enclaves in the United States and other societies more commonly associated with immigration.

Students of immigration have long been interested in one of the seemingly universal consequences of large-scale immigration, the ethnic community. Although they tend to agree on the ubiquitousness and general importance of such communities, the appearance of consensus fades once they move beyond the purely descriptive, relatively abstract theoretical level to considerations of the structures and functions of ethnic communities. Those following the assimilationist tradition, pioneered by Robert Park and the Chicago school of sociology, have tended to view immigrant communities as temporary—albeit important—way stations on the road to eventual assimilation.[3] Thus, they have analyzed the social and cultural dimensions of immigrant communities and their social or psychological role as support systems and/or intermediate structures that help to ease the passage of newcomers into the host society.

Those following a more recent, structural approach have tended to see immigrant communities as more permanent structures that are products of the host society's given economic opportunities or of specific characteristics of the newcomers or both.[4] Unlike the assimilation-

1. More specifically, foreigners represent the following percentages of the total population: in the Federal Republic of Germany, 7.4; the Netherlands, 3.8; Sweden, 4.8; Switzerland, 14.4; Belgium, 9.0; and France, 7.8.

2. See, for example, the titles of two recent books on the subject. Stephen Castles, *Here for Good: Western Europe's New Ethnic Minorities* (London: Pluto Press, 1984); Rosemarie Rogers, ed., *Guests Come to Stay: The Effects of European Labor Migration on Sending and Receiving Countries* (Boulder, CO: Westview Press, 1985).

3. Herbert Gans, *The Urban Villagers* (New York: Free Press, 1962); W. Lloyd Warner and Leo Srole, *The Social System of American Ethnic Groups* (New Haven, CT: Yale University Press, 1945).

4. This perspective is best presented by Alejandro Portes, "Modes of Structural Incorporation

ists, followers of this approach have focused on the economic characteristics of immigrant communities, especially their role in providing alternative employment to newcomers—within the community, rather than in the larger economy—and in providing important services to the larger society. Rather than facilitating the eventual integration of newcomers, such communities function to set them apart from the larger society.

Many of the differences between the two perspectives can be attributed to differences between the immigrant groups studied and the time of their immigration. The assimilationist perspective thus reflects the circumstances of some groups, especially of the immigrants from southern and eastern Europe who came to the United States between 1890 and 1924. The structuralist perspective reflects the experiences of other groups, often more recent immigrants of non-European origin, many of whom arrived as refugees.[5] Each perspective has been induced from a historically specific situation and appears appropriate for the empirical realities produced by concrete circumstances of contact. Can either perspective serve as a useful framework for understanding Europe's emergent immigrant communities?

In the following pages I will argue that the legal and political aspects of European migrations since World War II differ sufficiently from those of previous migrations to suggest that the process of settlement and the structure and role of immigrant communities may not correspond with either of the two perspectives. Following a brief examination of the differences that set European migrations apart from seemingly similar migrations elsewhere, I will analyze their impact on the formation and structure of immigrant communities. Finally, the longer-term consequences for relations between the immigrants and the host society will be considered.

In its socioeconomic aspects, large-scale European migration does not appear to differ significantly from migrations elsewhere.[6] Immigrants tend to have the least desirable jobs, and they experience higher rates of unemployment than native workers. They often live in inferior housing in decaying inner-city areas. Most of the children of immigrants attend the least academically oriented schools, where their rate of failure exceeds that of native children. As a consequence of school failure and discrimination by employers, their access to occupational training is severely limited.[7] The current extended period of slow economic growth in most of the

and Present Theories of Labor Immigration," in *Global Trends in Migration: Theory and Research on International Population Movements,* ed. Mary Kritz, Charles Keeley, and Silvano M. Tomasi (New York: Center for Migration Studies, 1981), pp. 279-97; Ivan Light, "Immigrant and Ethnic Entreprise in North America," *Ethnic and Racial Studies,* 7(2):195-216 (Apr. 1984).

5. See, in particular, Kenneth Wilson and Alejandro Portes, "Immigrant Enclaves: An Analysis of the Labor Market Experience of Cubans in Miami," *American Journal of Sociology,* 86(2):295-315 (Sept. 1980); Ivan Light, *Ethnic Enterprise in America* (Berkeley: University of California Press, 1972).

6. The literature on socioeconomic positions of immigrants tends to point out the immigrants' shared socioeconomic similarities across countries. For examples, see Stephen Castles and Godula Kosack, *Immigrant Workers and Class Structure in Western Europe* (London: Oxford University Press, 1973); Castles, *Here for Good.*

7. Carlos Castro-Almeida, "Problems Facing Second Generation Migrants in Western Europe," *International Labour Review,* 118(6):763-75 (Nov.-Dec. 1979); André Lebon, "Second Generation Foreigners in France," in *Guests Come to Stay,* ed. Rogers, pp. 135-58.

receiving countries has further exacerbated already existing tendencies of discrimination and prejudice among native
populations and institutions.[8]

These seemingly universal concomitants of large-scale migration are com-
pounded by important political and
legal differences that set the Western
European context apart. The long-term
presence of immigrants is an unanticipated consequence of temporary contract labor systems. Although the host
countries have attempted many policy
adjustments with respect to the prolonged presence of foreign populations,
the political and legal underpinnings
and temporary definitions of the original situation continue to define the
framework for the expectations and
actions of all participants.

## MIGRANTS OR SETTLERS?

The countries of destination, with the
possible exceptions of Sweden and
France, are not immigration countries.
That is, their legal, political, and most of
their social structures have not adjusted
to reflect permanent or long-term settlement.[9] Indeed, the two countries with
the largest number of immigrants—the
Federal Republic of Germany and
France—continue to hope that they can

solve some of their current problems by
enticing many foreigners to leave.[10] Nor
are the countries of origin emigration
countries. They are temporary export-
ers of labor and generally oppose any
large-scale settlement of their citizens
abroad. Although they may lobby for
more social rights and even political
participation for their citizens at the
local level in the host countries, they
oppose permanent legal and political
integration.

The migrants hardly consider themselves permanent immigrants or settlers.
The natural desire to return home observed among many migrants throughout history is constantly reinforced by
frequent visits to their countries of origin. Antiforeign manifestations and continuing legal and political barriers between immigrants and host societies
further serve to reinforce their home
orientations.[11]

### The myth of return

The myth of return is more than a
dream; it remains a powerful ideology
that serves a useful function for all
participants and is reinforced by existing legal and political arrangements
between host and sending countries.

8. In France, the *Front national,* led by Jean-
Marie Le Pen, has gained an impressive 10 percent
of the votes in recent elections on its anti-immigrant
platform. In West Germany, antiforeign political
parties have been less successful, but there is a
pervasive uneasiness about *Ausländerfeindlich-
keit* ("hostility toward foreigners").
9. Schools have not generally redesigned curricula to reflect the need to socialize foreign
populations; naturalization remains difficult, although it has been facilitated in France. For a
more detailed discussion, see Rosemarie Rogers,
"The Transnational Nexus of Migration," this
issue of *The Annals* of the American Academy of
Political and Social Science.

10. It is generally agreed that the return-
incentive schemes have only enticed those foreigners already planning to return shortly to do so. See
ibid.
11. In France a survey found that 90 percent of
those questioned wanted to leave. *Hommes et
migrations,* p. 177 (1 Sept. 1984). Similarly, in
Germany over 75 percent "intended to return";
however, they frequently made return dependent
on "the possibility [of finding] employment" or on
saving "enough to become independent." Ursula
Merhländer et al., *Situation der ausländischen
Arbeitnehmer und ihrer Familienangehörigen in
der Bundesrepublik Deutschland: Repräsentativ-
untersuchung* (Bonn, Bundesminister für Arbeit
und Sozialordnung, 1981).

Politicians and policymakers in the host societies point to public opinion data indicating that few migrants are interested in obtaining citizenship and argue that most will eventually return.[12] Sending countries benefit from the long-term absence of large numbers of their citizens, as long as they continue to send remittances home and remain abroad to relieve pressures on local labor markets and social and political infrastructures. Full integration of their citizens in the host countries would mean a permanent loss of remittances.[13] Migrants find needed psychological and social relief from the strains and stresses of immigrant life by dreaming of ultimate return. Their plans for the future inevitably center on the home country.

The myth of return is not likely to lose saliency since it is continuously maintained and reinforced by social and political structures that are part of the legal and political underpinnings of the original contract labor agreements between host and sending countries. These agreements, concluded between 1948 and 1968, were to ensure the temporary nature of migration, and they established institutional structures to achieve that end. The agreements continue to produce unanticipated and seemingly contradictory consequences.

*Institutional arrangements*

The recruitment agreements spelled out conditions of recruitment and em-

ployment. Although the conditions varied slightly from case to case, all placed some limits on the length of time—usually one year—and the type of job to be performed. They did not, however, place limits on the number of times work or residence permits could be renewed. To protect native workers from competition from cheaper foreign labor, the agreements also gave migrants work-related equality, that is, equality with indigenous workers in terms of wages and work-related social benefits, such as social security and accident and health insurance.

Postmigration social and political problems associated with more permanent immigration and settlement were not expected to become relevant. Beyond some provisions for housing for the predominantly single men, such issues as family housing, schooling, and the like remained largely unspecified or deliberately left in the domain of the sending countries. This permitted the sending countries to set up their own institutions to provide social and political services to their citizens abroad, a step that seemed at the time very much in accordance with the need to reintegrate these citizens into their countries of origin. The institutions were originally set up to support a putatively temporary labor system. As the duration of the emigrants' residence abroad lengthened, these institutions came to play increasingly important roles.[14]

Initially limited in size and scope and in the types of services they provided, the sending-country institutions have significantly expanded their original sphere of influence to meet the changes brought by long-term residency and family migration. In short, the bilateral

12. Few migrants and surprisingly few children of migrants want to become citizens of the host countries. Thus, in West Germany, only 6.6 percent expressed any interest in citizenship. There was little variation between nationalities. Merhländer et al., *Situation der ausländischen Arbeitnehmer,* pp. 554-59.

13. Barbara Schmitter Heisler, "Sending Countries and the Politics of Emigration and Destination," *International Migration Review,* 19(3):469-84 (Fall 1985).

14. Although the bilateral treaties have been superseded or are no longer in effect, the original structures remain very present.

recruitment agreements gave sending countries opportunities and, importantly, the right and obligation to establish service networks. This provides sending countries with direct structural links to their citizens abroad and, more important, it changes the conditions of settlement and with them the structure and dynamics of immigrant communities. Indeed, sending-country institutions and organizations must be considered an integral part of Western Europe's immigrant communities.

### HOST SOCIETIES AND IMMIGRANT COMMUNITIES

In the extant literature, immigrant communities are fequently identified by their geographic dimensions, their employment characteristics, and the existence of distinct social and cultural institutions. The immigrant scene in Western Europe displays all three characteristics. It is important, however, to determine their extent and try to discover other, heretofore less obvious characteristics.

### Geographic concentration

There can be little doubt that immigrants in Europe are not equally distributed within the host countries' borders. This is not surprising, considering that they were specifically recruited to work in particular industries located in particular regions. In France, for example, they have been concentrated in the Paris, Lyons, and Marseilles metropolitan areas. In Belgium, they have settled in Brussels and the Walloon industrial areas in the southern region of the country. In the Netherlands, the majority are found in the largest cities: Amsterdam, Rotterdam, and Utrecht. In West Germany they have been heavily concentrated in the Ruhr and Rhein-Main conurbations and in the industrial areas

of Baden-Württemberg and southern Bavaria. In Switzerland, foreign workers are found predominantly in the industrial cantons of Zürich, Geneva, and Basel.

Within these areas, immigrants have tended to live in particular inner-city neighborhoods. Neighborhood concentration, however, varies considerably across host countries and, more important, among the various immigrant groups. Indeed, the degree of residential concentration encountered is a product of available housing and the immigrant's national and social characteristics. Algerians, Moroccans, and Turks tend to live near each other. Not coincidentally, they are also culturally most distinct from native populations, encountering greater discrimination in Europe's generally tight housing markets. In addition, it is among them that the largest proportions of men who have immigrated alone are to be found, men who seek cheap housing. The savings permit them to send larger sums to their families at home.

### Employment

Even though we find some variation among host countries, the majority of immigrants are employed in medium to large firms in manufacturing, mining, construction, and the service sector. The majority partake of full social benefits and increasingly participate in trade unions.[15] Immigrants are rarely self-employed. Indeed, the laws of host coun-

15. Although trade union participation among immigrants is lower than that among native workers, in countries where trade union organizations are strong the migrants' participation rate tends to be only a few percentages points lower. See Barbara Schmitter, "Trade Unions and Immigration Politics in West Germany and Switzerland," *Politics and Society,* 10(3):317-34 (Spring 1981).

tries tend to restrict rather than encourage independent economic activity by foreigners. Although grocery stores, travel agencies, restaurants, and tailor shops—specializing in the alteration of used clothing—have increased in the past few years, they account for a minuscule share of foreigners' economic activity.[16] This suggests that, unlike in the United States, the vast majority of immigrants are neither relegated to secondary labor markets, as defined in the literature,[17] nor are they employed within an immigrant economy per se.

### Social institutions

When migrant workers first arrived, little contact between them and the host society's institutions was expected except that entailed by the employment situation itself. In retrospect, such expectations seem to have ignored the near impossibility, in advanced industrial welfare states, of maintaining strict separation between employment and such social institutions as trade unions and health and welfare service institutions. From the onset, immigrants had some contact with union representatives, health officials, and social workers. With increased length of residence and family migration, the institutional contacts expanded to include non-work-related institutions such as churches, local housing authorities, and school systems. These social service institutions of the host society have generally included immigrants among their clien-

tele. Their dependent employment status and their inclusion in the social benefits of advanced welfare states have meant that they were not likely to organize mutual aid societies or revolving-credit institutions, institutions that have been identified as the hubs of immigrant communities.[18]

This brief discussion of the factors commonly associated with immigrant communities suggests sufficient differences between the Western European experience and that commonly presented in the literature to prevent facile generalizations. Clearly, as newcomers with distinct social, cultural, and political characteristics, all immigrants encounter constraints in the host society. For example, they are not likely to be geographically dispersed, and, excepting the so-called brain drain, they are bound to occupy less desirable economic positions. What may be considered less desirable by the standards of a given host society varies considerably between societies. In Europe, even the less desirable jobs are not characterized by an absence of social benefits.

### SENDING COUNTRIES AND IMMIGRANT COMMUNITIES

In accordance with the original recruitment agreements emphasizing return to the countries of origin, the official representations of the sending countries—the embassies and consulates—have taken on a variety of functions not generally counted among their official tasks. These include a wide range of social and political services to their citizens for which they engage a large staff of specialists:

16. Great Britain differs significantly from this pattern. See Robin Ward and Richard Jenkins, eds., *Ethnic Communities in Business* (Cambridge: Cambridge University Press, 1984).

17. See Michael J. Piore, "The Shifting Grounds for Immigration," this issue of *The Annals* of the American Academy of Political and Social Science.

18. Raymond Breton, "Institutional Completeness and the Personal Relations of Immigrants," *American Journal of Sociology*, 70(2):193-205 (Sept. 1964); Light, *Ethnic Enterprise*.

social workers to help with family problems, teachers in charge of teaching home language and culture to immigrant children, education counselors to help citizens with school problems in the host country, and legal experts to give advice and provide representation in disputes over employment rights, welfare and social rights—in particular retirement and workman's compensation claims—and landlord-tenant disputes.

In addition to official government representatives, the European immigrant scene includes many quasi-governmental and independent formal organizations from the home country. Foremost among them are religious organizations, trade unions, political parties, and other interest groups.

Given the variety and number of existing institutions they encounter, and their own return orientation, migrants have generally been slow to create their own organizational life. Even though the number of social, cultural, and—in particular—recreational clubs and groups has increased in recent years, we must be careful to note that many of these are not independent. Many are subsidized and indirectly maintained by a sending country's government and/or formal organizations; others are initiated and supported by the host society's organizations.

There is a considerable variation in the combined home-country organizational network. The network includes government representations, quasi-governmental and independent organizations with headquarters in the countries of origin, and many immigrant self organizations. The differences have important consequences for the type of immigrant community we are likely to encounter among the various nationalities.

Although the sending countries share some characteristics, the differences between them are considerably greater than are the differences between the host countries. Such countries as Italy, Turkey, Yugoslavia, and Algeria have less in common than France, the Federal Republic of Germany, and Belgium. Among sending countries, Italy is the most economically developed overall, the most democratic, and the most experienced emigration country. Turkey, on the other hand, must be classified as authoritarian, far less developed, and lacking in substantial relevant prior experience with emigration. Algeria and Yugoslavia are both socialist and relatively new states. Spain, Portugal, and Greece have undergone great political transformations since they first agreed to export labor to the host countries. In short, sending countries differ in their historical experience with emigration; the relative importance they assign to emigration as a factor in their own economic development; and their political structures and processes.

Such differences among sending countries have led to three types of organizational networks aimed at providing social and political services and simultaneously ensuring the migrants' continued loyalty. The first, best illustrated by the Italian case, consists of multiple organizations that are integrated into a state-coordinated network of expatriate organizations. The second, typified by Turkey, consists of multiple, fragmented organizations. The third type, exemplified by the two socialist sending countries, Yugoslavia and Algeria, presents a single state-controlled organization that is highly integrated.[19]

Given that immigrant nationalities are not evenly distributed among host

19. Spain and Portugal have been establishing structures similar to that of Italy since the demise of their dictatorships.

countries and that sending countries are more likely to concentrate their organizational efforts in those host countries to which relatively large proportions of their citizens have migrated, it seems appropriate to take illustrations of these general observations from one receiving country, the Federal Republic of Germany. The Federal Republic is particularly instructive in that it is host to a large variety of nationalities. Thus, it provides illustrations for each of the sending-country organizational models.

SENDING-COUNTRY EXCLAVES:
WEST GERMANY,
AN ILLUSTRATIVE CASE

Following arrangements between the German government and the countries of recruitment—Italy, Spain, Portugal, Greece, Turkey, and Yugoslavia—the former agreed to provide those recruited with some help in adjusting to their new, presumably temporary environments. The agencies chosen for this task were the welfare organizations, which, although they are nominally private, form an integral part of the German welfare state.[20] The Caritas, an official agency of the Catholic Church, was put in charge of the overwhelmingly Catholic migrants from Italy, Portugal, and Spain; the Diakonisches Werk, the official arm of the Protestant church, took responsibility for the Greeks; and the Arbeiterwohlfahrt, a welfare organization with close links to the German trade union movement and the Social Democratic Party, took charge of Turkish and most Yugoslav migrants.

From the beginning, these organizations hired social workers from the sending countries, set up meeting centers for newcomers, and engaged in some symbolic activities—for example, setting aside a day to be the day of the foreigner—to raise the awareness of the German population. Most, if not all, of their activities were subsidized by the German government. As migration matured and foreign populations increasingly remained for extended periods, the welfare organizations and the churches came to act as advocates for the immigrants vis-à-vis the German government and local social and political bodies.[21]

These host-society-initiated immigrant organizations are relatively similar for all nationalities. Important organizational differences, however, appear between sending-country organizations. Thus Italians, Turks, and Yugoslavs working and living in West Germany encounter quite different home-country organizations.

*Italian organizations*

The Italian immigrant community represents a varied and highly integrated network of state and independent interest organizations. In addition to well-developed consular services, Italian organizations include the ubiquitous Missione cattolica and the *patronati,* the social welfare organizations attached to the three major trade union federations. According to Italian law, the *patronati* provide free advice and legal assistance to Italian nationals on all aspects of social insurance rights and claims. The offices of the *patronati* are staffed with Italian trade unionists who often provide advice and give assistance beyond their official tasks. Since the Italian government pays part of the travel costs

20. Dietrich Thränhardt, "Ausländer im Dickicht der Verbände" (unpublished manuscript, n.p., n.d.).

21. Churches and welfare organizations have advocated the granting of local voting rights to foreigners.

of citizens returning to vote in national elections, political parties are similarly active.

What makes the Italian situation remarkable, however, is not the variety of organizations, but their integration into a network of Italian organizations abroad—a network that is connected to the Italian Foreign Ministry. Thus, Italian organizations are arrayed into two major overarching associations, the National Union of Immigrant and Emigrant Associations and the Italian Federation of Emigrant Workers and Families. These in turn are represented in the Consultative Committee of Italians Abroad. That committee, in turn, coordinates the activities of Italian organizations within each consular district and is located within the Foreign Ministry.[22]

### Turkish organizations

In contrast to the Italian situation, Turkish organizational life is marked by its fragmentation and politicization. A latecomer to emigration, confronted with myriad political, economic, and social difficulties at home, the Turkish state was slow to develop an appropriate organizational structure for its citizens abroad. It was not until the late 1960s that the government decided to approach the subject by placing one department in the Ministry of Education in charge of organizing a program for Turkish children abroad. Consulates in areas with large Turkish concentrations have only relatively recently added social, cultural, and educational services to their tasks.

Unlike the Italian organizations, the Turkish organizational network replicates in Germany the political divisions

of the home country. The network includes an array of extremist groups, many of which are outlawed in Turkey. Thus we encounter the fascist National Movement Party, with 111 local organizations and 26,000 members; the Islamic Cultural Center, with 18,000 members; and the Islamic Union, with 20,000 members. All are extremely nationalist, Islamic fundamentalist, and strictly opposed to any integration of Turks living in Germany.

Left-wing organizations are numerous, comprising mini-parties and Maoist splinter groups. Organizations on the left include the Federation of Workers Clubs of Turkey and the Federation of Progressive Peoples Organizations of Turkey. Although the former in particular has been controlled by Communist interests—the Communist Party is outlawed in Turkey—these organizations do attempt to carry Turkish immigrants' interests to the German government and the German public.

### Yugoslav organizations

In many ways the Yugoslav minority in West Germany is the least visible. This is particularly surprising given the not-so-dormant hostility between ethnic groups in the émigré population, especially between Croatians and Serbs. The Yugoslav government has been successful in keeping tight control over its "citizens living temporarily abroad."[23] In addition to the local consulates, Yugoslav emigrant life centers around the Yugoslav Clubs—an arm of the government—which are charged with promoting so-called Yugoslav socialist patriotism. These clubs are found in all cities where Yugoslavs have settled and pro-

22. For a more detailed discussion, see Barbara Schmitter, "Sending States and Immigrant Minorities: The Case of Italy," *Comparative Studies in Society and History*, 26(2):325-34 (April 1984).

23. This expression is consistently used by Yugoslav officials in reference to their citizens abroad.

vide migrants with an impressive array of leisure, culture, educational, sports, and entertainment programs. Given the absence of competing political parties and state control over religious, regional, and ethnic organizations, there are no independent self organizations. Furthermore, the Yugoslav social workers employed by the Arbeiterwohlfahrt are designated by Yugoslav authorities and delegated to work in Germany.

*Organizational impact*

The majority of migrants are not likely to participate extensively in any formal organizations. Yet such organizations not only represent the structural outlines of immigrant communities, but they also have long-term consequences for the future of relations between the host society and immigrants. In the Italian case, the well-developed Italian organizational network may serve a positive function for Italian migrants, free to move into and out of German—and other European Community—labor markets. The Italian organizational network ties Italians to Italy and to a larger European community.

The Turkish case is more problematic. The inability of the state to take effective control over its citizens abroad, and the increasing hostility encountered by the Turkish minority in particular, have meant that many Turks are completely alienated from either the host or the sending societies and that they seek refuge in extremist organizations.[24] Neither option is potentially integrative.

24. Turkish workers often resent their government, which they perceive as interested only in foreign exchange. See Ekmel Zadil, "Die Auswirkungen de Arbeitskräftewanderung in der Türkei," in *Ausländerbeschäftigung und Internationale Politik*, ed. R. Lohrman and K. Manfrass (Munich: Oldenburg Verlag, 1974), pp. 207-32.

The Yugoslav case presents a good example of what one might call state-organized exclaves. Although by the usual measures—language ability, education, housing preference—the Yugoslav minority appears as the best integrated and least troublesome of immigrants, this is at least partially due to the Yugoslav state's unambiguous policies of control and return supported by excellent organizational networks.

CONCLUSION

In this article, I have attempted to give some evidence that the long-term consequences of migration in post-World War II Europe cannot be equated with those occuring under different legal and political conditions. As long as the myth of return is sustained by structures and policies of the host and sending countries for varying but important ideological reasons, integration is not a likely option for any nationality as a group. It is certainly possible for individuals to choose to renounce their citizenship and seek that of the host country, but such a step is often difficult.

As long as migrants maintain institutional and ideological attachments to their countries of origin, a goal that continues to be supported by sending and host states, their political and social ties to the hosts will remain tenuous at best. In that sense, immigrant communities in Western Europe tend to resemble exclaves, rather than enclaves, some with well-traveled and solid bridges—others with more tenuous ones—to the social and political institutions of the home countries. Whatever the host countries' future policies concerning their foreign populations, any full and genuine effort to integrate them must first confront the exclaves.

ANNALS, *AAPSS*, 485, May 1986

# Migration Policies of Sending Countries: Perspectives on the Turkish Experience

*By* SABRI SAYARI

ABSTRACT: During the 1960s and early 1970s, Turkey participated heavily in the process of labor migration from the Mediterranean basin to Western Europe. In addition to the policy preferences of advanced industrial European states and the demand for jobs in Europe by large numbers of Turks, Turkey's migration policies played a significant role in the expansion of the migratory flow. Turkish policymakers sought to use labor migration abroad to fulfill several objectives such as reducing unemployment and increasing the volume of foreign-exchange reserves through remittances. The migration of Turkish workers to Western Europe produced some significant results concerning these primary objectives. The policy of exporting workers, however, has also had important unintended consequences and problems for Turkey.

*Sabri Sayari has been a professor of political science at Bogazici University, Istanbul. He received his Ph.D. from Columbia University and has held visiting teaching and research appointments at a number of European and American academic institutions. Between 1982 and 1984, he was the holder of a Danish Social Science Research Council grant to study Turkish migrant workers in Denmark. At present, he is a visiting scholar and consultant at the Rand Corporation, Santa Monica, California.*

A N important by-product of the economic expansion experienced by Western European states during the late 1950s and 1960s was the large-scale migration of workers from the Mediterranean basin to western and northern Europe. Turkey was a latecomer to the postwar European migration process, but it quickly became one of the main suppliers of migrant workers. During the heyday of migratory flow from Turkey to Western Europe, between 1961 and 1973, nearly 800,000 Turkish workers were officially recruited for specific jobs by European employers. In the same period, thousands of other Turks joined them unofficially, coming into Western Europe on tourist passports and staying on after finding employment. Today, an estimated 2 million Turkish workers and their dependents constitute one of the largest ethnic groups in the total stock of immigrant workers in Western Europe. Nearly 80 percent of these Turks reside in West Germany. In addition to this very large concentration, there are many in the Netherlands, France, Belgium, Austria, Switzerland, and the Scandinavian countries.[1]

Given that until 1961 Turkey had little involvement in the transnational migration of workers, what factors account for its having become a leading source of immigrant labor for Western Europe? The present article addresses this question. It argues that while the migration process was started and termi-

1. The approximate distribution in the early 1980s is as follows: West Germany, 1.55 million; the Netherlands, 150,000; France, 135,000; Belgium, 64,000; Austria, 65,000; Switzerland, 36,000; Sweden, 18,000; Denmark, 17,000; and Norway, 2700. At present, there are also more than 200,000 Turkish migrant workers in the Arab countries, with the largest concentrations in Libya—106,000—and Saudi Arabia—53,000.

nated by the Western European states, the volume of migration was significantly influenced by Turkey's migration policies. The first section provides an overview of migration from Turkey to Western Europe. In subsequent sections, the objectives, results, and unintended consequences of Turkey's efforts to promote migration abroad are discussed.

MIGRATION PROCESS

The migratory flow of workers from Turkey to Western Europe began in the early 1960s. The migration process was initiated by the West German government and West German employers. Gradually, other Western European states followed West Germany's lead and recruited Turkish workers throughout the 1960s. For all practical purposes, labor migration from Turkey to Western Europe came to an end in 1973 and 1974. Alarmed by the recessionary economic trends following the 1973 oil crisis, rising unemployment, and faced with growing public opinion pressures against further inflow of migrant workers, West Germany restricted the entry of new migrants from outside the European Economic Community (EEC). Again, most of the other Western European countries followed the West German example and implemented similar measures. Collectively, these measures marked the end of Turkish worker migration to Europe. The workers' dependents, however, have continued to move to European destinations under family-reunification schemes in the host countries.

The first group of Turkish migrant workers who came to Western Europe were neither unemployed in Turkey nor part of the traditional category of peasant emigrants facing bleak economic prospects at home. Most of them were skilled workers and artisans who had been employed in major Turkish cities such as Istanbul, Ankara, and Izmir. In the later phases of the migration process, there was a notable change in the social composition of the Turks who joined the migratory waves. Along with the increasing number of females, most of whom had been housewives in Turkey, there was also a steep rise in the number of peasant farmers who came from Turkey's rural areas. Evidence from surveys shows that these rural migrants owned some land and worked on it. They were not the poorest, non-land-owning peasants,[2] but, unlike their predecessors, the majority of these later emigrants had little or no previous exposure to modern forms of urban social and economic organization.

Migration from Turkey to Western Europe accelerated rapidly during the course of the 1960s, as information about the economic and social benefits of employment in Europe trickled back to Turkey. Its impact was most strongly felt in the social networks of the pioneering emigrants—among their relatives and friends and in their local communities. New recruits for Western European employers usually came from these social networks. The beachheads established by the initial groups of workers in West Germany became centers of reception for new migrants from Turkey. Turkish immigrant enclaves in West Germany and elsewhere in Europe had their origins in the preferences of the newly arriving Turks to settle in areas close to other Turkish migrants. These were usually in the inner rings of cities, where cheap housing and easy access to public transportation could be found.

## Motives for migration

By the mid-1960s, increasing numbers of Turks were attracted to the idea of becoming migrant workers. Most of them planned to work in Europe for only a few years; they expected to return home afterward. The dominant motive that shaped their interest in migration was the expected economic return from employment in Western Europe based on higher wages offered by the European firms. As Turks already employed in Europe began sending home remittances in sums that were considered to be extraordinary by relatives and friends in Turkey, the economic rewards of migration became self-evident. The numbers of potential migrants rapidly increased when the Turkish workers in Europe began their annual summer vacation trips to Turkey. Coming back with expensive gifts for relatives and friends, wearing European-made clothes and expensive personal items, and using their savings to buy new land or housing, the vacationing migrants provided further concrete evidence of the material gains to be had from jobs abroad.

A number of surveys conducted on Turks departing for European destinations has highlighted the primacy of economic factors in the decisions to migrate.[3] The survey respondents generally ranked items such as saving money or securing their families' future high on the list of reasons for becoming migrant workers. Along with the anticipated economic gains from migration, these responses revealed disillusionment with economic conditions in Turkey.

2. Suzanne Paine, *Exporting Workers: The Turkish Case* (London: Cambridge University Press, 1974), pp. 71-89.

3. For a discussion of the results of several surveys, see ibid., pp. 87-88, 200.

Despite significant strides toward development in the postwar period, Turkey remained economically the least advanced country in southern Europe. Between 1960 and 1978, per capita gross national product grew at an annual rate of 3.6 percent. Despite this gain, per capita income had reached only $850 by 1980, far below that of Spain, Greece, or Portugal, not to mention advanced industrial Western European states.

An important stumbling block in Turkey's efforts to attain higher economic growth rates has been the steep population rise. With a 2.6 percent annual increase, Turkey's population rose from 20.9 million in 1950 to 45.2 million in 1980. The impact of this demographic trend was felt most strongly in the labor market and population pressures on land. The entry of thousands of new workers into a labor market that could annually meet the demand for only about one-third of these job seekers created severe unemployment—and underemployment—problems in the Turkish economy. In the rural areas, high fertility rates combined with mechanization of the agricultural sector accentuated population pressures on land. The movement of approximately 7 to 9 million people from the countryside to the cities between 1950 and 1975 was partially due to growing economic difficulties encountered by Turks living in the rural areas.

It would be erroneous, however, to view the individual preferences for emigration exclusively in terms of economic variables. In-depth interviews with one group of migrant Turks show that migration to Europe is based on the desire to improve the migrants'—and their dependents'—quality of life.[4] While economic

rewards are viewed as the principal means to this goal, there are also other specific values attached to migration. One such highly valued objective is the attainment of higher social status or prestige, not necessarily in the host society but in the context of the home community in Turkey. Expectations of upward social mobility are based on greater wealth, as well as on living in a more modern environment, acquiring greater knowledge about the world, and providing advanced education for one's children. Another value related to quality of life and attached to migration is the goal of living in a more stimulating environment than that of the rural small towns and villages in Turkey. For some migrants, the desire to live without the traditional obligations of their home society constitutes an important aspect of their search for a better quality of life.

The individual preferences of many Turks to migrate to Europe can be viewed, therefore, as a human strategy for upward social and economic mobility. Research among the migrant workers reveals that most are motivated by a desire to shape their own destinies and view migration as a means to search for new alternatives. Their decisions to migrate were not simply prompted by the mechanistic and impersonal interaction of environmental forces, as commonly depicted in the traditional push-pull theories or chain-migration models. Rather, their behavior was based on a rational choice that, in turn, reflected realistic expectations of economic and social rewards. Although many Turkish workers came from a traditional sociocultural environment, they chose to migrate with a view toward fulfilling such funda-

4. These observations are based on my research among Turkish migrants in the Danish city of Aarhus. The study was conducted between 1982 and 1984; it was funded by a grant from the Danish Social Science Research Council.

mentally modern aspirations as improved quality of life, higher social
status in Turkey, education for their children, and so on. These goals were sufficiently valued that information about
the negative aspects of the migrant worker's experience—poor housing conditions, social isolation and loneliness,
manifestations of anti-immigrant behavior, and the like—did not deter millions
of Turks from seeking jobs abroad
through both legal and illegal channels.

## TURKEY'S MIGRATION POLICY

Combined with the labor-recruitment policies of the Western European
states, the growing demand in Turkey
for employment abroad created a favorable milieu for transnational migration.
However, without Turkey's policy of
promoting migration, the migratory
flow to Europe would probably have
been much less extensive. The term
"policy" is used here in a general sense.
It includes permissive indifference—or
the absence of specific legislation to
control and shape a social phenomenon—
as well as attempts to regulate the phenomenon to secure desired outcomes.[5]
Turkey's migration policy has included
elements of both. In some instances, its
objectives were not clearly articulated
by policymakers. Nevertheless, Turkey's
promotion of labor migration to Europe
was based on two major and several
minor considerations.

The first major policy concern was to
use migration as a means for alleviating
the pressures on the domestic labor
market. Given the high unemployment

and underemployment rates, "exporting
workers" to Western Europe became an
increasingly attractive policy objective
to Turkey.[6] Consequently, Turkey welcomed the decisions of European employers to include Turks in the pool of
migrant workers from the Mediterranean basin. To promote the process of
migration, Turkey signed a bilateral
labor-recruitment agreement with West
Germany in 1961. Similar agreements,
covering general stipulations for recruitment, employment, and wages, were
signed with Austria, the Netherlands,
and Belgium in 1964, with France in
1965, and with Sweden in 1967. A somewhat less comprehensive agreement was
signed with Switzerland in 1971. No
labor agreement was signed with Denmark, but one concerning the welfare of
Turkish migrants did go into effect in
late 1970. As one observer notes, the
timing of these agreements showed Turkey's strategy of maintaining a certain
continuity in its efforts to export labor
by "falling back on other countries if
one showed signs of saturation and
diminished absorption ability."[7]

The second major objective of Turkey's migration policy became explicit
more gradually, as it was discovered
that the remittances of the Turks employed in Europe could play an important role in coping with the perennial
foreign-exchange crises of the Turkish
economy. Since the early 1950s, when
ambitious industrialization projects
with heavy dependence on imports first
began to have negative repercussions on
the Turkish economy, Turkey had encountered serious balance-of-payments

5. Aristide R. Zolberg, "International Migration Policies in a Changing World," in *Human
Migration: Patterns and Policies,* ed. William H.
McNeill and Ruth S. Adams (Bloomington: Indiana University Press, 1978), p. 243.

6. The term "exporting workers" is borrowed
from the title of Paine's *Exporting Workers.*
7. Sefik Alp Bahadir, "Turkey and the Turks in
Germany," *Aussenpolitik* (First quarter 1979), p.
105.

problems. When it became evident that the remittances of the Turkish migrants could help cover the normally huge trade deficits—a consequence of migration that had not been clearly foreseen by policymakers in the early 1960s—government efforts to encourage the outflow of migrant workers were intensified. The Second Five-Year Development Plan, covering the period from 1968 to 1972, underlined the official recognition of the importance attached by Turkey to the remittances of migrants and specified the measures that were intended to raise their volume.[8]

In addition to these two main policy objectives, Turkey's official support of labor migration to Western Europe also rested on several secondary considerations.[9] One of these concerned the expectations of the policymakers that the migrants working in the industrialized settings of Western Europe would acquire new skills and training as a result of their experiences abroad. This policy objective was perceived to be of particular significance in the case of Turks coming from rural origins and without any previous exposure to an industrial work environment.

Another expected benefit from the official promotion of labor migration pertained to the impact of migration on the migrant's home community. When the migratory flows to Western Europe began, Turkish policymakers believed that migration would have a favorable impact on the migrant's local community in the form of new investments in small or medium-sized investments, transfer of technology and machinery, and new enterprises when the migrant returned. Again, this consideration was especially relevant for the rural migrants, as migration to Western Europe was expected to contribute to rural development in Turkey.

Finally, although never articulated very openly, outward migration from Turkey was looked upon favorably by some policymakers as a means of slowing down the rush to the cities in Turkey from the rural areas.[10] Hyperurbanization of Turkish cities during the 1960s and 1970s created problems in providing housing, municipal services, and jobs. In view of these problems, migration to Western Europe was perceived as serving a useful function in reducing some of the pressures of internal migration within Turkey.

## The influence of domestic political pressures

Along with these considerations, the actions of Turkish policymakers concerning worker migration to Europe were influenced by pressures from the Turkish public. As the economic and social opportunities offered by employment in Western Europe became apparent, the main political actors involved in migration policymaking—political parties, bureaucracy, labor unions, and employers' associations—increasingly came under pressure from the potential migrants to continue promoting the policy of exporting labor.

In the highly clientelistic environment of Turkish politics, the demand for

8. Turkey, State Planning Organization, *Second Five Year Development Plan 1968-1972* (Ankara: State Planning Organization, 1969), p. 134.

9. For the perspectives of policymakers on these issues, see Nermin Abadan-Unat et al., eds., *Migration and Development,* (Ankara: Ajans-Turk Press, 1975).

10. This is suggested in a study based on a survey of Turkish policy officials; see Ned Levine, "Antiurbanization: An Implicit Development Policy in Turkey," *Journal of Developing Areas* (July 1980).

getting on the official lists for worker recruitment emerged as a new and important source for political patronage. Parliamentary deputies and party officials actively worked on behalf of their constituents to find a place for them on the lists of applicants prepared by the Turkish Employment Service for jobs in Europe. Reacting to similar demands from their members, labor unions pressured the government to expand the volume of migration and to secure a more permanent status for Turks already employed in various European countries. Under the circumstances, it would have been politically risky for any elected Turkish government to oppose these demands. Later on, as new issues related to the Turkish workers in Europe—family reunification, visa restrictions, and so forth—came up for public discussion, similar pressures from the electorate became an important input in policymaking.

### The consequences of migration policy

It would be safe to assume that Turkey's policy orientation toward labor migration would have remained the same even in the absence of these domestic political pressures. The policy of promoting migration has paid off handsomely in two critical areas of the Turkish economy, namely, employment and foreign exchange. By siphoning off approximately 800,000 workers from the Turkish labor market since the early 1960s, migration abroad has eased some of the burdens on the economy with respect to the unemployment problem. This fact has played a significant role in Turkey's efforts to redirect the flow of migrant workers to the Arab countries since 1973 and 1974, when European labor recruitment came to an end.

The contribution of workers' remittances to the Turkish economy has been even more prominent. Remittances represented 14 percent of Turkey's foreign currency earnings in 1964; by the early 1970s that figure had increased to nearly 70 percent. In 1972, these remittances equaled 84 percent of export earnings and approximately 5 percent of the gross national product.[11] However, the volume of remittances sent home by Turks employed abroad has varied over the years, largely in accordance with the discrepancy between the official and real exchange rates of the Turkish lira. When this discrepancy was substantial, as in the period between 1974 and 1978, there was a sharp drop in the volume of remittances sent through official channels. Yet, even the unofficial transfer of foreign-exchange earnings by migrant workers through the black market has proved useful for the functioning of the Turkish economy. During the late 1970s, when Turkey faced its most severe economic crisis of recent times, the transfer of migrants' remittances via the black market helped to pay for about $1.5 billion worth of smuggled imports. Much of these consisted of badly needed equipment and primary inputs, without which Turkish industry would have probably collapsed.[12]

This vital role played by remittances in the economy has made remittances the cornerstone of Turkey's migration policy. In this respect, Turkey's policy responses fit the pattern set by other labor-exporting Mediterranean countries. As in Yugoslavia, Greece, and Spain, various schemes—some with little success—have been used by Turkey to direct the migrants' savings from

11. Paine, *Exporting Workers*, p. 106.
12. William Hale, *The Political and Economic Development of Modern Turkey* (London: Croom Helm, 1981), p. 232.

European into Turkish banks, preferably through official channels. These measures have ranged from special interest rates for foreign-currency saving accounts in Turkey to import privileges for migrants. A new bank was also established in 1975 to participate in financing the so-called workers' companies, which are manufacturing plants that would have as their principal stockholders Turks working abroad. This particular scheme initially received much acclaim in Western Europe; many viewed it as a possible incentive for facilitating return migration. However, the experience of the workers' companies has been disappointing for all parties concerned. The plan did not attract as many participants as anticipated, and many of those migrants who did become stockholders ended up with companies that ran into financial problems and bankruptcy.

With respect to the secondary objectives, Turkey's migration policy has produced mixed results. The expectation that the migrants would return to Turkey with newly acquired skills has not been fully realized. While some of the migrant workers have received new occupational training in the host societies, many were placed in jobs for which they were overqualified. Similarly, the goal of achieving rural development in Turkey through migration abroad has had only mixed results. In the first place, many returnees tend to settle in Turkey's major cities rather than in their original communities. Second, those who do settle in their home towns and villages generally tend to invest their savings in real estate rather than in economically productive enterprises.

Viewed in a broader context, however, migration abroad has become an important source for social change in Turkey. Employment in Western Europe has exposed large numbers of Turks to modern economic, social, and political processes. It has enabled them to expand their knowledge about these processes through firsthand experience in advanced, postindustrial societies. This learning experience has already affected the lives of many migrants; its impact on Turkey is beginning to be felt with the increasing number of returnees.

A notable aspect of migration-induced social change concerns the attainment of upward social mobility by the migrants in their home society. While in Europe, Turkish workers are generally accorded a very low social status, but their social standing in Turkey improves markedly. The signs of their upward social mobility are visible in both rural and urban Turkish society. For example, patron-client relations in rural areas have undergone major changes in recent years. On the basis of their newly acquired economic power, migrants who used to be the clients of the local rich farmers are no longer in dependent positions in such relationships. Another significant indicator of the same phenomenon is the changing pattern of arranged marriages in the rural communities. Children of Turkish migrants in Europe have become the preferred choice of nonmigrant families. In the cities, on the other hand, signs of migrants' upward social mobility are best exemplified by new trends in urban housing. Many Turks working abroad now own apartment flats in the richest neighborhoods of Istanbul, Ankara, and other major Turkish cities. During the summer months, the seaside resort areas near Istanbul—once accessible only to the city's well-to-do families—are filled with the trailer camps of the vacationing Turkish workers from Europe. These and similar changes attest to the improvement in the social and economic status of Turkish migrant-worker families.

*Unintended and unforeseen
policy consequences*

Turkey's efforts to promote labor migration to Western Europe have also had numerous unintended and unanticipated consequences. The most important of these concern the emergence of frictions with the host countries and the EEC, the cultural-revivalist trends among the Turkish migrants in Europe, and the problems related to return migration and second-generation migrants.

Since the early 1970s, the policy preferences of Turkey and Western European host countries concerning migration have been in conflict. The decisions of European countries to stop the inmigration of workers from outside the EEC area was bitterly opposed by Turkey. The latter's reaction to restrictive migration policies was particularly strong in the immediate aftermath of the legislation enacted in West Germany and other Western European states. When it became evident that pressures on individual countries would not lead to the removal of visa restrictions on Turks, Turkish policymakers concentrated their efforts on working out a solution through the EEC.

The basis for this strategy was the agreement signed by Turkey and the EEC in Ankara in 1963. The Ankara agreement, which gave Turkey associate membership status in the EEC, also provided for the free movement of Turks within the EEC upon Turkey's ascendancy to full membership. However, during the protracted negotiations between the EEC and Turkey regarding full membership, the issue of free move-

ment for Turkish workers turned out to be one of the major obstacles to Turkey's entry into the EEC. As one observer put it, the objective of the EEC in the early phases of these negotiations was "to bring Turkey into membership without bringing in the Turkish workers."[13] Turkey, on the other hand, viewed the Ankara agreement as a means for achieving, among other political and economic goals, the main objective of its migration policy. Later on, as the EEC began to show growing reluctance to accept Turkey as a full member, the likelihood of resolving this problem diminished even further. The last signed interim agreement between Turkey and the EEC in 1976 did not include any changes in the EEC's stand on the issue, although it did specify a number of measures favorable to Turkish workers already employed in the EEC member states.

The treatment of Turkish migrant workers in Western Europe also contributes to friction between Turkey and the host countries. Since the departure of the first group of migrant workers, the Turkish press has regularly carried news about real or alleged discriminatory acts against Turks in Europe. More recently, there has been a rise in the number of such reports as Turkish workers, particularly those in West Germany, have become the principal targets of racial and religious hostility. The news media in Turkey, as well as the European editions of several major Turkish newspapers, have extensively publicized these incidents. From time to time, Turkey has brought this problem to the attention of the host governments through diplomatic channels. Given the growing anti-

13. Ray C. Rist, *Guestworkers in Germany: The Prospects for Pluralism* (New York: Praeger, 1978), p. 101.

immigrant sentiments in Western Europe, the problem of racially motivated hostile acts against Turkish migrant workers remains a potential source of conflict in Turkey's relations with Western Europe.

Religious and ethnic revivalism among Turkish migrants in Western Europe constitutes the second major unforeseen consequence of Turkey's migration policy. The growing reaffirmation of cultural traditions and primordial loyalties in Turkish immigrant enclaves represents a radical departure from official state policies in Turkey concerning religion and ethnicity. Turkey's experience with secularism since the early 1920s is unique among Islamic states. The cultural revolution carried out by Atatürk following the establishment of the republic in 1923 drastically undermined the role of Islam in Turkish politics and society for nearly three decades. Since the late 1940s, Turkey has experienced a gradual Islamic revival, but official secularist policies have continued to play an important role in many areas of Turkish society. Possibly the most prominent example of this continued secularism concerns the national education policy, which is based on secular institutions and principles.

The large-scale migration of Turkish workers to Western Europe has posed an important challenge to the secularist principles of the Turkish state. Once settled in Europe, many Turks adopt a discernibly more Islamic orientation. This phenomenon is related to a variety of social and psychological concerns felt by the emigrants: the need to overcome the sense of homelessness in a foreign environment, the search for means of maintaining cultural ties with the home society, the belief in the value of an Islamic education in learning about proper social conduct and moral values,

and so forth. However, an equally important factor pertains to the fact that by virtue of living in Europe, the migrants can freely carry their commitment to Islam to its most conservative extremes. As a result, in an interesting and unexpected way, Western Europe—particularly West Germany—has become the center of intense activism by religious sects and movements, some of which are proscribed in Turkey.

The revival of Kurdish ethnic consciousness among the migrant workers has followed a similar pattern. Turkey's Kurdish ethnic minority—which constitutes approximately one-fifth of the country's total population—has participated heavily in the outflow of labor. In addition to providing them with economic benefits, migration has enabled many Kurds to reinforce their ethnic allegiances. Again, this has resulted from a mix of personal psychological needs and the absence of legal constraints in the host societies on free expression of Kurdish ethnic interests. In some Scandinavian states, such as Sweden and Denmark, the ethnic mobilization of Kurds from Turkey has been facilitated by governmental policies concerning educational programs. For example, the provision of instruction in Kurdish in Swedish elementary schools has played a central role in the resurgence of ethnicity among Sweden's Kurdish migrant workers from Turkey. As in the case of religious revivalism, the growing saliency of this ethnic resurgence stands in sharp contrast to official state policies in Turkey concerning ethnicity.

The third area of unintended and unforeseen consequences of Turkey's migration policy is related to problems of return migration. During the 1960s and 1970s, relatively small numbers of Turkish workers chose to return home. Their general inclination was to prolong their stay in Europe without making a firm commitment either to permanent settlement in the host countries or to resettlement in Turkey. The adoption of restrictive immigration measures by the European countries contributed to the prolongation of this critical decision; many who might have otherwise left chose to stay on, fearing that they might not be able to come back to Europe at a later time.[14] For its part, Turkey did little to encourage return migration. Wary of the economic and social consequences of large-scale return migration, Turkey sought to delay it as long as possible.

The 1980s have witnessed gradual increases in the volume of returnees. Some of the migrants have decided to return home to reap the benefits of their long years of labor in Western Europe. Others have been more or less forced to return, due to unemployment in the host countries.[15] The return bonus offers made by West Germany and increasing anti-immigrant sentiments in Western Europe in general have also contributed to the increasing return flow.

Changing trends in return migration have highlighted Turkey's unpreparedness to deal with problems of reintegration. Returning migrants experience considerable strains in adjusting to Turkish society. Adjustment is particularly stressful for their children. Having spent the early part of their adolescence abroad, they are now trying to adapt to the widely different social and educational environment of Turkey—a country that they know, for the most part, only from the stories told by their parents. In the absence of advance planning, Turkish policymakers have only belatedly realized the complexities of cultural reintegration processes.

## CONCLUSION

In his analysis of international migration movements, Zolberg notes that "the preferences of 'those who send' and 'those who receive' have shaped international migrations to a much greater extent than the preferences of 'those who go.' "[16] His observation is particularly relevant in the case of Turkish labor migration to Western Europe. As the preceding analysis has emphasized, the process of migration was started by the decisions of the European states to recruit labor from Turkey. Their initiative met with a positive response from increasing numbers of Turks who chose to work in Europe to improve their economic and social status. The migration of Turkish workers came to an end with the introduction of restrictive immigration legislation in the labor-importing countries. While the opening and closing of the gates of migration were determined by the host countries, Turkey's migration policies had a major impact on the flow of workers to Western Europe. Based largely on economic considerations, Turkey's efforts to promote labor migration abroad have met their primary objectives. However, the country now faces a number of problems related to the unforeseen consequences of its migration policy.

14. Rosemarie Rogers, "Incentives to Return: Patterns of Policies and Migrants' Responses," in *Global Trends in Migration: Theory and Research on International Population Movements*, ed. M. Kritz et al. (New York: Center for Migration Studies, 1981), p. 340.

15. See Czarina Wilpert, "Returning and Remaining: Return among Turkish Migrants in Germany," in *The Politics of Return: International Return Migration in Europe*, ed. Daniel Kubat (Rome: Centro studi emigrazione, 1984), pp. 101-12.

16. Zolberg, "International Migration Policies," p. 279.

ANNALS, *AAPSS*, **485**, May 1986

# Islamization in Western Europe: Political Consequences and Historical Parallels

*By* WILLIAM SAFRAN

ABSTRACT: This article deals with Islamic postwar immigrants to Western Europe, specifically North Africans—Maghrebis—in France and Turks in West Germany. It explores the relationship between economic status, ethnic consciousness, and religion and discusses the response of the host society to the Islamic reality. In this exploration a comparison is made with the immigration, several generations earlier, of Jews from Eastern Europe. Whereas Jewish immigrants, as individuals, were able more easily to adjust to their new environment and to advance economically, Muslim immigrants have encountered greater difficulties and have tended to remain economically underprivileged much longer. Conversely, it is argued, the Muslim communities have been able more effectively to maintain ethnocultural cohesion and collective political security because of the convergence of a variety of factors: the massive number, and urban concentration, of the postwar immigrants; the spread of pluralist ideology; the continuing connection with, and protection from, homeland governments; and other contextual elements. The article concludes with an evocation of appropriate policy responses by the French and German governments to the Muslim presence.

---

*William Safran is professor of political science at the University of Colorado at Boulder. He holds the B.A. and M.A. degrees from the City University of New York and a Ph.D. from Columbia University. He has done extensive research and writing on French and Western European politics, in particular on parties, social forces, and economic and ethnic policies. He is the author of* Veto-Group Politics *and* Ideology and Politics: The Socialist Party of France, *and coauthor of* Comparative Politics. *The revised edition of his* French Polity *was published recently.*

T HE phenomenon of immigrant workers in postwar industrial democracies has given rise to an impressive number of books and articles. Most of them have concentrated on the following themes: the imperative of rapid economic development and the shortage of workers, both of which occasioned a quest for cheap foreign labor; the exploitation and underclass status of immigrant workers; the tensions between the immigrant workers and the indigenous working class; and the ambivalence of the governments of the host countries, which could not clearly decide between rotation and resettlement, or between a policy of integration and de facto apartheid. Since most of the discussions have been informed by the assumption—often associated with the Left—that immigrants are a mere substratum of the working class as a whole and that, if they remained in the host countries, they would ultimately be dissolved into it, relatively little attention has been paid to noneconomic aspects of the immigrants' identity or relation to the host society.

The present article is an attempt to explore the relationship between immigrants and natives, particularly the impact of a community with an alien culture and an exotic religion upon the Christian, secular, Western, and modernizing majority. In this exploration, the postwar Muslim migration northward from the Middle East and North Africa will be compared with the prewar Jewish immigration westward from Poland, Russia, and Rumania. The title of this article is suggestive rather than strictly descriptive, for although it concentrates on the Turkish workers in West Germany and the Maghrebi—that is, Algerian, Moroccan, and Tunisian—workers in France, I am aware that there

are immigrants in other industrial countries as well, and that France and West Germany harbor numerous non-Muslim immigrants.

Muslim workers coming from the Middle East and North Africa after World War II have a great deal in common with Jews who emigrated from Eastern Europe two or three generations earlier. Both groups were motivated by a quest for better economic prospects; belonged to non-European cultures and practiced non-European religions and were, therefore, considered difficult to assimilate; chose Germany and France as the major European countries of settlement; and posed a challenge to the majority's traditional self-definition of its society.

The comparisons undertaken here must be tentative because they are diachronic and because the cultural and religious aspects of the immigrants and the implications of their presence for native culture are elusive matters. Nevertheless, such a comparison is analytically useful because it points at once to the existence of universal patterns in the relationship between immigrant and host society and to the importance of time and context in shaping such relationships. These are not merely functions of economy and class but of evolving culture and ethos, of changing definitions of society, and of international relations.

Among the major problems are the unreliability of demographic data; the imprecision of definitions of legal or illegal immigrant, guest worker, and alien; incomplete, and often conflicting, information about the number and nature of Islamic institutions; the absence of credible survey data on attitudes of immigrants, especially for earlier periods; and the difficulty of determining the relationship between categoric membership in the Islamic—or Jewish—community and degrees of religious observance. There are other problems, among them the following:

— a lack of concern by trade unions, employers, and governments with religious questions or religious memberships, especially in France, with its official commitment to separation of church and state;

— the difficulty of relating questions of language to questions of religion;

— the inability of Europeans to understand Islam—or Judaism—in its own terms; and

— the underlying, if sometimes unarticulated, assumption that Islam—or normative Judaism—does not combine comfortably with modernity in general and European culture in particular.

### THE ISLAMIC ASPECT
### OF THE IMMIGRANTS

According to most estimates, about half of the postwar immigrants to France, and more than a third of the immigrants to West Germany, are Muslims. The foreignness and the alien social patterns, the economic and housing conditions of the Maghrebis and Turks have long been matters of concern to governments, trade unions, employers' associations, and researchers; and a variety of approaches has been considered to help integrate these immigrants and their children economically and linguistically. Yet the Islamic aspect of these immigrants has been widely ignored. The typical French study of immigrants devotes little if any attention to religion; similarly, studies and government poli-

cies in West Germany convey the impression that Islam is not particularly relevant to the Turkish immigrant problem.[1]

Freedom of religion is guaranteed in West Germany. In addition to the established religions—Roman Catholicism, Lutheranism, and Judaism, which together comprise some 54 million people, or about 88 percent of the population—there are the free religions. The members of these latter and the rest who identify with no religion—together constituting about 7 million people—include the Turks, virtually all of whom are Muslims. Official German yearbooks devote extensive space to the two major Christian denominations and their institutions and give some attention to the religious communities of the Jews—which include about 30,000 members—and lesser Protestant sects. By contrast, the yearbooks tend not to deal with Muslims at all, except that they refer to the fact that more than 1.8 million of them live in the Federal Republic, that there is religious pluralism, and that Islamic institutions exist.[2] In the large German cities in which many Turkish immigrants live there are semipublic offices for the *Religions-*

1. See, for example, Bernard Granotier, *Les travailleurs immigrés en France* (Paris: Maspero, 1973 and 1979); Paulette Calame and Pierre Calame, *Les travailleurs étrangers en France* (Paris: Editions Ouvrières, 1972); Juliette Minces, *Les travailleurs étrangers en France* (Paris: Seuil, 1973); Nerman Abadan-Unat, ed., *Turkish Workers in Europe 1960-1975* (Leiden: E. J. Brill, 1976). In each of these volumes, the discussion of Islam is confined to three to five pages.

2. See *Facts about Germany, 1984* (Gütersloh: Bertelsmann, 1984), pp. 307-11, and *Jahresbericht der Bundesregierung 1983* (Bonn: Presse- und Informationsamt, 1983), pp. 596-97, which do not mention Islam at all; and *Taschenbuch des öffentlichen Lebens, Bundesrepublik Deutschland 1978* (Bonn: Festland Verlag, 1978), in which the extensive section on religion contains a single entry to the effect that there are Muslims in West Germany.

*gemeinschaft Islam,* but it is difficult to get from them precise information about the number of Muslims and the number and location of mosques.

Such cavalier treatment of the Islamic presence might be explained somewhat differently with regard to France and West Germany. In France, there have been, since 1906, no official census figures for religion; Islamic religious institutions have been characterized by relative underdevelopment and organizational weakness; and, finally, left-wing political parties and intellectuals, government, and trade unions have shared the conviction that Islamic or any other religious consciousness is artificial, temporary, and in the long run irrelevant, and that the Arab identity of Maghrebi immigrants can somehow be politically and analytically divorced from their Islamic identity.

In Germany, a combination of two factors has prevented both officialdom and the mass of society from taking Islam seriously: the myth of return *(Heimkehrillusion),* which in turn has led to assumptions of the temporary nature of all Islamic institutions; and the difficulty of accepting Islam as a religion that can be properly fitted into the Germanic cultural climate. The presupposition that was maintained for many years that the immigrants were guests who would be rotated back to their native countries had begun to assume an unrealistic air by the end of the 1970s. An increasing number of foreign workers remained in Germany, brought their families, and produced offspring. Thus, while the total number of foreign workers grew from 329,356 in 1960 to nearly 2 million in 1978, the number of dependent children grew much faster: from fewer than 25,000 in 1965 to about 250,000 in 1977, of whom more than 110,000 were in the school-aged group, between 6 and 18 years old.[3] In 1976, 17 percent of all live births in West Germany were to guest-worker families.[4] Whether such figures constitute sufficient proof that the Federal Republic is evolving into a culturally and ethnically pluralistic society is a matter of controversy.[5]

German authorities have shown some ambivalence about whether their educational policies should reflect, or promote, this pluralism. On the one hand, the need to function minimally in the German economic system has inclined the authorities to provide basic education in the German language; on the other hand, the fiction that the children of guest workers would eventually leave— a fiction that had gained some substance when, in the early 1980s, about 300,000 Turks took advantage of the offer of a generous lump-sum payment to return to their native country—suggested that they might well be excluded from typically German educational curricula and that whatever education they received should relate strictly to their homeland culture. Moreover, in order to make it easier for the guest workers to return home, their children would be systematically exposed to native culture and language. German educational policy went in several directions simultaneously:

1. It became integrationist and assimilationist, treating immigrants as new Germans.

3. In addition, there were over 700,000 children residing in Turkey whose parent or parents worked in Germany and who were therefore potential immigrants. Cf. Ray C. Rist, *Guestworkers in Germany* (New York: Praeger, 1978), p. 86; Abadan-Unat, ed., *Turkish Workers in Europe,* pp. 11, 393.

4. Figures from Ray C. Rist, "Guest Worker Children in Germany," *Comparative Education Review,* pp. 355-69 (Oct. 1979).

5. Rist, *Guestworkers in Germany,* p. 245 and passim.

2. It regarded the immigrants as foreigners and subjected them to a special educational regime that would fit them out for return.

3. It provided a curriculum that would acknowledge the existence and legitimacy of a hyphenated German and that would be genuinely pluralistic.

Many Germans have appeared to accept the idea of cultural pluralism in principle, and school policies seem to be increasingly consonant with such acceptance. One of these policies is the Bavarian double solution: the mainstreaming of Turkish children and the provision of several hours a week of Turkish language and Islamic studies. This solution was given a considerable institutional boost when the government of Northrhine-Westphalia decided that, beginning in the school year 1983-84, elementary school pupils born in Germany would be given the option of choosing Islamic religious instruction.

There is an increasing number of stories pointing out the long tradition of Islam in Germany. According to one such story, the first mosque in Germany was built by Frederick William I in 1732 in Potsdam for a group of Muslim soldiers serving in the Prussian army.[6] Another story mentions that an Islamic community center was built in Berlin in 1924, and a German translation of the Koran was published in 1938.[7] There are now said to be more than 150 mosques and Islamic prayer rooms throughout the Federal Republic, including large mosques or Islamic community centers or both in Berlin, Munich, Frankfurt,

Stuttgart, and Hamburg.[8] There is some uncertainty about whether these institutions are meant to serve the Turkish immigrant population on a permanent basis and whether they are indicative of a full acceptance of Islam by German society. Some of the Islamic institutions, such as the Islamic centers of Aachen and Munich, were built with Libyan money, primarily for the use of Arab university students and perhaps for the secondary purpose of promoting Arab political interests, and they have not attracted Turkish workers.

A more serious question is whether all this evidence of Islam is indicative of the acceptance of Islam as the equal, in institutional terms, of the well-established Christian religions. The fact that Islamic subjects are taught by imported teachers perpetuates the view that Islam is a foreign religion ill suited to the German context. Religious devotion, in that context, is associated with Gothic spires and organ music and not with carpeted prayer halls, minarets, and the call of the muezzin. Some Germans glorify Islam because it represents the exotic or romantic rather than because they are committed to pluralism; others, because they wish to fawn upon Arabs or express their continuing hatred of Jews in a more acceptable fashion. Many of the pro-Islamic Germans are members of the upper classes who do not often encounter, or compete with, Muslim Turks and who do not require an ethnic underclass for their status satisfactions.

With a history of colonialism extending over vast Islamic domains, France has been much more receptive to the presence of Muslims than has Germany.

6. "Islam in the Federal Republic of Germany," *Kulturchronik*, p. 44 (Apr. 1983).

7. "Islam in Germany," *Rabetat al-Alam al-Islami*, 3:12, 41-44 (Oct. 1976).

8. Most of these are Sunni; there is a Shiite center in Hamburg. See "Jeder nach seiner Fasson," *Scala*, no. 4, pp. 40-41 (Apr. 1980).

Naturalized army veterans of North African origin (*harkis*) have been living in France for at least two generations, and the first mosque was built in Paris immediately after World War I. But the Maghrebis then numbered no more than 20,000 or 30,000; most of them, moreover, were thoroughly assimilated to French culture (*francisé*) and not particularly religious. After World War II, the number of Maghrebis increased rapidly. Between 1962 and 1973, the number of French citizens of the Islamic faith tripled from 67,000 to 200,000. By 1985, there were more than 2.5 million Muslims in France—including more than 700,000 citizens—making Islam the second most popular religion, after Roman Catholicism.[9]

This numerical strength has not translated precisely into the organizational strength of Islam, nor is it as yet reflected in the overall influence of that religion in France. There are now several voluntary associations—the growth of which has been particularly marked since 1981—for promoting the study of Arabic and Islamic culture, but there are only about three dozen mosques—roughly a third of them in the Paris region—and 200 to 300 prayer halls. It has been difficult to convince the municipal authorities to grant permits for the construction of mosques, and to persuade the national authorities to provide Muslims with significant access to television and radio programs to transmit their culture.[10] In the Paris suburb of Mantes-la-Jolie—where at least half of the inhabitants are Muslims—when the municipal government participated in the construction of a mosque, some citizens objected because "this mosque was a terrible sign of the installation of Islam in a conquered land."[11]

The resistance of much of the native majority to Islam has several sources. For many trade union leaders, hostility to Islam reflects a dislike for all organized religion; for ultranationalists, anti-Arab and anti-Islamic attitudes intermingle. The ultranationalists often evoke historical themes relating to the building of the French nation, such as the halting by Charles Martel of the Muslim invasion in the eighth century.[12] Associated with that historical evocation are images of Islamic hordes, followed by wives and numerous children, again invading Europe, converting infidels by the sword, and bringing in polygamy, harems, and feudal family relations.

The problem of the Islamic image in France must be attributed in part to the ambivalence of the Maghrebis' orientation to their own religion—in other words, of the relationship between their Arab ethnicity and their Muslim faith. Many Maghrebi workers behave like other immigrant proletarians in stressing their ethnic identity more than their religion. Ethnicity is emphasized because it is viewed as the major factor of their underprivileged economic condition; it includes their ghetto upbringing, their physiognomy, and their marginality. The Arab identity is inculcated by a father's telling his son never to forget "that you are an Arab, and that they [the

9. Figures from Jean Benoit, *Dossier E . . . comme Esclaves* (Paris: Editions Alain Moreau, 1980), pp. 105-6.

10. There has been some success with the media. Since the mid-1970s, there have been Islamic-culture programs, and the 1981 legislation permitting private radio stations has enhanced the possibilities for such programing.

11. "Immigrés: Le dossier explosif," *Express,* 4 Feb. 1983, pp. 46-63.

12. See Georges Mauco, *Les étrangers en France et le problème du racisme* (Paris: Pensée universelle, 1984), p. 190.

French] have killed a million of our people in Algeria."[13]

The Arab—or Maghrebi—identity, however, cannot be easily separated from the Islamic one. Although most Maghrebi workers are not particularly religious—and some have even begun to observe such Christian customs as Christmas celebrations—they continue to adhere to basic Islamic practices such as male circumcision, the observance of Ramadan fasts, and the abstention from eating pork. Moreover, the Maghrebis' self-definition according to their national origin, which is initially more important than religious identification in the secular environment of urban France, soon leads to a greater identification with Islam for several reasons.

1. Identification with Islam implies a membership in a large and influential extraterritorial community and is therefore seen as most effective in preserving Maghrebi identity.[14]

2. It gives a sense of purpose to people not fully accepted by French society.

3. It provides a form of psychological security.

Similarly, normative Islam—there is as yet no Westernized or Reform Islam—cannot be easily separated from Arab culture. It is difficult to imagine an imam wearing the upturned collar of a Christian clergyman, the Koran being studied without some knowledge of Arabic, and Koranic schools failing to focus on Middle Eastern or North African historical and political themes. Hence, to many of the French, Islamic orientations of immigrants may be in-

dicative of a form of political double allegiance.

MUSLIMS AND JEWS:
A DIACHRONIC COMPARISON

A look at the situation of Muslims in France and West Germany recalls in many ways that of the Jews who had settled in these countries earlier. Like the Muslims, Jews had come in search of a better economic future; were viewed as an alien, indigestible presence; and were the object of distrust. Jewish men then, like Muslim men today, were labeled by their European hosts as dirty, given to criminality, and tending to lust after native girls. In some ways, Jews were better off than Muslims are today. First, they were economically more adaptable, often coming equipped not only with intense ambition but also with commercial and artisan's skills. Second, they were able to assimilate much more quickly than present-day Turkish or Maghrebi immigrants. They came in smaller numbers, were less ghettoized, and consequently less able to maintain communities that were tightly knit and strong enough to perpetuate a cohesive ethnic culture; they were for the most part literate and came with linguistic affinities—in the form of Yiddish—and a certain receptivity to the culture of their adopted domiciles.

Since the time of Napoleon, Eastern European Jews had developed an admiration for German and French literary traditions and political ideas. Although the Orthodox Judaism with which most of them came looked oriental in juxtaposition to Christianity, models of a westernized—Reform—Judaism were already provided by the native Jews of Germany and, to a lesser extent, France. Moreover, these native Jews, often em-

13. Ahmed Boubeker, "Quartier cousin: Les immigrés de la deuxième génération," *Esprit*, pp. 28-48 (Apr. 1983).

14. Minces, *Travailleurs, étrangers*, pp. 438-39.

barrassed by the outlandish manners of their newly arrived coreligionists, did their best to help them adjust.[15] Finally, Jews were driven by circumstance to make much greater personal effort at Germanizing or gallicizing themselves than has been required of Muslim immigrants. There was no myth of the Jews' return—other than in an abstruse, millennial sense—and no cultural contact with home governments. On the contrary, the governments of Russia and other Eastern European countries, which had often turned a blind eye to the persecution of Jews, or, worse, had instigated pogroms and forced conversions, were glad to be rid of their Jews. Unlike the postwar Turkish immigrants, Jews who came to Germany quickly opened shops or factories and began to achieve middle-class and lower-middle-class status when the Gentile petite bourgeoisie was still weak.[16] The children of many of the Jewish immigrants easily became professionals, in contrast to the descendants of the Turks and Maghrebis, who have tended to remain in an underclass condition, immigrants of the second generation.

On the other hand, Jewish prewar immigrants suffered from a number of disadvantages that postwar Muslim immigrants have been spared. The rapid *embourgeoisement* of the Jews improved the fortunes of individuals, but in the long run it enhanced neither the political power nor the security of the Jewish community. In the first place, *jus sanguinis*—descent rather than place of birth—was the dominant basis for granting citizenship, and naturalization was far more difficult—even in France, a country of immigration—than it was to become after World War II.

Second, the Jews provoked widespread resentment among a variety of groups. The peasantry resented Jews because they often constituted the middlemen and were accused of sharp business practices. Today the indigenous working class resents the Muslim immigrant because he or she is viewed as a scab, whereas the working-class and trade-union ideologues and other elements of the political Left resented the Jews because they were viewed as the harbingers of capitalism.

Third, the cultural adaptability of the Jews, the progressive westernization of Judaism, and the creeping secularism of the Jewish immigrants all conspired to reduce both the Jewish birthrate and communal cohesion. In contrast, the relative so-called backwardness of the Muslim immigrants must in the long run enhance their collective security. Both the proletarian status and the Islamic culture of Middle Eastern and North African immigrants contribute to the fact that these immigrants have numerous children. Although, to be sure, large family size helps to keep the Muslims poor in the short run, it also enlarges the size of their communities. This development will ultimately be reflected in a significant growth of political power, particularly on local levels, as soon as France and Germany follow the Swedish and Dutch examples and grant immigrants the right to vote in municipal elections.

15. See Steven E. Aschheim, *Brothers and Strangers: The East European Jew in German and Jewish Consciousness, 1800-1923* (Madison: University of Wisconsin Press, 1982), chaps. 1-3; Jack Wertheimer, "The Unwanted Element: East European Jews in Imperial Germany," *Leo Baeck Institute Yearbook,* 26: 23-46; Paula Hyman, *From Dreyfus to Vichy: The Remaking of French Jewry, 1906-1939* (New York: Columbia University Press, 1979), esp. pp. 63-88, 114-52.

16. Jacob Lestchinsky, "Jewish Migrations 1840-1956," in *The Jews,* ed. Louis Finkelstein (Philadelphia: Jewish Publication Society, 1966), 2:1549-50.

The presence of a community of more or less well-established native Jews in Germany and France was advantageous to immigrant Jews in the sense that it provided an institutional infrastructure, a degree of solidarity, and a role model. By contrast, native Muslim communities in these countries are small, and their voluntary associations and philanthropic activities are underdeveloped. However, philanthropy is today less necessary than it was a century earlier, since the welfare state is now fully in place, providing for immigrants as well as natives. Moreover, there is no evidence that the *Kulturkampf* that once raged between native and eastern Jews in Germany and France is now paralleled by a religious conflict within the Islamic community in West Germany, within the immigrant Maghrebi community in France, or between the latter and the more than 400,000 naturalized French Muslims, many of whom had established themselves in the country a generation or two earlier. And there is less reason for such conflict, because there are relatively few native, acculturated, and *embourgeoisé* Turks in Germany or Maghrebis in France who worry about having their status jeopardized by the influx of new immigrants. On the contrary, the settled and naturalized Muslim intellectuals often find that the greater immigrant presence provides them with new professional roles as intermediaries or academic interpreters.

More important, religion is a far less significant source of tension and hostility for postwar Muslim immigrants than it was for prewar Jewish immigrants. Several generations ago, liberal Protestants agreed with conservative Catholics and Protestants in affirming "the exclusively Christian character of German

society, nationality, and culture";[17] in France, too, membership in the national community was—at least since the revocation of the Edict of Nantes—often equated with membership in the Catholic Church. Hence, to the extent that the Germans and French were believing Christians, they viewed Judaism with hostility. It was old-fashioned, particularistic, and identified with those who rejected the Savior; thus the uniqueness, isolation, and poverty of Jewish communities in Europe until the modern era were signs of divine disfavor.

In contrast, the Muslims do not bear the stigma of deicide and there is no exact Muslim parallel to the image of the wandering Jew. Islam seems too exotic to native Europeans, and the presence of its adherents in Germany and France is too recent, for the majority and for the leaders of the Christian establishment to have developed a distinct theological hostility or a mass paranoia about Islam or Muslims. The Catholic integralism that once lurked behind the *mission civilisatrice*—and that was often cloaked in the ideology of universalism—must compete today with a host of secular ideologies as well as with a Muslim integralism in which Islam "functions at once as ideology, religion, morality, and guide of social and individual conduct."[18]

Muslim residents in Western Europe are less embarrassed and insecure about Islam than were the Jews about their Judaism before the advent of Hitler. There is no instance of Muslim self-

17. Uriel Tal, *Christians and Jews in Germany: Religion, Politics, and Ideology in the Second Reich, 1870-1914* (Ithaca, NY: Cornell University Press, 1975), p. 163.
18. Adil Jazouli, "Jeunes Maghrébins en France," *Etudes,* 360(5):609-20 (May 1984).

hatred quite comparable to the Jewish self-hatred that led Otto Weininger, a young Viennese Jewish intellectual, to commit suicide in the early years of the twentieth century; and there are no postwar Muslim parallels to the nineteenth-century vogue of upwardly mobile Jews embracing Christianity. There is not yet a Western European diaspora intellectualism among Muslims that would produce cultural oversensitivities—in part because Islam is globally too powerful, and in part because Christianity as a European household religion has been morally eclipsed, as a result of the actions and inactions of its leaders during the war, and has been organizationally and financially weakened, as a result of loss of believers. This explains the fact that whatever proselytizing efforts the Christian churches have made among Muslims—and they are not very noticeable—have not been successful.

What adaptation there has been among Muslims is not to Christianity but to modernity: a change in eating and dressing habits; a desire for material possessions; an interest in a better lot for one's children; a diminution of the distrust of women; a more private pattern of religious observance; and a general decline in religiosity.[19] On the other hand, there is the pull of Islam, reflected in the presence of more than 40,000 converts to that religion in France and between 2000 and 10,000 in Germany.[20] These converts comprise not only natives married to Muslim immigrants but are said also to include ex-Christian theologians and university graduates who have viewed Islam as an attractive third way between capitalism and communism.

Despite the virtual halt in Muslim immigration since the mid-1970s and the departure of several hundred thousand Muslims from Germany and France, the Muslims' presence in these two countries is likely to be a permanent feature and, with it, the implantation of Islam. Today, Islamic consciousness is clearly coupled with the consciousness of economic deprivation; but even if the material situation and class status of the immigrants should change for the better, Islam will maintain itself, because religion and ethnicity have been shown to outlive the objective economic conditions with which they have been associated. If the fate of the Jews in Germany serves as a parallel, the successful socioeconomic integration of Turks in the Federal Republic might breed as much resentment as lack of integration would because these Turks would be accused of posing or passing as Germans. If they renounced their Islamic religion in favor of Christianity and Germanized their names, they would not necessarily win acceptance as genuine Germans—largely because of their un-German looks—and would, in addition, be considered traitors by the masses of unassimilated, and still solidly Muslim, Turks. A similar situation might arise in France, except that racism and xenophobia would be partially transferred from the Maghrebis to blacks from sub-Saharan Africa, whose presence acts as a buffer.

19. Granotier, *Travailleurs immigrés* (1973), p. 139; "Etre musulman dans une société française: Entretien avec Michel Serrin," *Projet*, no. 171-72, pp. 50-56 (1983).

20. *Quid 1983* (Paris: Laffont, 1983), p. 619; "Islam in the Federal Republic of Germany," p. 45.

## PROSPECTS AND SCENARIOS

Before World War I, many Jews in Germany dreamed in vain of a tolerant religious pluralism—in which the thesis would be accepted that state and nation were distinct and where Jews would be permitted to claim both Jewish peoplehood and German citizenship.[21] More than two generations—and the murder of 6 million Jews—later such a distinction has come to be progressively legitimated, so that Turks in Germany and Maghrebis in France are acquiring a triple choice among return, assimilation, and biculturalism.

The prospects of assimilation of Turks and Maghrebis into their host societies and even of a merger of Muslim and native cultures are not very good, owing to the massive number of the immigrants and the immigrants' tight network of social relations associated with urban concentration, lower-class status, the persisting myth of return, and the continuing cultural and family ties with countries of origin. In the nineteenth century, a member of a minority wishing to live in Germany or France had to make a complicated adjustment; for Jews, this often required that they attempt to follow the dictum of Moses Mendelssohn to "be a German on the street and a Jew at home." Today it is not easy for Turks to be Germans on the street, when their foreign accent, their gestures, and their occupational status mark them off from other Germans. It is sometimes just as difficult to be Turkish at home, since many aspects of life that used to be essentially private—education, welfare, and leisure-time pursuits—tend increasingly to be in the public domain.

One might reasonably expect a gradual westernization of selected religious and social attitudes and practices: a

greater role for women; a partial displacement of Islamic fatalism by the Protestant work ethic required for upward mobility; the printing of the Koran and other Islamic books in French and German; and perhaps, ultimately, the use of the languages of the host countries in Muslim prayer. By and large, however, it is likely that the pressure to assimilate will slacken and that biculturalism and the legitimacy of the hyphenated Frenchman or German will be increasingly acknowledged.

There are many reasons for expecting pluralism to become more firmly established in France and West Germany, and with it, the partial Islamization of their societies. To begin with, the Jacobinism of the leaders and heirs of the French Revolution and the racist organicism of German Romantics, the two major ideologies that, in theory or practice, glorified the culturally homogeneous nation-state, have been discredited. A century ago, many Eastern European Jews had been convinced that "civilization comes from the West; one must go and meet it."[22] Postwar Muslim immigrants do not have such an idealized view of the *civilisation* of France or the *Kultur* of Germany, owing to the colonial record of the one and the barbaric behavior of the other, the deflation of the military mystique of both countries, and the decline of the global importance of the French and German languages.

A second factor is the evolution of the society of the host country. The presence of Turks and Maghrebis may no longer be as offensive to the prevailing conception of society as that of Jews had once been. Being essentially urban, Jew-

21. See Max Kollenscher, *Zionismus und Staatsbürgertum,* 2nd ed. (Berlin: Zionistisches Zentralbureau, 1910), pp. 3-6.

22. Quoted in Monika Reinharz, ed., *Jüdisches Leben in Deutschland: Selbstzeugnisse zur Sozialgeschichte, 1780-1871,* (Stuttgart: Deutsche Verlagsanstalt for Leo Baeck Institute, 1976) p. 50.

ish immigrants of the nineteenth century had offended many a French citizen because they did not understand "treasured simple French virtues best incarnated in the peasant";[23] and they offended many a German who harbored romantic notions—later successfully exploited by Hitler—about the peasantry as an anchor of social stability. The fact that a large proportion of Turkish immigrants to Germany and Maghrebi immigrants to France are of peasant origin has little do with the greater official and academic sympathy toward them, simply because in the face of rapid urbanization the immigrants' threat to peasant virtues is not very compelling.

Third, there is a degree of transnational concern with the treatment of Muslim and other immigrants that was sadly absent in connection with the German treatment of Jews during the Nazi period. That concern is embodied in multilateral agreements between the European Community and the countries supplying immigrant workers, resolutions emanating from the Council of Europe, and various covenants produced by the United Nations and its agencies.[24] All these have helped to develop standards for the equitable treatment of minorities and a pluralistic approach to their cultures and have served as a system of surveillance and pressure.

One scholar of ethnicity has argued that "cultural power"—that is, the capacity of a minority culture to maintain itself—depends on its ability not only to adapt to rapid technological change but also to mobilize its economic power and its external political support. "In the

western world," he asserts, "most cultural minorities have a homeland."[25] This was not true of Jews until 1948; it is, however, true of the Muslim immigrants in France and Germany. Home governments—notably Turkey, Algeria, and Morocco—supply teachers and educational material, often on the basis of bilateral agreements, and are fully capable of utilizing their political and sometimes economic clout.

To be sure, racism persists; the old Jew-hatred, based on phobias about the excessive Judaization *(Verjudung)* of French or German society, is now often supplanted by a phobia and hatred of Muslims. In France, this hatred has led to beatings and murders of Maghrebis, and in Germany, to insults and stonings of Turks, bombings of their stores, and the refusal to rent rooms to them or serve them in restaurants.[26] While many Germans have tried to suppress their experiences under Hitler—and few would publicly label the Turks as subhuman—"the attitudes and behavior developed then must still have some effect in shaping prejudices."[27] These are sometimes reflected in the recycling of Nazi terminology that was once used in connection with the persecution of Jews.[28] Thus far, the overtly political expression of anti-Muslim sentiments has been confined, in West Germany, to manifestos

23. Hyman, *From Dreyfus to Vichy,* p. 67.

24. See James Fawcett, *The International Protection of Minorities,* Minority Rights Group Report no. 41 (London: Minority Rights Group, 1979).

25. Antony E. Alcock, "Government Attitudes to Cultural Minorities," in *The Future of Cultural Minorities,* ed. A. Alcock (New York: St. Martin's Press, 1979), pp. 109-10.

26. "Raus mit dem Volk," *Spiegel,* 15 Sept. 1980, pp. 19-26.

27. Stephen Castles and Godula Kosack, *Immigrant Workers and Class Structure in Western Europe* (London: Oxford University Press, 1973), p. 25.

28. For example, *Deutschtum, Fremdartigkeit, abendländischer Kulturraum, deutsche Eigenart,* and *Ausrottung.*

against *Ueberfremdung* ("overforeignization") and, in France, to the support of the extreme rightist *Front national.* But these are not likely to lead to the kinds of policies applied earlier to Jews—forcible conversion, expropriation, mass expulsion, or wholesale murder—because the host countries in question are democratic, because international public opinion—and especially that of the Third World—would mount vocal protests, and hence because such policies are in the present context inelegant, if not technically unfeasible.

Nothing illustrates the contextual difference better than the change in official attitudes regarding racism and discrimination. Whereas before the rise of nazism little was done to protect Jews and other minorities against job discrimination or hate campaigns, after World War II several Western European governments sponsored specific legislation to protect minorities. The French made the dissemination of race hatred and the libeling of ethnic groups a punishable offense; the British government introduced antidiscrimination bills;[29] and in 1985 the West German Parliament discussed legislation to outlaw the public denial of the historicity of the Holocaust. Of course, some of these measures have little more than symbolic value, but they may have a restraining impact on the actions of citizens.

Juxtaposed to the racism of certain segments of society there are governments that, at least publicly, promote pluralism. These are abetted by labor unions and mass political parties, especially on the democratic Left, that must, for reasons of principle and long-term

political calculation, come out in support of the economic and cultural rights of immigrants, even in the face of racist pressures within the indigenous rank and file.

One of the manifestations of the difference between prewar attitudes toward Jews and postwar attitudes toward Muslims is the presence of mass movements concerned with supporting immigrants, fostering understanding, or fighting racism. Before the advent of Hitler, there was no German equivalent of the Mouvement contre l'antisémitisme et le racisme et pour la paix; there were no mass demonstrations protesting violence against Jews, and no German equivalent of the movement, inaugurated early in 1985 in France, that preaches solidarity with foreigners. Since the inauguration of the Bonn republic, there have been organizations for Christian-Jewish collaboration; efforts at rebuilding synagogues, often in places where few Jews remain; the opening of institutes for Judaic studies at universities; and a miscellany of official measures that accord Jews a kind of *Denkmalsschutz,* or protection of a historic relic.

The changing context is reflected in the orientations and organizational patterns of the immigrants. Before the rise of fascism, the majority of Jewish immigrants—and virtually the whole Jewish establishment except for the small Zionist segment—were optimistic about the prospects of the cultural integration of the Jews in France and Germany. By contrast, most of the leaders of the Turks in Germany and the Maghrebis in France are participating in attempts to preserve the Muslim identities of their respective communities. Thus the Amicale des Algériens en Europe, the membership of which ranges from 60,000 to

29. See Gary Freeman, *Immigrant Labor and Racial Conflict in Industrial Societies: The French and British Experience, 1945-1975* (Princeton, NJ: Princeton University Press, 1979), pp. 53-57.

100,000 in France,[30] promotes the retention of Algerian consciousness, in part because of a lack of optimism about the prospects of complete Maghrebi assimilation in France and in part because, if there were such assimilation, it would impair the flow of remittances to the immigrants' families in Algeria.

In sum, the low economic status, the alien culture, and the persistence of racism and its opposite—the growth of tolerance and pluralistic thinking—all stimulate the Muslim immigrants and their descendants to keep their eyes turned to their countries of origin and to maintain their culture while fully expecting to remain where they are.

In view of the anticipated growth of the absolute number of Muslims in France and Germany and of their proportion of the population as a whole—a growth that is not likely to be counterbalanced by a complete cultural attrition—it is possible to prognosticate the adjustments of the host societies and government policies and the evolution of new patterns. These would include the following:

— the institutionalization, on a countrywide basis, of weekly free periods for Muslim elementary school children, to be used for supplementary instruction in Islam, Arabic, Turkish or any combination of these;

— the growth of Koranic schools and institutes, culminating—in West Germany—in Islamic confessional schools parallel to the existing Roman Catholic and Lutheran ones and, ultimately, in the establishment of Islamic theological faculties at universities;

— an increased effort at introducing the indigenous students to the diversity of cultures by intercultural experiences that would go beyond such current superficial practices as the recounting of Anatolian folklore in German schools or having mothers bring recipes for *couscous* to French ones;[31]

— the formal recognition, or establishment, of Sunni Islam in West Germany, and in both countries, the appointment of Islamic clergy—imams—to serve as military chaplains;

— a possible adjustment of Sunday closing laws to provide for alternative days of rest for devout Muslims and perhaps even a selective toleration of polygamy.[32]

— the provision of regular state-supported programs on Muslim culture and religion on radio and television; and

— a more sensitive approach to the presentation of the country's history, such that there will be fewer references to "our ancestors the Gauls" or "our forebears the Teutonic knights."

31. See Robert Solé, "Les immigrants dans l'école," *Le Monde,* 10-11 Feb. 1985.

32. In May 1985, a federal court in West Berlin ruled that the polygamous marriage of a Jordanian Muslim, resident in the Federal Republic since 1961, was not in conflict with public morals and was protected by the Basic Law, but that—since polygamy was "extrinsic to the European cultural sphere and does not correspond to the concept of equality between man and woman"—his second wife "would not automatically be granted immigrant status." *Week in Germany* 10 May 1985.

30. Mark J. Miller, "Reluctant Partnership: Foreign Workers in Franco-Algerian Relations, 1962-79," *Journal of International Affairs,* 33: 219-37 (Fall-Winter 1979).

Such developments might well be accompanied by increasing talk about a possible symbiosis of Muslim and French or German culture, the dissemination of such slogans as "Islamo-Christian civilization," and the proliferation of associations of Christian-Muslim cooperation. In any event, these developments would add up to a partial Islamization that would, in turn, lead to a redefinition of French and German societies and transform them into "more pleasant pluralistic places."[33]

33. Irving Louis Horowitz, Preface, in Rist, *Guestworkers in Germany,* p. ix.

ANNALS, *AAPSS*, **485**, May 1986

# Immigration Policy in France and Germany: Outputs versus Outcomes

*By* JAMES F. HOLLIFIELD

ABSTRACT: This article looks at the successes and failures of immigration policy in France and Germany. Particular attention is given to comparing immigration and foreign-worker policies—outputs—and the results of these policies—outcomes—in each state since the suspension of immigration in the mid-1970s. The analysis of the French and German experiences suggests that the gap between outputs and outcomes results from the inability of the state fully to control the migratory process. Inevitably, many foreign workers will choose to settle in the country in which they work. Stopping the movement of workers into and out of the country and suspending immigration tends to speed up the process of settlement and increase family and seasonal immigration. The principal lesson for other industrial democracies is that suspending immigration and exporting workers is not an effective way to solve employment problems.

---

*James F. Hollifield is assistant professor of politics at Brandeis University. He recently received his Ph.D. in political science from Duke University. Prior to joining the Brandeis faculty, he taught at Duke University and Davidson College. He also has studied and taught in France at the Université de Grenoble and the Institut d'études politiques in Paris. He has written on the topic of immigration in both French and English, and his most recent work is* The Political Economy of Immigration.

POLICYMAKING in industrial democracies is a continuous struggle between competing groups over the allocation of resources and opportunities. This struggle is more intense during periods of rapid social and economic change, when every group is searching for that factor or combination of factors that will give it an advantage. Since the economic crisis that began in 1973, the fight for jobs has intensified and governments have been pressed to find a solution to the problem of unemployment. One solution has been to stop immigration and expel foreign workers, who have little political power.

Prior to 1973, many Western European governments regarded foreign labor as a valuable economic resource. The introduction of foreign workers into national labor markets was seen as the best way to overcome labor shortages and fully utilize productive capacity in an era of economic expansion.[1] In states where the labor shortage was seen as particularly acute, such as France and the Federal Republic of Germany, the government attempted to recruit foreign workers.

After the oil shock in 1973 and the recession that followed, immigration policy in Western Europe changed radically. Foreign workers came to be seen as a political and economic liability. Efforts were made to stop further immigration and, wherever possible, to encourage foreigners to return to their countries of origin.

This article focuses on the changes in immigration policy in France and Germany in the 1970s. Particular attention is given to explaining the gap that has developed between policies—outputs—

and the results of the policies—outcomes—in each country.[2] Given the relative political vulnerability of immigrants, it seems that governments would have little difficulty in expelling them in order to reduce unemployment. Yet, immigration and foreign employment in France and Germany have remained relatively high in the past ten years. How do we explain this failure to simply export unemployment?

A CONCEPTUAL FRAMEWORK
FOR THE ANALYSIS OF
IMMIGRATION POLICY

In any democratic society, the outcome of public policy depends in part on the ability of government to achieve agreement between competing groups. Therefore, explaining the gap that exists between outputs and outcomes in the area of immigration requires understanding the activities of those groups capable of influencing the formulation and implementation of policy. Employers, workers, and the state all have an interest in immigration policy. Workers, represented by their trade unions, want to protect wages and working conditions. Therefore they will try to control the number of foreign workers and the conditions under which these workers will be employed. Employers may need foreign labor when it becomes difficult or impossible to recruit national workers for menial jobs. The question arises, therefore, To what extent can a government design and implement immigration policies that either incorporate the demands of major economic interest groups, bypass them in favor of some higher national interest, or simply allow

1. See Charles Kindleberger, *Europe's Postwar Growth: The Role of Labor Supply* (Cambridge, MA: Harvard University Press, 1967), pp. 7 ff.

2. The distinction between outputs and outcomes is explained in David Easton, *A Systems Analysis of Political Life* (New York: John Wiley, 1965), pp. 351-52.

the market to solve—or aggravate—the problem?[3]

To a certain extent, the effectiveness of immigration policy is a measure of the strength of the state, its ability to prevent employers from hiring undocumented workers, and change the structure of the labor market. It could be argued that the smaller the gap between policy outputs and outcomes, the greater the ability of the state to control employers' hiring practices and change market outcomes.[4] At least three factors can affect the making of immigration policy: (1) interest group pressures; (2) public opinion, which may be expressed through social unrest or traditional political institutions; and (3) the relatively independent assessment by policymakers of the need for foreign labor.

The influence of each of these factors will depend in part on institutional arrangements. For example, the influence of interest groups depends on their access to a variety of institutions, ranging from parties, legislatures, and bureaucracies to neocorporatist institutions, such as the Conseil économique et social in France or the standing advisory councils—Beirat—in Germany. In recent years in Western Europe, extreme right-wing political parties have emerged—or reemerged—and formed new constitu-

encies organized primarily around the issue of immigration. The National Front parties in France and Britain have both succeeded in capitalizing on racism and xenophobia.[5] Finally, among the factors that can affect the content of immigration policy is the relatively independent decision by government to encourage or discourage immigration. For example, in France just after World War II, economic planners and other elements of the government decided to recruit immigrant workers, on the basis of projections of demographic trends and future demand for labor.[6]

The economic downturn in Western Europe after the oil shock led to the first sustained rise in unemployment in the postwar period. This increase sent trade unions scrambling to protect jobs and wages, and foreign workers were among the first casualties in this new struggle. Some employers, on the other hand, felt a need to maintain the supply of cheap foreign labor. They therefore lobbied to keep the immigration valve at least partially open. At the same time, governments came under increasing pressure, manifested in public opinion, to stop immigration and protect the jobs of national workers from foreign competition.

With the suspension of immigration and with attempts to encourage immigrants to return to their countries of origin, foreign labor came to be viewed as a kind of shock absorber for industrial economies. According to this argument, foreigners could be hired when times were good and fired when times

3. This point is similar to the argument about distributional conflict made in Mancur Olson, *The Rise and Decline of Nations* (New Haven, CT: Yale University Press, 1982), pp. 41-47.

4. Policy can only affect markets at the margins; however, in a mixed economy, this marginal influence can be very important. It is the degree of marginality that is important and must be defined. See, for example, Charles Lindblom, *Politics and Markets* (New York: Basic Books, 1977), esp. pp. 170-88; F. G. Castles, "How Does Politics Matter? Structure or Agency in the Determination of Public Policy Outcomes," *European Journal of Political Research,* 9:119-32 (1981).

5. On politics and racial conflict in Western Europe, see Gary Freeman, *Immigrant Labor and Racial Conflict in Industrial Societies* (Princeton, NJ: Princeton University Press, 1979).

6. Georges Tapinos, *L'immigration étrangère en France* (Paris: Presses universitaires de France, 1973), pp. 14-17.

were bad.[7] It is interesting, therefore, to determine how well or how poorly foreigners have played the role of shock absorber in France and Germany, the two largest importers of labor in Western Europe. Is it possible for the industrial state to use immigrants for making labor and employment policy? What factors may intervene to prevent such use of foreign workers?

### THE OBJECTIVES OF IMMIGRATION POLICY

Unlike Germany, France has a long tradition of immigration.[8] The reason for the receptivity of the French state to immigration is clear. From the Napoleonic Wars until the 1950s, France was faced with a constantly declining population. During the twentieth century, various French governments under pressure from pronatalist groups and struggling with the ghost of Malthus have turned to immigration as a way of increasing the population. Thus, unlike Germany and most other receiving countries, the rationale for recruiting immigrant workers after 1945 was not only to provide additional manpower for economic reconstruction and expansion, but also to give a needed boost to the population.[9]

7. In Germany, foreign workers have been labeled *Konjunkturpuffer*, which is a reference to their role as shock absorber in the economy. For an analysis of the conjunctural role of foreign labor, cf. Michael Piore, "Economic Fluctuation, Job Security, and Labor-market Duality in Italy, France and the United States," *Politics and Society* 9(4):379-407 (1980); Wolfgang Franz, "Employment Policy and Labor Supply of Foreign Workers in the Federal Republic of Germany: A Theoretical and Empirical Analysis," *Zeitschrift für die gesamte Staatswissenschaft*, 137:590-611 (1981).

8. Tapinos, *L'immigration étrangère en France*, pp. 1-10.

9. See Alfred Sauvy, "Besoins et possibilités de

Although contemporary migrations in Germany are not without historical antecedents, immigration is a relatively new phenomenon.[10] In Germany the supply of labor in the immediate postwar period was more than adequate, thanks to the nearly 3.1 million refugees who poured into the Federal Republic from the East. The construction of the Berlin Wall in 1961 changed all this. For the first time since 1945, the German government found itself confronted with a potentially severe labor shortage. It sought to avert this problem by recruiting a temporary foreign work force, primarily from the Balkan and Mediterranean countries of southern Europe. Although there had been some movement of Italian workers into the German labor market in the 1950s, the *Gastarbeiter* ("guest-worker") phenomenon did not begin until the 1960s.

France and Germany progressively lost control of the migratory process in the late 1960s and early 1970s. In France, the preferred immigration of southern European Catholics gradually gave way to a new flow of immigrants from North Africa. In Germany, ever larger numbers of foreign workers and their families chose to settle. In both countries, foreign labor became a structural component of labor supply, with foreigners taking over certain categories of low-paying, low-skill jobs in manufacturing, construction, and the service sector. The gap between policy outputs and outcomes was growing, and public opinion

l'immigration en France," *Population*, 2-3: 209-34 (1950).

10. Industrialization in the nineteenth century did draw immigrants from peripheral areas of central and eastern Europe. See G. Stopler, *German Economy, 1870-1940, Issues and Trends* (New York: Reynal & Hitchcock, 1940), p. 40.

was increasingly hostile to continued immigration.

Well before the oil shock in 1973 and the economic crisis that followed, the governments of France and Germany were aware of the political and social consequences of large-scale immigration. In order to avoid growing xenophobic reactions, the governments attempted (1) to regain control of the migratory process, namely, of the recruitment, placement, and integration of foreigners, and (2) to create a better social infrastructure to house, educate, and care for the resident foreign population.

To achieve the first objective, new regulations were put into effect governing the recruitment and placement of foreign workers. In Germany, the employers' option to recruit foreign workers privately was eliminated in November 1972, compelling them to use official recruitment commissions. At the same time, the government increased substantially the recruitment fees *(Anwerbepauschale)* required from firms using foreign labor.[11]

In France, similar government attempts to eliminate the private recruitment of foreign workers proved to be more controversial, since for the first time the proposal was made to link work permits with residence permits. Trade unions opposed the regulation because it was seen as giving employers much greater power over workers. By threatening to fire a worker, an employer could effectively jeopardize the right of the worker to remain in the country. In this respect, the French authorities were following the example of the Germans, who had always insisted on linking residence and work permits, except for family members.

To achieve the second objective, both governments required employers to provide adequate housing for new foreign workers. Thus employers were obliged to contribute to the development of the social infrastructure needed to maintain a large foreign work force. In France, these measures met with objections from both trade unions and employers' associations, forcing the government to back down and liberalize the procedure for admitting foreigners to the work force.[12] In Germany, however, there was a growing consensus that the uncontrolled recruitment of foreign workers had to be stopped.[13]

In 1973, the poltical-economic climate in the industrial democracies changed dramatically. Rising energy costs contributed to inflation and to an economic slowdown that led to increased unemployment. The governments of labor-importing countries responded by (1) suspending immigration and the recruitment of foreign workers; (2) encouraging workers to return to their countries of origin; and (3) attempting to integrate into the host society those workers and their families who had been working and living in the

11. See Organization for Economic Cooperation and Development, *SOPEMI, Continuous Reporting System on Migration, Report for 1973* (Paris: Organization for Economic Cooperation and Development, 1974), p. 17. See also Nikolaus Notter, "Le statut des travailleurs étrangers en Allemagne Fédérale," *Droit social,* 4: 223-30 (Apr. 1973).

12. See J. Bunel and J. Saglio, "Le CNPF et la politique d'immigration," *Economie et humanisme,* 221:41-50 (Jan.-Feb. 1975); Marie-Claude Henneresse, *Le patronat et la politique française d'immigration: 1945-1975,* Thèse de 3ème cycle (Paris: Institut d'études politiques, 1978), p. 417.

13. Klaus Unger, *Ausländerpolitik in der Bundesrepublik Deutschland* (Saarbrücken: Verlag Beitenbach, 1980); see also, Ray C. Rist, *Guestworkers in Germany: The Prospects for Pluralism* (New York: Praeger, 1978), pp. 120-32.

country for a specified period of time.[14] These were the main policy changes adopted in Germany in 1973 and in France in 1974. The new policies were based on two objectives: to avoid competition between foreign and national workers for scarce jobs in tight labor markets; and to avoid ethnic conflict, by assimilating those foreigners who could not be expelled for legal and/or humanitarian reasons.

Some notable differences between the French and German policies remained. First, the suspension of immigration in Germany was more categorical and more severe than in France. German authorities insisted that at no time had any commitment been made to allow the permanent settlement of guest workers.[15] Hence, they saw no inconsistency in unilaterally halting immigration and exporting unemployed foreign workers.

In addition, German policy maintained a sharper distinction between residence and work permits for family members. This distinction became increasingly important in light of the rise in family immigration after 1973.[16] The

hope was to prevent the spouses and children of foreign workers from entering the labor market; this goal was to be achieved by granting them temporary residence permits but not work permits.[17]

In France, too, attempts were made to discourage the entry of new migrants, particularly family members, into the labor market. Nevertheless, the Ministry of Labor admitted substantial numbers of new migrants, including family members, into the labor market after 1974.[18] Thus, the French ban on new immigration was less categorical than the German. French authorities, recognizing foreign labor to be a structural component of labor supply, were willing to grant exemptions to the new regulations.[19]

Throughout the 1970s, both countries sought to reinforce the ban on immigration through cooperation with the sending countries. Numerous bilateral agreements were worked out with the major sending countries in order to regain control of the migratory process and assist in the reintegration of those migrants who chose to return. In France, four cases are of particular interest. The

14. Since 1973 and 1974, length-of-residence requirements for obtaining permanent resident status have changed frequently. For a general review of this and other problems associated with foreign-worker programs in Western Europe, see Mark J. Miller and Philip L. Martin, *Administering Foreign-Worker Programs* (Lexington, MA: D.C. Heath, 1982).

15. Bundesanstalt für Arbeit, *Ueberlegungen zu einer vorausschauenden Arbeitsmarktpolitik* (Nuremberg: Bundesanstalt für Arbeit, 1978), pp. 75 ff.

16. On the evolution of family immigration and other migrant flows in France and Germany after the suspension, see Georges Tapinos, "Enquête sur les perspectives des migrations à long terme en R.F.A. et en France," *Studi emigrazione*, 50:213-45 (June 1978).

17. See Elmar Hönekopp and Hans Ullman, *The Effect of Immigration on Social Structures* (Nuremberg: Institute for Labor Market Research, 1980). An attempt was also made to limit the development of immigrant enclaves by imposing numerical limits on foreigners living in administratively defined districts *(Kreise)*. However, these limits were in place only for a short period because of the difficulties of enforcement.

18. Admissions to the labor market have been at 40,000 or above annually since 1976, according to statistics from the Ministry of Labor.

19. Secrétaire d'état aux travailleurs immigrés, *La nouvelle politique de l'immigration* (Paris: Documentation française, 1977). Exemptions account for only 14 percent of total worker immigration controlled by the National Immigration Office in 1974 and 1975. See Henneresse, *Le patronat et la politique d'immigration*, pp. 433-44.

Portuguese continued to enjoy a some-what privileged status among immi-grants, because of agreements that made Portugal a most favored supplier of for-eign workers. These agreements helped to eliminate the clandestine flow of Portuguese workers and their families into France. Similarly, migrants from the *franc zone* of West Africa benefited from a special status. The movement of workers between France and its former colonies in West Africa has been rela-tively free.[20] Moroccans also received special consideration because of their importance as a source of labor for the mining industry. Finally, Algeria, which was one of the most important sending countries, unilaterally suspended emi-gration in 1973 because of incidents of violence against Algerian nationals in France. Until then, Algerians had been able to move more or less freely into and out of France.[21]

The unilateral suspension of immigra-tion by Germany abrogated most prior agreements with the sending countries. Since 1973, however, the German gov-ernment has placed great emphasis on as-sisting the sending countries with the re-integration of returning migrants. Thus agreements with Greece and Turkey es-tablished funds in those countries to aid returnees. Until very recently, however, Germany did not have a general return policy applicable to all foreigners.

The policy of paying foreigners to return was first proposed in France in early 1976 to provide more incentives for those foreigners who wanted to leave but could not afford to make the move. In addition to a one-time payment of a modest sum, foreigners could also avail themselves of retraining programs set up in cooperation with the sending coun-tries. The number of foreigners who took advantage of return assistance from 1977 to 1979 was roughly 76,000. More than two-thirds of these returnees were from the Iberian peninsula.[22] By 1980, over 1000 foreign wokers were benefiting annually from retraining pro-grams. In the German case, official repatriation assistance was approved in the fall of 1983. The current German policy offers a substantial sum of money to foreigners in order to encourage them to return.

*Integration into host countries*

Apart from stopping immigration and encouraging foreigners to return, French and German immigration poli-cies also were directed toward integrat-ing migrants who chose to stay. Prob-lems associated with the integration of the large foreign populations in France and Germany are numerous. Policy out-puts in this area can be divided into three basic categories, each with serious political ramifications: (1) the rights of foreign workers, including civil and vot-ing rights; (2) family reunification and the problems of the second and third generations; and (3) social welfare.

In both France and Germany, the po-litical activities of foreigners have been circumscribed by legislation that limits

20. See Bruno Courault, *Contribution à la théorie de l'offre de travail: Le cas de l'immigra-tion en France, 1946-1978,* Thèse d'état (Paris: Université de Paris I, 1980), pp. 300-301.

21. On the Franco-Algerian case, see Miller and Martin, *Administering Foreign-Worker Pro-grams,* pp. 44-48. The Franco-Algerian accords of 1980 brought renewed cooperation between Alge-rian and French authorities, primarily on the ques-tion of reintegration and retraining of returnees.

22. See André Lebon, "Sur une politique d'aide au retour," *Economie et statistique,* 193: 37-46 (July-Aug. 1979).

rights of association and restricts occupational and geographical mobility. Such regulation has contributed to the insecurity of foreigners by making their rights subject to administrative discretion rather than constitutional law. Legislation concerning rights of association was ostensibly designed to maintain public order and allow the expulsion of foreigners who threaten that order. In France many of these restrictions were dropped after the election of the Socialists in 1981.[23] Foreigners in both countries have been allowed to form associations to promote their interests and to consult with national and local authorities on policy questions that affect them. Neither country, however, has been willing to extend the franchise to foreigners. Thus, participation in political parties by foreigners is extremely rare in both countries.

Yet, foreigners do have the right to participate fully in trade-union activities and have had some success in making their voices heard on the shop floor.[24] In recent years, with the entry of second-generation immigrants into the labor market and with first-generation immigrants having lived in the country for an extended period, foreign workers have become more militant. They are often in the vanguard of striking workers in declining industries, such as steel and automobile production.

Perhaps the biggest challenge to the policy of controlling migration is the increase in family immigration. Both France and Germany have experiment-

ed with regulations designed to limit it. The governments have tried preventing foreigners who arrived relatively recently from bringing in family members; refusing to grant work permits to family members, or granting them only after a predetermined period of residence; and restricting family immigration to cases where the head of household can provide adequate housing for all family members. These regulations have changed frequently in both countries, often as the result of pressure from human rights organizations and church or other groups supporting immigrants.

Family immigration rose significantly in both France and Germany, once the admission of new foreign workers was halted. The suspension of new worker immigration accelerated the settlement of workers, who then sought to reunite their families in the host country. As a result, the problems of providing housing, education, health care, and recreational facilities for the second and third generations became more acute in the late 1970s and 1980s.

The development of immigrant enclaves in large cities has contributed to the political salience of the immigrant problem and has led to a deterioration in ethnic relations. The presence of large culturally, linguistically, and sometimes racially distinct populations in the cities has focused public attention on immigration. One area of public concern is the impact of immigration on welfare programs. Anti-immigration groups argue that too many immigrants have become wards of the state and, as such, are a drain on public finances, notwithstanding evidence that immigrants contibute more to the budget in taxes—because of their higher employment rates—than they take out in the form of unemployment benefits, health care, education, or

23. For details of the new policy of the Mitterrand government, see Jean-Pierre Garson and Yann Moulier, *Les clandestins et la régularisation de 1981-1982 en France,* Working paper (Geneva: International Labour Office, 1982), pp. 18 ff.

24. See Mark Miller, *Foreign Workers in Western Europe, An Emerging Political Force* (New York: Praeger, 1981), pp. 147-79.

social security.[25] As the second and third generations attain school and working age, however, the integration of immigrants and their families is likely to become more complex and more expensive.

## EXPLAINING POLICY OUTCOMES

We might expect the French state to have an advantage in making and implementing policy because of the centralized nature of public administration and the relative autonomy of the bureaucracy from pressure groups.[26] But, in fact, it is the German state that enjoys important structural advantages in policy implementation. Interest groups in Germany are more closely linked to the state and more likely to support changes in policy.[27] This is important, especially as far as immigration policy is concerned, because without the compliance of key economic groups it is difficult to enforce a ban on immigration. The neocorporatist character of policymaking in Germany should make it easier for the state to gain the support of employers in implementing a ban on the importation of new foreign workers. These differences in state-society relationships between France and Germany are a reflection of differences between the two economies. In France, production traditionally has been decentralized into smaller firms, whereas in Germany production has been concentrated in much larger ones. Controlling the use of foreign labor in large manufacturing industries is easier than controlling it in small shops.

Officially, the decision to suspend immigration was welcomed by the employers' associations in both France and Germany. In France, however, the positions of both major employers' associations, the Comité national du patronat français and the Confédération générale des petites et moyennes entreprises were somewhat ambiguous. Even though the leaders of these organizations were in favor of the ban, some of the member groups, such as the Fédération nationale du bâtiment, were reluctant to give up an important source of cheap labor. These groups lobbied for exemptions to the new regulations, but with marginal results.[28] Some firms in mining and construction, which had difficulty hiring national workers, were given exemptions. Small businesses in France had almost always been denied legal access to foreign labor; nevertheless, the influx of family members and seasonal workers provided a new source of foreign labor for employers in the small-business and tertiary sectors.[29]

In the German case the principal employers' association—the Bundesvereinigung Deutscher Arbeitgeberverbände—backed the new policy and even went so far as to oppose the integration of the resident foreign population.[30] This position seemed counter

25. Anicet Le Pors, *Immigration et développement économique et social* (Paris: Documentation française, 1976), pp. 89-136.

26. Reference here is to the etatist tradition. See Andrew Shonfield, *Modern Capitalism* (London: Oxford University Press, 1965), pp. 71-87.

27. On this point, see, for example, Claus Offe, "The Attribution of Public Status to Interest Groups: Observations on the West German Case," in *Organizing Interests in Western Europe,* ed. Suzanne Berger (Cambridge: Cambridge University Press, 1981), pp. 123-58.

28. Henneresse, *Le patronat et la politique d'immigration,* pp. 414-84.

29. Cf. Garson and Moulier, *Les clandestins et la régularisation,* pp. 43-47; Olivier Villey, "Le redéploiement actuel de la main-d'oeuvre étrangère passé le premier choc de la crise," *Travail et emploi,* 8:47-55 (Apr.-May 1981).

30. Unger, *Ausländerpolitik in der Bundesrepublik,* p. 182.

to their interests in maintaining a supply of cheap labor. However, as in France, it was politically difficult for any group openly to oppose the ban on immigration. Employers in both France and Germany could continue to count on some access to immigrant labor due to the increase in family immigration and the entry of second- and third-generation immigrants into the labor market. In France, most of these new immigrants went into the service sector, whereas in Germany the manufacturing sector continued to be the heaviest user of foreign labor.[31]

Trade unions supported both governments' efforts to stop immigration. Again, however, the French unions were more divided over the issue than were their German counterparts. The leaders of the Communist union, the Confédération générale du travail, tried to promote greater solidarity between national and foreign workers. Their fear was that the government and employers might use foreign workers to divide the working class.[32] They were reluctant to support fully the government's policy for fear of alienating foreign workers, whose support they needed in order to fight plant closings in declining industries. At the same time, conflicts between national and foreign workers inside and outside the factories demonstrated the tensions that existed among the rank and file.[33]

Trade unions in both countries were concerned mainly with promoting a policy that would reestablish state control of the migratory process. Such a policy would ensure that all workers were protected, while stabilizing levels of foreign employment. The German unions initially took a somewhat tougher stance against immigration and particularly against the permanent settlement of guest workers. By the end of the 1970s, however, the Deutscher Gewerkschaftsbund fully supported the policy of stopping immigration, encouraging return migration wherever possible and integrating into German society those workers and their families who chose to settle.[34]

Some groups, particularly in Germany, opposed the new policies on humanitarian and constitutional grounds. Church groups and organizations for the support of foreign workers lobbied successfully for better working conditions and extensions of residency and work permits. However, both the French and German governments moved quickly to legitimize the new policies. In France, the Conseil économique et social issued a report calling for the elimination of all uncontrolled migration.[35] In Germany, a coordinating committee within the Ministry of Labor was convened to help establish a consensus for implementing the ban on immigration. Both the Conseil économique et social and the coordinating committee brought together major

31. Data from the Ministry of Labor's surveys of foreign workers in France show that foreign employment in the manufacturing sector declined while rising in the service sector; the increase from 1973 to 1976 was 11 percent. In Germany, foreign employment in manufacturing increased by 7 percent from 1978 to 1980. See Winfried Schlaffke and Rüdiger von Voss, eds., *Vom Gastarbeiter zum Mitarbeitzer* (Cologne: Informedia Verglag-Gmbh, 1982), p. 352.

32. See Léon Gani, *Syndicats et travailleurs immigrés* (Paris: Editions sociales, 1972), pp. 68-69; see also André Vieuguet, *Français et immigrés, le combat du P.C.F.* (Paris: Editions sociales, 1975).

33. Miller, *Foreign Workers in Western Europe,* pp. 149-59.

34. See Unger, *Ausländerpolitik in der Bundesrepublik,* pp. 180-85.

35. Le rapport Calvez, "La politique de l'immigration," *Avis et rapports du Conseil économique et social,* 23 May 1975, 349-75.

groups concerned with the issue of immigration. Within this neocorporatist institutional context, these groups voiced their support for banning immigration.

We now have a reasonably clear picture of some of the pitfalls of using immigration to solve problems of unemployment. Policymakers hoped that suspending immigration would reduce unemployment among national workers by creating more vacancies. However, they failed to foresee the full consequences of a complete suspension of immigration, particularly the difficulty of controlling different migrant flows and reducing stocks of foreign labor.

Figures 1 and 2 show the impact of return policies and the suspension of immigration in each country. During the 1960s, the foreign population in Germany grew rapidly, eventually surpassing 7 percent of the total population in 1980. In France, the foreign population reached a peak of 8 percent of the total population in 1977.[36] With respect to foreign employment, although Germany started at much lower levels than France, it quickly caught up with and surpassed the latter in the late 1960s. In Germany, foreign employment has fluctuated between 9 and 10 percent of total employment since the 1970s, while in France it has been in the range of 7 to 8 percent.[37] Because of the German em-

phasis on recruiting young males of employment age, employment rates among the foreign population were much higher in Germany than in France. As can be seen from Figure 2, the upward trend in foreign employment was reversed in both countries in 1973. The trend continued to fall in France until 1975. In Germany, the downward trend lasted until 1977. Certainly some of the drop can be attributed to the change in policy. However, labor market conditions deteriorated—more in France than in Germany—as a result of the international recession. Thus, some of the decrease in levels of foreign employment can be attributed to a decline in the overall demand for labor in both economies.

Unemployment rates among national and foreign workers since 1973 show substantial unemployment in both groups. The rate of unemployment among foreigners in France reached a high of almost 10 percent in the early 1980s. In Germany, the foreign unemployment rate fluctuated between 4 and 5 percent until 1980, after which it rose dramatically, reaching almost 12 percent in 1982.[38] Only in the past few years has foreign unemployment been significantly higher than unemployment among indigenous workers. Apart from the deterioration of the job market in both countries in the early 1980s, part of the rise in unemployment among foreigners was due to the entry of family members and the second generation into the work force.

36. Data on the foreign population in France are taken from two sources. In the curve in Figure 1, data before 1967 are extrapolated from census data, which tend to underestimate the foreign population. Hence, data before 1967 are discontinuous with data after 1967. The German data are more reliable.

37. Measuring stocks of foreign workers in France is difficult. For a discussion of some of the problems, see Courault, *Contribution à la théorie de l'offre de travail,* pp. 323 ff. Data for France prior to 1975 in Figure 2 are based on estimates using the Ministry of Labor's foreign-worker surveys. The data after 1975 come from household

surveys of the Institute national de la statistique et des études économiques, cited in Organization for Economic Cooperation and Development, *SOPEMI.*

38. See various reports of the Système d'observation permanente des migrations internationales (SOPEMI). Pierre Bideberry, *Le chômage des travailleurs étrangers* (Paris: Inspection générale des affaires sociales, 1974).

FIGURE 1
EVOLUTION OF FOREIGN POPULATIONS IN FRANCE AND GERMANY, 1945-85

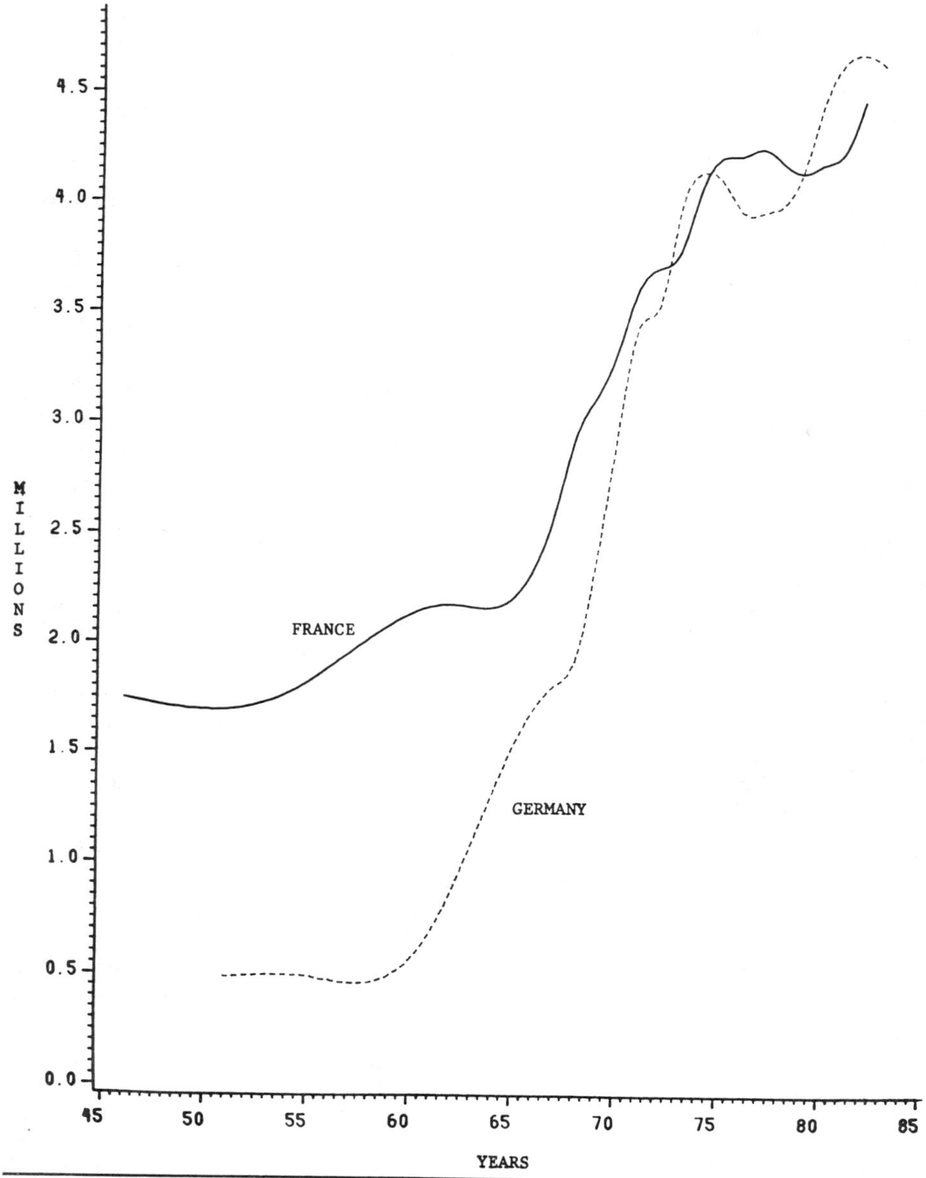

SOURCE: For France, Institute national de la statistique et des études économiques and Ministere de l'interieur, Paris; for Germany, Statistisches Bundesamt, Wiesbaden.

German policy appears to have been more effective than French policy. This can be attributed partially to the tighter control exercised over foreign workers in Germany and to the concentration of workers in certain manufacturing indus-

FIGURE 2
**EVOLUTION OF THE NUMBER OF FOREIGN WORKERS
IN FRANCE AND GERMANY, 1945-85**

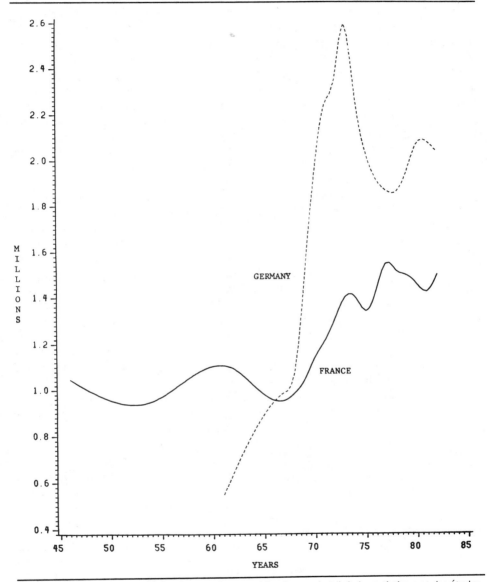

SOURCES: For France, Ministère du travail and Institut national de la statistique et des études économiques, Paris; for Germany, Bundesanstalt für Arbeit, Nuremburg.

tries, which made it easier to regulate the use of foreign labor. In France, centralization of administration and a strong state do not appear to have helped in the implementation of the ban on immigration.

With respect to the foreign populations, the policies instituted in 1973 in Germany and 1974 in France seem to have had the opposite effects of those intended (see Figure 1). Although they did help to stabilize the foreign population and reduce it in Germany in the short term, in the long term the suspension of immigration contributed to an increase in the foreign population. By stopping the inflows of workers, the new policies inadvertently created new inflows of family members and, in the case of France, seasonal workers.[39] Family and seasonal immigration took the place of worker immigration in France in the late 1970s and early 1980s. The argument has been made that the cutoff also led to increases in clandestine immigration.[40] Because of its complexity, the migratory process does not lend itself easily to regulation. Once started, migration has its own dynamic and is to a certain extent self-perpetuating.[41]

Several other factors beyond the state's control contributed to increases in the foreign population. First, immigrants have higher birthrates and lower mortality rates than the indigenous population, which means that the foreign populations in France and Germany

have been growing naturally.[42] Second, since the ratification of the Rome Treaties, workers within the European Economic Community have had freedom of movement. The policies discussed earlier do not apply to migrants from countries of the European Economic Community. The flow of European labor has had a greater impact on Germany than on France, since Germany has been the principal repository of surplus Italian and Greek labor.[43]

Third, a large percentage of foreign workers who have entered the French and German labor markets legally since 1973 have been political refugees. In France, which has a tradition of welcoming political refugees, most have come from Southeast Asia, Central and Latin America, and the Middle East. The number of refugees, however, has remained below 20,000 per year since 1973. In Germany the increase in the number of applications for political asylum in the late 1970s, primarily from Turks, led to the adoption of a series of measures designed to stop abuses. Among the steps taken by the government was the denial of work permits to applicants for asylum during their first year of residence.

Finally, as in all labor-importing countries, clandestine immigration has been a problem in France and Germany, both before and after the cutoff. Although the problem is much smaller in Western Europe than in the United

39. According to the National Immigration Office's statistics, seasonal workers entered at an average annual rate of 122,500 from 1974 to 1980, compared to a rate of 137,000 for the period 1968-73. The average annual rate of immigration of family members went from 70,500 for the period 1968-73 to 50,000 for the period 1974-80.

40. Garson and Moulier, *Les clandestins et la régularisation*, p. 6.

41. On this point, see W. R. Bohning, *Les conséquences économiques de travailleurs étrangers* (Paris: Organization for Economic Cooperation and Development, 1974); see also E. Reyneri, *La catena migratoria* (Bologna: Societa editrice il mulino, 1979).

42. This is due to the lower average age of immigrants. See Tapinos, "Enquête sur les perspec-

tives des migrations à long terme en R.F.A. et en France," passim.

43. Compared to other nationalities, migrants from the European Economic Community have had little impact on employment or population in either country since the 1960s, but the impact of European migrations on France may be much greater when Spain and Portugal are admitted to the European Economic Community.

States, it is by no means trivial.[44] During the 1970s, the French and German governments imposed increasingly severe sanctions on employers who hired undocumented workers. By far the most dramatic attempt to deal with the problem of clandestine immigration was the amnesty offered by the Mitterrand government in France in 1981 to foreign workers and their families living in an irregular situation. The objective was to reduce the insecurity of foreigners residing in France, while at the same time maintaining a strict ban on new immigration. At least two preconditions limited the effects of the amnesty: only foreigners who entered the country before 1 January 1981 could apply; and all applicants had to present evidence of employment, preferably a contract to prove that they had been employed for at least one year.[45] Despite these preconditions, 82,493 workers had obtained adjustments of status (régularisations) under the new procedures by the end of 1982.[46] Thus, a large part of the apparent increase in foreign employment and the foreign population in France after 1981 is attributable to the new policies of the Mitterrand government.

CONCLUSION

In the postwar period, immigration has become one of the most intractable issues on the policy agenda in the advanced industrial democracies. This arti-

cle has attempted to explain the gap between policy outputs and outcomes by distinguishing between formulation and implementation of immigration policy. Translating immigration policy outputs into outcomes has been particularly difficult in France and Germany since 1973, primarily because of misconceptions about the conjunctural role of foreign labor and a misunderstanding of the dynamics of the migratory process.

It has proved much more difficult to stop immigration than to start it. There is little doubt that the influx of foreign workers into the French and German labor markets in the 1950s and 1960s helped sustain phenomenally high growth rates during that period. The motive for recruiting foreign labor was primarily economic and, in the French case, demographic. The decision to suspend immigration was motivated largely by political and social considerations. Immigrant labor was still useful for many firms even after the recession of the 1970s, but it was no longer politically acceptable to have high levels of immigration while there was high unemployment among national workers.

Most of the major interest groups in France and Germany agreed with their governments' decision to suspend immigration. However, certain types of firms in both countries continued to hire foreign workers. The tertiary sector in particular benefited from the new flow of foreign labor composed primarily of family members, political refugees, and, in France, seasonal workers. Hence the dynamics of the migratory process, from the recruitment of temporary workers to the settlement of these workers and their families, posed serious problems for the implementation of new policies designed to stop the influx of foreigners. The new immigrants arriving in the late

44. Estimates of the number of undocumented workers in the United States range from 2 million to 12 million. In Germany in 1975, there were estimated to be 200,000 undocumented workers, and in France the number of foreigners who have taken advantage of the amnesty program is on the order of 100,000.

45. Garson and Moulier, Les clandestins et la régularisation, pp. 36-37.

46. Organization for Economic Cooperation and Development, SOPEMI p. 12.

1970s and early 1980s probably saw living conditions and job prospects in France and Germany as being good enough to warrant the move. In the end, regulations designed to stop this new wave of immigration had to be liberalized in the face of criticism on constitutional and humanitarian grounds. It proved impossible to prevent family reunification or to stop family members from entering the labor market. The reasons for this failure probably have as much to do with the pluralist nature of politics in French and German society as with the dynamics of the migratory process.

The principal lesson to be learned from the French and German experiences is that immigration is almost always a permanent phenomenon. While it may be possible and desirable to use foreign labor to deal with manpower shortages, it is difficult to get rid of foreign labor when it is politically expedient to do so. Inevitably, many foreign workers choose to settle, and in relatively open and democratic societies like France and the Federal Republic of Germany, expelling these workers en masse is not acceptable. Importing labor has long-term political, economic, and social consequences that make the use of foreign workers as shock absorbers very problematic.

ANNALS, *AAPSS*, **485**, May 1986

# Migration to the United Kingdom and the Emergence of a New Politics

*By* B. GUY PETERS and PATRICIA K. DAVIS

ABSTRACT: Britain has had three different types of guest workers. One has been the Irish with continuing rights in the United Kingdom. Another has been guest workers as found in most other European countries. The largest group has comprised residents of former Commonwealth countries who come to live permanently. This article examines the latter group as they become partially assimilated into the British society, economy, and polity.

*B. Guy Peters is the Maurice Falk Professor of American Government at the University of Pittsburgh. He is the author of several books, including* Can Government Go Bankrupt?, *with Richard Rose, and* The Pathology of Public Policy, *with Brian W. Hogwood, and numerous scholarly articles.*

*Patricia K. Davis, presently enrolled in the graduate program in political science at the University of Pittsburgh, spent 1985 at the University of Strathclyde in Glasgow.*

MANY textbook descriptions of the United Kingdom discuss the homogeneity of the British population. Even if the persistent—and sometimes violent—struggle of the Scottish, Irish, and Welsh populations in the United Kingdom against the dominant English population had not given the lie to such a characterization, the growing nonwhite population in Britain would have. The latter has grown to almost 5 percent of the total population from a minuscule fraction at the end of World War II. A series of immigration acts since the early 1960s has greatly slowed the flow of nonwhite immigrants into the United Kingdom, but the higher birthrates of these immigrants have resulted in an increasing percentage of immigrants and their descendants in the population. Immigrants and their offspring, and the manner in which they have been treated, have raised a number of social, political, and legal issues for British society. Further, unlike the presumption for many of the guest workers in other European countries, the majority of these immigrants will probably never return permanently to the countries of origin.

FOREIGN WORKERS IN BRITAIN

The question of the migration of foreigners into the United Kingdom is more complex than that of the migration of *Gastarbeiters* into most other European countries. This is in large part because there are three distinct types of migration into Britain, only one of which appears similar to that occurring in other countries. The first is the continuation of now well-established patterns of migration from Ireland to the other British isle. Migration continued after the Republic of Ireland gained its independence in 1922, and Irish citizens can enter and leave the United Kingdom with virtually no formalities. Although some Irish families continue to migrate and remain in the United Kingdom permanently, many Irish men work in the United Kingdom for a significant portion of the year and return home during holidays to their families. Irish citizens in Britain are considered neither British nor foreign, and they have the right to vote in British elections and even to sit in Parliament.[1] The Irish in the country are in effect quasi citizens of the United Kingdom while remaining citizens of another nation at the same time.

A second group of immigrant workers is more similar to that found in other European countries. They come to work in Britain, primarily from Mediterranean countries, with or without their families. This pattern has been less common in Britain than in other European countries because of increasing legal restrictions on persons entering Britain in order to obtain a job. In addition, the generally lower rates of economic activity in Britain have meant less demand for migrant labor than in such countries as West Germany or Switzerland, with higher rates of economic growth and lower levels of unemployment. Finally, to the extent that there has been a need for immigrant labor to do jobs that the British themselves no longer want to do, much of that need has been filled by immigration from the former British colonies, as discussed later. There is, despite all that, a significant Mediterranean population in Britain. These people constitute a major labor source for some businesses, such as hotels, restaurants, and other components of the tourist industry. Some of the comedic episodes of *Fawlty Towers* may represent some-

1. Richard Rose, *Politics in England,* 4th ed. (Boston: Little, Brown, 1986).

thing approaching reality for a significant portion of the tourist industry.

The third, and by far the largest, group of foreign workers in the United Kingdom are immigrants from the Commonwealth and especially the "New Commonwealth and Pakistan," as the census category reads. These are immigrants from the Indian subcontinent, the West Indies, Hong Kong, and to a lesser extent Africa, especially African Asians such as those expelled from Uganda. The entry of members of these groups into the United Kingdom has been fundamentally different from the migration of guest workers into most other European countries in many important respects.

*Permanence*

The first major difference is that many of those coming to the United Kingdom come with the intention of settling, and some—those with British citizenship or patrial rights obtained during the period of colonial rule—have a virtual right to enter and settle.[2] Rather than migrating to work for a short period of time and then gradually becoming settled or semipermanent residents of the host country, as has been the case in most Continental countries, many or most foreign workers entering Britain came ready, willing, and able to remain. These are not the semi-settlers found in other European countries, but real settlers, intending to remain from the time they arrive. Increasing legal restrictions on New Commonwealth—as contrasted to the old, largely white Commonwealth—immigration have slowed the influx. The 1971 Immigration Act revoked the right of settlement for any

New Commonwealth citizen except those who could prove that they were dependent on some person already settled and as well that they would be maintained and accommodated by this person. Immigration from the New Commonwealth has, however, by no means been stopped, as any visit to Heathrow Airport will quickly demonstrate. Some 24,800 people from the New Commonwealth were accepted for settlement in 1984, as compared with 37,900 in 1970; the number of West Indian immigrants dropped from 15,000 in 1969 to 3,000 in 1982.

The permanent nature of the settlement by the New Commonwealth immigrants has constituted the major political issue surrounding immigration, as some political leaders and perhaps more citizens have felt the nature of British society and culture to be threatened. It is evident that Britain has become a multiracial society, and the changes are profound and, to many, threatening. This is the way in which, as one set of authors puts it, "the empire strikes back," and the former glories of being a colonial power have now imposed a major social and political question into British life.[3]

*Acculturation*

A second difference is that Britain is not a strange and foreign land to many of those who immigrate. It is, rather, the mother country. Even for those who were born and raised after the end of the colonial period, there are substantial cultural and linguistic ties. Thus, unlike the immigrant to many European countries, the new immigrant to Britain enters already at least partially acculturated. To some degree that acculturation may be false, based on outdated or inaccu-

2. Jonathan Power, *Immigrant Workers in Western Europe and the United States* (Oxford: Pergamon, 1979), pp. 107 ff.

3. Centre for Contemporary Cultural Studies, *The Empire Strikes Back* (London: Hutchinson, 1982).

of just what living in
y like. Even in those
owever, there is signifi-
le information and a lin-
guistic ᴜ. ᴀat may put the immigrant
from the New Commonwealth at an advantage relative to the recently arrived
*Gastarbeiter* in many European countries. Further, the new immigrant is
likely to move into an ethnic enclave
populated by relatives who are in the
country on a permanent basis; thus he or
she will immediately have a more extensive social support system than that
greeting many other immigrants, who
have more tenuous ties to their new host
country.

The problems of acculturation for
nonwhite youth are more salient. Unlike
their parents, they often are not immigrants, and find themselves caught between two cultures. Interestingly, this
means that they do not share with their
parents the same illusions about life in
Britain.

*Economic mobility*

Third, many immigrants to the United
Kingdom from New Commonwealth
countries and their second and now even
third generations are not in poorly paid,
manual jobs that the inhabitants of the
host country do not want to do. Many
are shopkeepers or restaurateurs. They
are increasingly entering the liberal professions, to serve not only members of
their own groups but the larger community as well. Also, as restrictions on entry have been tightened, an increasing
number of those entering the United
Kingdom from the New Commonwealth
come with professional qualifications,
especially in medicine. The National
Health Service would be extremely hard
pressed were it not for the immigration
of physicians from the Indian subconti-

nent, since many native British physicians have emigrated to the Old Commonwealth, the European Community,
or the United States.

This pattern of employment and upward economic mobility for immigrants
varies markedly among the immigrants
groups, however. Many immigrants
from the Indian subcontinent and from
East Asia—Hong Kong, for example—
have been quite upwardly mobile and
successful in business, the professions,
and, to some extent more recently, in the
civil service. Immigrants from the West
Indies have been much less successful
and have extremely high rates of unemployment, even when compared to the
generally high rates of unemployment in
the economy as a whole. As in the United States, the rate of unemployment is
especially high for black—in this case,
West Indian—youths. Further, those
West Indians who are employed fit the
more common Continental guest-worker pattern of employment in poorly paid
and relatively undesirable occupations.[4]
Thus, some of the political and racial
tensions in Britain may arise between
different immigrant groups rather than
between immigrants on the one hand
and the indigenous white society on the
other. This was clearly evidenced by the
riots in the Wandsworth section of Bir-
mingham, as well as in parts of London,
in the summer of 1985. The principal
targets of the burning and looting, largely by West Indian youths, were the businesses of Indian and Pakistani merchants. This may have been in part
because those targets were convenient,
but it also may indicate a deeper hostility
toward those merchants.[5]

4. David J. Smith, *The Facts of Racial Disadvantage* (London: PEP, n.d.), pp. 64-77.

5. This pattern appears similar to the attacks
on Indian merchants and professionals by blacks
in South Africa during the same summer and hos-

Even within the Indian and Pakistani communities, however, there are marked differences in abilities—especially linguistic—that can serve as the basis of becoming a more successful member of the society. Survey evidence indicates that about 40 percent of men and 60 percent of women from these communities have little or no facility with the English language.[6] These Asians tend to have employment experiences that more closely approximate the experience of the West Indian population. If they are employed at all, it is in poorly paid manual jobs. They tend to live in substandard housing, usually in enclaves of other immigrants who have similar problems in coping with the dominant society, and they have few opportunities for upward mobility.

*Politicization*

Finally, in part because of the immigrants' permanence and the perception that they are thus fundamentally altering the nature of British society, immigration and the presence of the immigrant population appear to have become more significant political issues in the United Kingdom than in many other European countries. This can be seen in part in the principal political parties, especially on the right wing of the Conservative Party when it was led by Enoch Powell.[7] To the embarrassment of most of the party, an openly racist candidate, running as a Conservative, won one parliamentary seat in 1964. Political tensions have also been manifested in the development of a stricly anti-immigrant—especially immigrants of color—party, the National Front. In the 1983 general election, the National Front ran candidates in 60 constituencies and, although their candidates received on average only a few hundred votes—0.1 percent of the total—they did raise the issue of immigration and race politically.

Unlike countries using *Gastarbeiters* in their industries and service jobs, the British public cannot reasonably expect their immigrant population ever to return home or even to sustain the myth of return. Further, with relatively higher birthrates, even without further immigration the portion of the population comprising people of color will continue to increase relative to the rest of the population. Although it has arisen in a different manner, the United Kingdom now has a racial situation more similar to that of the United States than to those of its European neighbors.

## COPING WITH A MULTIRACIAL SOCIETY

Given these differences from guest workers in other societies, one might expect a rather different pattern of relationships between the dominant society and its migrant workers, or, perhaps more appropriately, its new citizens. This is largely, but by no means entirely, true. It would appear that the differences have resided mostly on the side of the immigrants rather than the dominant society. In particular, a significant portion of the immigrant population has attempted to integrate into British society and even politics.

But there have been important differences in the host country itself. Perhaps

---

tility toward Jewish merchants by other immigrant groups in American cities in the late nineteenth and early twentieth centuries.

6. Colin Brown, *Black and White Britain: The Third PSI Survey* (London: Heinemann, 1984), pp. 137-49.

7. Douglas E. Schoen, *Powell and the Powellites* (London: Macmillan, 1977).

the most important is that, because of the legal status of most of the immigrants as long-term residents and sometimes as citizens, their political problems must be treated as questions of civil liberties and political rights; their political problems would be treated quite differently if there was an expectation that they would eventually be sent home or were aliens. Again, the situation more closely parallels that of the United States, with a nonwhite population that is far from fully integrated into the economic or social mainstream but that has the right to press demands through the courts and the political system. The parallel is perhaps closer to the Hispanic population in the United States than to the black population. This is so because, despite the generally legitimate status of the majority of the immigrant population in the United Kingdom, there are still some illegal residents who may deter the formation of more vocal supportive political movements. The use of the legal process to press claims for racial minorities is further complicated by the absence of a formal constitution that undergirds the provision of guarantees of equal treatment. Of course, there is now substantial legislation prohibiting discrimination, but the potential power of constitutional provision is lacking.

With this brief background on the origins and status of the immigrant populations in the United Kingdom we can begin to look at several specific issues in which the political system is forced to respond to those populations. Again, we would expect these responses to be quite different from responses of countries where guest workers were originally presumed to be only passing through and where they often have less than clear-cut legal status.

## Policing and internal controls

One of the most fundamental issues that arises in the treatment of immigrant populations is their relationship with the police. As in the United States, there have been numerous charges of discriminatory treatment of the nonwhite population by the police. This has been especially true for the West Indian population, particularly for West Indian youths. While almost one-third of Asian respondents to a survey indicated that they believed their racial group was treated worse by the police than was the white population, almost two-thirds of the West Indian population believed they were treated worse.[8] Less than 10 percent of the Asian population believed they were treated unfairly by the courts, while almost 40 percent of the West Indians surveyed did. On the other hand, over two-thirds of the white population believed that the criminal justice system treated minorities the same as the rest of the population, while 20 percent thought that the police—but almost none the courts—treated minorities worse.[9]

The issue of the relationship between the police force and the immigrant populations came to light most explosively in a series of urban riots. These first occurred in 1981 in Brixton and Moss Side, and they produced the inquiry that came to be known as the Scarman Report, after Lord Scarman, who headed the inquiry. In the summer of 1985, relationships between police and West Indian youth appear to have contributed to another outbreak of urban violence. The police soon became the object of much of the violence in these outbreaks.

It appears clear that there are a number of issues about policing in the minor-

8. Brown, *Black and White Britain,* p. 276.
9. Ibid.

ity communities that have an important impact on the civil rights that the minority populations in Britain have in practice. One of the most important of these is the enforcement of the immigration acts themselves. Here the presence of a number of illegal immigrants comes into play, because, when attempts are made to detect and deport those illegal residents, the rights of the legal immigrants and of citizens come to be threatened.[10] Further, even though they may be long-term residents in the United Kingdom, most of the New Commonwealth immigrants are still subject to deportation if, in the eyes of the home secretary, their presence is not conducive to the public good. To put teeth into the immigration acts, especially that of 1971, the police were given broad powers of arrest without warrant in the case of suspected illegal entry or other violations of the immigration laws. In most instances, appeal against deportation was allowed only after the person had left the United Kingdom.

Aside from the harsher sanctions, such as deportation, concern over the presence of illegal immigrants has produced internal controls in the United Kingdom, which the rather conservative newspaper *Financial Times* once likened to the pass laws in South Africa.[11] People whose origin is obviously in the New Commonwealth may be required to produce their passports in a number of sometimes embarrassing or intimidating settings to prove that they are in the country legally. These powers to control immigrants have extended to police raids on premises where suspected illegal immigrants are housed and to rather

extensive investigations of the marital status of people attempting to enter the United Kingdom as dependents of those legally in the country.

It is obvious that any country has the right to enforce its laws and to make decisions about which noncitizens to allow to stay and which to debar or expel. In this instance, however, it is the manner in which the immigration laws have been enforced that has caused controversy, and this is claimed to be a part of a general pattern of policing that is in any case at least mildly discriminatory against minorities, whether legally resident or not.[12] This perception of discrimination contributes to the continuing tensions between the police and the immigrant communities.

Another of the important issues about policing as it affects the minority or immigrant community in the United Kingdom is the composition of the police force itself. As of 1982 only approximately three-tenths of 1 percent of the members of the metropolitan police force in England and Wales were of Asian or West Indian descent, as contrasted with almost 5 percent of the population.[13] As in most instances when the representativeness of public organizations is at issue, such a difference in figures need not represent overt discrimination in recruitment. It may simply reflect differences in educational attainment—especially important in the case of West Indians—and different career preferences.[14] These figures do, however, represent a problem for the police when they are working in minority en-

10. Paul Gordon, *Policing Immigration: Britain's Internal Controls* (London: Pluto Press, 1985).

11. *Financial Times*, 22 Mar. 1978.

12. John Benyon, ed., *Scarman and After* (Oxford: Pergamon, 1984).

13. John Benyon, "The Policing Issues," in *Scarman and After*, ed. Benyon, pp. 102-4.

14. B. Guy Peters, *The Politics of Bureaucracy*, 2nd ed. (New York: Longman, 1984), pp. 74 ff.

claves where they have to deliver a service but may not be particularly well trusted or welcomed by the resident population. Much of the impact of government services in general may be in how they are delivered and by whom. A virtually all-white police force may not have the most positive image or the most effective service-delivery organization for many areas of British cities.

Associated with the issue of the racial composition of the police force is the question of the attitudes maintained and displayed by the members of the force. In any modern society policing is a difficult task, and interaction patterns with members of groups within the society may lead to stereotyping. We have already pointed out that a large segment of the minority population in Britain does not believe that it is treated equally or fairly by the police. Further, a large number—over half of the West Indian respondents—did not believe that they would be protected from racial attacks by the police. Since the 1981 urban riots and the Scarman Report on those riots, there has been a great deal of concern about police training in community relations.[15] However, it would appear that, at least as perceived by the members of the minority communities, there is still a way to go before relationships between the police and immigrant populations will be as both groups might like them.

*Claims on the welfare state*

Another important issue in the rights of immigrant groups in the United Kingdom is their access to the programs of the welfare state. In some ways their access may be more limited than would be true if they were citizens of other member nations of the European Com-

munity, even though they may be permanent residents of the United Kingdom. There are reciprocal arrangements with other members of the Common Market guaranteeing services, but the provision for services for immigrants from outside the Euopean Community is at times less certain.

One important factor in controlling access to the programs of the welfare state is that immigrants are at times required to present their passports in order to gain access to certain public services such as care from the National Health Service, supplementary benefits, or even elementary education. They thereby prove that they are in the country legally and may be entitled to the services. While attempts are made to make this policy nondiscriminatory by inquiring about everyone's eligibility for social services, it appears clear that such screening can be a way of reducing access or, increasingly, a way of charging for services provided people who are not ordinary residents of the United Kingdom. Rather than being an overt means of reducing such access, the effect may be more indirect. As with other forms of stigmatization associated with social services, this may simply deter some qualified persons from applying. Interestingly, however, the vast majority of respondents to a survey believed that immigrants were treated the same as the white population by the Department of Health and Social Security and by National Health Service hospitals.[16] It would appear that although passport checks and other controls do present barriers of some sort to the use of social programs, the actual delivery of services provided by those programs is conducted in a very evenhanded manner.

15. Benyon, "Policing Issues."

16. Brown, *Black and White Britain*, p. 235.

Another problem that arises in the utilization of welfare state programs by immigrant populations is that the cultural patterns of those populations may not be respected in the delivery of the services. Examples of this type of problem are numerous: conservative Muslims not wanting to send their daughters to school with male students, attempts to make Sikhs remove their turbans for admission to schools, questions regarding bilingual education or education in the original native tongue, and so forth. These issues point to the even larger question of the extent to which a multiracial Britain also aspires to be a monocultural Britain. They also point up the crucial difference between a country in which immigrant workers are to be a permanent part of the society and one in which there is no such expectation, even if circumstances eventually produce rather different results.

*Housing*

Although housing programs are certainly a component part of welfare state programs, perhaps especially in the United Kingdom, they deserve special attention because of the relationship of those programs to residential patterns and the preservation of traditional cultural patterns. The total nonwhite population of the United Kingdom is approximately 4 percent of the entire population. However, almost half of all Asians and West Indians live in enumeration districts—census areas of approximately 165 households each—that are more than 12 percent nonwhite, and one-fifth live in districts that are over 30 percent nonwhite. While this degree of concentration or segregation is not as great as in many American cities or in several settings in Continental host countries, the develop-

ment and persistence of these ethnic enclaves will amost certainly contribute to the persistence of a multicultural society, as well as a multiracial one. This is especially the case in large cities and most of all in some of the old industrial cities in the north of England, of which Bradford is perhaps the best example.

Ethnic enclaves also allow the greater development of indigenous middle and professional classes within the host country as doctors, lawyers, and other professionals—largely of Asian descent—have a better-developed clientele base than they might otherwise have. In addition, the existence of these enclaves begins to provide the immigrant population a political power base; for example, the current lord mayor of Bradford is of Asian descent. Thus, in the case where guest workers are to be long-term residents, the existence of ethnic enclaves both allows for the preservation of some of their cultural background and provides for the beginnings of the economic and political integration of those groups into the dominant society.

The development and perpetuation of these ethnic enclaves in British cities have been in part products of the preferences of the immigrant population and in part the result of decisions made by local and central government. Although they have now been resident long enough to work their way into council— public—housing, the initial housing experience of many immigrants was that of private rental accommodations. These accommodations tended to be in concentrated areas within cities and therefore tended to concentrate the immigrant population. In the mid-1980s a higher proportion of the Asian, Indian, and Pakistani segments of the population are owner-occupiers than is true for the white population, while a higher proportion of West Indians than of the white indigenous population are council tenants.[17] These housing patterns tend to reflect the relative economic success of these two components of the immigrant population. Further, given that the Indian owner-occupiers tend to buy houses or flats near each other and that council housing in the cities is frequently of very high density, both of these patterns have tended to concentrate these segments of the population within certain parts of cities. Especially for the property owners, these housing patterns further emphasize the permanence of the stay of these immigrants.

## CONCLUSION

The immigrant populations of the United Kingdom have altered British society and politics in a significant and

17. Ibid., pp. 96 ff.

apparently permanent manner. Unlike migrant workers in other countries who are ambivalent about staying or who have become settlers almost by accident and whose relationship to the political and legal system of the country is often tenuous, most immigrants—especially those from Commonwealth countries— came intending to remain and most have remained. Some can claim rights approaching those of citizens, even upon arrival, or they can gain substantial civil and political rights once settled. They have transformed a society stereotypically viewed as homogenous into one in which race must be considered a major dimension of social and political life and an important issue. This issue goes beyond riots by youths in the equivalent of the American ghettos to include much broader issues about the distribution of rights and benefits in a welfare state that provides a wide range of such rights and benefits.

ANNALS, *AAPSS,* **485,** May 1986

# Immigration: Issues of Ethnicity, Class, and Public Policy in the United States

*By* ROBERT L. BACH

ABSTRACT: This article argues that the incorporation of immigrants into the advanced industrial states may be best understood in the context of recent theoretical debates over the changing character of racial and gender inequality. Specifically, it attempts to draw parallels between the conditions of working-class minorities and women born in the advanced economies and the economic progress of new immigrant groups. Shifting from a focus on individualized discrimination, emphasis is placed on the structural divisions within each immigrant group. For example, the bifurcation of the black community, resulting from the relative success of its middle class and the persistent decline of the underclass, is mirrored in the differentiation of immigrant and refugee groups. In contrast to the success stories of a few immigrant entrepreneurs or reconstituted fragments of an uprooted capitalist class, the majority within these immigrant and refugee groups are forming part of a restructured working class found throughout the advanced industrial states. This emphasis on the restructuring of the working class identifies grounds for a political framework based on a broad coalition of interests among those of various backgrounds who work for low and modest wages.

*Robert L. Bach is an associate professor of sociology at the State University of New York at Binghamton. With Alejandro Portes, he recently wrote the book* Latin Journey: Cuban and Mexican Immigrants in the United States *(1985). He is currently engaged in three research projects: U.S.-Cuban Relations and Cuban Migration; The Incorporation of Southeast Asian Refugees in the United States; and Women in the Garment and Electronic Industries.*

NOTE: Research upon which part of this article is based was funded by grants from the Rockefeller Foundation and the Ford Foundation. The opinions expressed are solely those of the author.

SINCE World War II, the world has been witness to an unprecedented movement of people from less developed regions to the advanced industrial states. Throughout most of this period, the expectation was that many—perhaps a majority of those who were not refugees—would return to their countries of origin. In Europe an expectation accompanying the widespread use of guest-worker programs was that when labor was no longer needed the migrants would depart. In the United States, immigration law and policy are based far more on the assumption that immigrants come to stay. Still, even here the possibilities of return have been promoted through a guest-worker program—the Bracero Program, terminated in 1964; and the circulatory nature of much of the illegal flow and the significant rates of return migration even among those presumed to be permanently resettled have worked in this direction.

In the 1970s, however, following economic crises in both the United States and Western Europe, it came to be generally recognized that large numbers of immigrant groups were not going to return home. They were becoming large, new, seemingly permanent ethnic minorities. Recognition of this transition from immigrant to ethnic group fostered both a revival of old views and efforts to develop new perspectives on immigrant adaptation. In the United States, the theoretical shifts are now fairly well known. Older theories of assimilation, though severely criticized for years, were resurrected under the guise of neoclassical labor market theories. Other observers focused on the characteristics of the new groups, emphasizing their distinctive cultural or ethnic traits, to discover the differences between them and the native-born population. Still others focused on the structural conditions of the labor market, identifying separate economic functions for immigrant as opposed to native-born workers.

The purpose of this article is not to review these familiar, if controversial, views of immigrant adaptation. Rather, the object is to advance a conceptual framework that brings together a variety of similar, yet disconnected, observations on the conditions in the United States faced by both immigrants and native-born blacks and women. Many writers have noted a general similarity in the conditions of immigrants, blacks, and women—especially as members of a secondary labor market. The commonality is deeper than generally observed, however, and it provides a basis for a conceptual framework that integrates the political and economic interests of each group. My aim is to make explicit what many researchers have reported in a variety of ways, namely that there has been a convergence of views on the nature of inequality in the United States that requires a reconceptualization of the role of discrimination in the current period. This conceptual shift supports a reorganization of the way in which we think about the incorporation of immigrants into their host societies.

### LINKS BETWEEN IMMIGRATION AND RACIAL AND GENDER INEQUALITY

There are several reasons for constructing a framework for a discussion of immigration that takes as its point of departure a commonality between immigrants and minorities in the U.S. economy. The most important may be historical. A few years ago, William Julius Wilson noted in the pages of this journal that civil rights supporters were puzzled by recent developments in the black community.[1] Despite gains in antidis-

1. William Julius Wilson, "The Black Community in the 1980's: Questions of Race, Class, and

crimination legislation and the promotion of affirmative action programs, the situation of black Americans was deteriorating, and politically they were being abandoned even by their liberal white allies.

A similar concern has puzzled those engaged in the age-old debate over the economic progress of immigrants: why do some immigrant groups advance economically more rapidly and further than others? In fact, why do some of these newcomers surpass even native-born minority groups? The puzzle is actually a paradox. On the one hand, a prestigious literature on immigration has argued that newcomers advance quite rapidly and even surpass their respective native-born ethnic groups within the first generation.[2] This literature had great influence on the Select Commission for Immigration and Refugee Policy, leading it to accept the premise that the nation did not have to worry that immigration would lead to long-term divisions in the population. This argument has never been reconciled with an impressively large, if politically less influential, set of research results that details the multiple problems, constraints, and barriers that immigrants face as they enter the United States. In particular, it did not mesh with studies that demonstrated that immigrants entered the lowest sectors of the labor market, where their opportunities for advancement were structurally limited.

The reasons for the puzzle in both literatures are the same. There have been profound shifts in the nature of inequality in the United States and a realignment of political and intellectual views of the importance of racial, ethnic, and gender discrimination. In Wilson's view, a careful examination of the issues shows that this puzzlement is due to the lack of an appreciation of the variations in the black experience, especially the differences that emerged during the 1960s and 1970s between blacks in the middle class and those among the working poor or underclass. The changes in inequality and in views of discrimination had a similar impact on ethnic and gender inequality, specifically posing an alternative to both the conservative and liberal understanding of discrimination.

As is well known, the conventional conceptualization of discrimination as an explanation for the subordinate, unequal positions of minorities focuses attention primarily on the individual. Discrimination exists in those situations where individuals with equal characteristics and experiences receive unequal rewards. These rewards are typically measured either by earnings or by promotions and hirings. The primary controversy between the liberal definition of discrimination and the conservative one is whether unequal outcomes are sufficient to establish the existence of discrimination, or whether intention and conspiracy to discriminate have to be manifest. In recent years, of course, conservatives appear to have triumphed: the prevailing view seems to be that discrimination exists only in cases where one person intentionally rewards another unequally, based on sex, race, ethnicity, age, or nativity.

While this debate raged, a very different conceptualization of the nature of discrimination and inequality was devel-

Public Policy," *The Annals* of the American Academy of Political and Social Science, 454 (Mar. 1981).

2. For example, see Barry R. Chiswick, "The Economic Progress of Immigrants: Some Apparently Universal Patterns," in *Contemporary Economic Problems,* ed. W. Fellner (Washington, DC: American Enterprise Institute, 1979), pp. 357-99.

oping. Part of the reason for this conceptualization was the increasing difficulty of establishing—and finding—individuals who had similar or equal backgrounds. As advances were made by relatively small numbers of middle-class blacks, professional women, and immigrants in gaining some protection against the worst excesses of individualized discrimination, the outstanding feature of inequality became the very different locations in the economy occupied by these groups. For example, the debate on gender inequality—once totally dominated by classical concerns over individualized discrimination, or equal pay for equal work—became a much more complex and compelling argument about the differential job structures for men and women. Simply stated, few working women occupied the same jobs that men did and, therefore, few were even subject to individualized forms of discrimination.[3]

For blacks, economic transformations made a similar structural or compositional argument possible. Decline in Rust Belt manufacturing, increase in the demand for skills requiring access to education unavailable to many working-class blacks, and concentration in the central cities have separated a major portion of the black population from jobs in which they could compete for equal pay. As a result, individualized discrimination could become a problem for only a comparatively small segment of the population.

The connection between immigration and the shifting conceptualization of inequality and opportunity for minorities and women can best be traced through the history of the debate over immigration policy reform. The last major reforms of U.S. immigration law took place in the 1960s, when the struggles of the civil rights movement against discrimination were extended to the nation's doorsteps and provoked a significant realignment on the issue of who should be able to enter the United States.

The 1965 amendments to the immigration law were equally swayed by antidiscrimination sentiments. The primary objective of these amendments was to end the National Origins Quota Act, which included a virtual ban on immigration from the Pacific region and clearly discriminated against non-European immigrants. In fact, as I have argued elsewhere,[4] the reform of the immigration law in 1965 followed quickly—and was fundamentally linked with—the passage of the Civil Rights Act.

Like the spectacular gains served by the civil rights legislation, however, these long-awaited immigration reforms faced a far different and more complex set of circumstances in the second half of the 1960s. The change in the composition of the immigrant population added considerable heterogeneity to both the class composition and the national origin of the influx. After 1968, the proportion of both Latin American and Asian immigrants rose rapidly and soon sur-

3. The National Research Council defines the problem as follows: "A second type of wage discrimination . . . arises when the job structure within a firm is substantially segregated by sex, race, or ethnicity, and workers of one category are paid less than workers of another category when the two groups are performing work that is not the same but that is, in some sense, of comparable worth to their employer." Donald J. Treiman and Heidi Hartmann, *Women, Work, and Wages: Equal Pay for Jobs of Equal Value* (Washington, DC: National Academy Press, 1981), p. 9.

4. Robert L. Bach, *Western Hemispheric Immigration to the United States: A Review of Selected Research Trends* (Washington, DC: Georgetown University, Center for Immigration Policy and Refugee Assistance, 1984).

passed the traditional European flow. The occupational backgrounds of Latin Americans were generally lower than those of earlier European immigrants. The new emphasis on family reunification added a strong working-class component to the influx. The heterogeneity of occupational origins made background experiences and skills a new source of differentiation among the various nationalities and became an important source of subsequent uneven economic progress in the United States.

Two additional changes in the structure of immigration added to this heterogeneity. First, in the 1970s there was a large, self-sustaining influx of undocumented workers. The movement of Mexican workers to the United States became a silent invasion of persons arriving in a precarious, politically defenseless position. This undocumented influx was not limited to the Mexican flow. By the 1980s, there was a rapid increase in the diversity of national origins of those being apprehended by the Immigration and Naturalization Service.

Second, by the late 1960s, the Cuban refugee flow had reached an unprecedented volume. Refugee resettlement on so large a scale brought the goals of foreign policies directly into established communities where minorities and whites coexisted. Broader, more encompassing political realities began to influence and separate groups at a local level. Special government interest in the Cuban population created the possibility, and certainly the perception, that the Cubans in America were receiving preferential treatment.

The experience with Cubans served as the basis for theoretical and programmatic insights into refugee resettlement until 1975. Then, the fall of American-backed regimes in Southeast Asia pro-duced a new wave of refugees. The diverse national and class origins of this new influx added considerable complexity to the immigrant population and changed the perception of what constituted a resettlement effort. In particular, the program had to change significantly to accommodate the Southeast Asians' very different social and class origins.

Another major change in this post-reform period resulted from the economic crisis of the 1970s and the restructuring of the U.S. economy. Inflation, housing, education, and employment became problems and reshaped the context for the reception of immigrants. New restrictionist pressures at the national border coincided with increased interest in differential group progress in the United States. For example, some writers on the topic advocated a strategy of economic selectivity at the border, to ensure the most productive and efficient integration of newcomers into the labor market.[5] Instead of civil rights concerns over equitable access or family reunion, the overriding principle became economic efficiency and reduced costs to social welfare programs. The new immigrant-related policy converged with increased pressures on the working class and the poor.

By the late 1970s, many observers still committed to social reform continued to concentrate on earlier battles over constitutional rights and did not fully recognize the newer forms of discrimination and inequality. As support for affirmative action programs for blacks declined and pressure for an Equal Rights Amendment for women waned, well-

5. Pastora San Juan Cafferty, Barry R. Chiswick, Andrew M. Greeley, and Teresa A. Sullivan, *The Dilemma of American Immigration: Beyond the Golden Door* (New Brunswick, NJ: Transaction Books, 1983).

meaning interest in immigration reform remained restricted to broad legislative changes. The Select Commission on Immigration and Refugee Policy, for instance, still accepted as one of its primary charges the task of ridding the United States of all vestiges of a discriminatory admissions policy.

A primary consequence of this legacy of antidiscrimination battles over control of the border was that, while each new wave of immigrants posed novel legislative problems, the condition faced by immigrants in the United States lost its political attractiveness. For example, the treatment of Cuban and Haitian newcomers met with criticism in 1980. The unequal treatment and the policy ambiguity that accompanied the influx of Cubans and Haitians fit well the traditional, liberal concern over constitutional rights, legislative reform, and human dignity. Once these entrants settled, however, there was a noticeable drop in agitation and even in attempts to service them as they encountered severe difficulties in entering the local labor market, locating shelter, and gaining access to assistance programs.[6] More attention was devoted to the immediate problems of individual rights at the border than to the less tractable problems of unemployment, underemployment, institutional racism, and abuse in the minority ghettos of major U.S. cities.

## COMMUNITY PERSPECTIVES

In the 1970s, the changing conditions of inequality produced a switch in emphasis to group solidarity and achievement. Black scholars turned to a black

6. Alejandro Portes and Alex Stepick, "Unwelcome Immigrants: The Labor Market Experiences of 1980 (Mariel) Cuban and Haitian Refugees in South Florida," *American Sociological Review*, 50:493-514 (Aug. 1985).

perspective, which focused on black achievements, racial solidarity, militancy, and hostility to whites. The feminist movement was similarly radicalized, and came to target economic and political equality with men as its goals.

Some immigrant groups adopted similar positions. For example, segments of the Cuban-American community transformed their economic and political goals into chauvinistic expressions of separatist pride and self-aggrandizement. From this Cuban-heritage view, the Cuban community in Miami is not an ethnic minority group but a community in temporary exile. While in such a state, it will maintain relatively distinct economic activities strongly defended by political and ideological boundaries.

Much of this kind of community or nationalistic argument served an important purpose—to counter the subtle racism of individualistic assimilationist views that stressed the breakup of community, the lack of skills, and the weakness of certain groups. The racism was replaced by a new affirmation of ethnic viability and pride that also de-emphasized the internal differentiation of the community—in particular, social class. For example, a Mexican-heritage view— stressing solidarity of persons with a common Mexican heritage—obscured the class divisions within the Chicano community. In the Cuban-American community of Miami the interests of a reconstituted upper class had effectively captured and defined the political orientation of all Cubans there, despite the considerable heterogeneity of economic and social conditions among them. In the Asian communities on the West Coast, entrepreneurial middlemen and highly educated professionals and technicians cast a generalized image of an aggressive, upwardly mobile population.

Overall, these community views pitted artificially—and erroneously—constructed homogeneous groups against each other. The analytical discussion was formulated in comparative group terms, black as opposed to white, men to women, and immigrants to native born. Little attention was devoted to inequalities inside each community or to problems with the economy that stratified each community. The result was the same, even when the economy was an explicit concern. This is best illustrated by the dual-labor-market perspective to the study of immigration.

Applied to immigration, this perspective has two fundamental premises: that the development of modern industry leads to a division of the labor market into primary and secondary jobs, and that immigrants constitute the best labor force for the secondary jobs. The first premise has made a major contribution to understanding the structural differentiation of job opportunities. The second, however, reinforces the mistakes of the community perspective. The important element in the thesis is explicit reliance on a contrast between the motivations of immigrants and those of the native born. Native-born workers are said to resist accepting dead-end, low-wage jobs because they have career goals and rely more on the social ranking of their jobs for a definition of their self-worth. In contrast, it is averred, immigrants take marginal jobs that produce only supplemental earnings. The reason given is that labor migrants are target earners, whose primary motivation is simply to maximize temporary earnings and then return home. As immigrants settle, however, these motivations change, and the immigrants develop goals that more closely resemble those of the native born.

Even from this brief summary it is clear that the primary analytic contrast places immigrants, conceived to be a homogeneous group with shared motivations, against the native-born population, similarly viewed as an undifferentiated group. Such a view not only embodies the group perspective, but reverts to even earlier, orthodox assumptions and stereotypes of groups' characteristics. For example, as I have argued elsewhere,[7] Piore draws explicitly upon sociological theories of racial inequality deeply rooted in outmoded concepts of the culture of poverty. He writes that for immigrants "the hallmark of the culture of poverty becomes the absence of culture and community."[8] Moreover, he argues that in the transition from migrant to settled ethnic minority, the migrants' culture of poverty "is an autonomous process that occurs within the immigrant community independently of whatever contact that community has with the larger cultural environment."[9] The result is that these migrant subcultures create problems that retard economic advancement, through deviant forms of social adaptation, unstable households, or inflated consumer expectations.

This perspective suffers from at least two shortcomings. The first constitutes an act of commission, the second, an act of omission. Piore likens immigrants' motivations to those of housewives, students, and peasants, who are seen as seeking only supplemental earnings. This trivializes the contribution of immigrant workers, not only to the economy but to their households and places of

7. Robert L. Bach, "Review Essay," *Journal of International Affairs,* 33(2):339-50 (Fall-Winter 1979).

8. Michael J. Piore, *Birds of Passage: Migrant Labor and Industrial Societies* (Cambridge: Cambridge University Press, 1979), p. 72.

9. Ibid., p. 77.

origin. Ironically, given his focus on the functions of immigrants for the economy, it also misrepresents the magnitude of immigrants' contributions and roles in specific sectors of the economy.

Second, and more important for the argument here, this motivational perspective ignores the socioeconomic heterogeneity of both immigrant and native-born groups; and the fact that a large portion of the immigrant flow simply does not correspond at all to the image of the secondary labor market worker is overlooked. As Portes and Bach have argued,[10] the majority of legal immigrants represent a middle-class influx, comprised of professionals, technicians, and those with above-average education. In addition, although motivations certainly change as immigrants remain in the United States—for surely whenever material conditions in one's life change, goals and motivations also change—it is the heterogeneous character of each group and the very conditions of resettlement that are the important factors in determining how immigrants' perceptions change and whether these new perceptions, in turn, have an effect on economic progress.

The overall problem with the dual-labor-market conception is that it fails to explain the paradox of immigrants' economic progress. Those who argue that the primary contrast is between immigrants and the native born encounter problems in explaining the apparently remarkable progress of some immigrant groups and especially the success of a relatively small segment of each group. This is especially true when the successful immigrant group is nonwhite and

when broad charges of individualized discrimination are hard to substantiate.[11]

The increased significance of refugee flows for the progress of the immigrant population as a whole also creates problems for a community perspective. For the most part these problems come about because research on refugees falls victim to the now-familiar orthodox views of their collective character. Refugees are presumed to be different from labor immigrants because they have different motivations: labor migrants are target earners, while refugees are permanent settlers. Such broad, gross stereotypes have been advanced not only by orthodox economists but also by those who have focused on the administrative necessity of finding a way to distinguish migrants from refugees.[12]

The critical point, however, is that such a view reproduces the entire problem with group comparison based on overall characteristics. First, comparisons are based on group traits, and there is no empirical evidence that motivation, based on such undifferentiated group membership, exists. Second, since the motivations among members of each group are heterogenous, large segments of both the labor-migrant and refugee populations share reasons for migrating and set similar goals in the United States. Third, the emphasis on motivation advances a group-psychology view in total isolation from the material conditions faced by these groups in the United States. As biased as the first two tendencies are, the

10. Alejandro Portes and Robert L. Bach, *Latin Journey: Cuban and Mexican Immigrants in the United States* (Berkeley: University of California Press, 1985).

11. See, for example, Morrison G. Wong and Charles Hirschman, "Labor Force Participation and Socioeconomic Attainment of Asian-American Women," *Sociological Perspectives,* 26(4): 423-46 (Oct. 1983).

12. Robert L. Bach, "The New Cuban Exodus: Political and Economic Motivations," *Caribbean Review,* 11(1):22-25, 58-60 (Winter 1982).

third is inexcusable. Such views are based on a lack of the requisite thorough appreciation of these structural conditions and, thus, are unsupportable. They are tantamount to assuming that once a group is labeled refugee it becomes isolated from the prevailing pressures that all workers face in the receiving economy.

## STRUCTURAL DIVERSITIES

By the early 1980s, the diversity of minority groups and the vastly different conditions they face in the United States had produced another switch in perspective among many students of racial, ethnic, and gender inequality. It became clear to observers of the black community that civil rights legislation had benefited primarily middle-class blacks. For the black majority, the situation in ghettos and working-class neighborhoods was not improving. Inadequate schooling, substandard and overcrowded housing, lack of access to jobs and job training created a new form of segregation—segregation by class.

For working-class women, the situation was similar. Entry into the labor force was far from the panacea that had been promised by the forecast of equal rights. In fact, working women were faced with increasing obligations in the labor force, which they now had to combine with obligations in the household.[13]

As students of these group experiences pursued their respective concerns,

they independently derived comparable expressions for the idea that class differentiation within communities was the primary source of differences between communities. Here, specifically, the literature on blacks and immigrants converged. As students of the black experience began addressing the differential modes of adaptation,[14] researchers of the immigrant experience focused on differential modes of incorporation.[15] In sharp contrast to individualistic perspectives that blame the victim and promote a culture of poverty—popular among some researchers of the black experience—and assimilation theory and the concept of inadequate human capital—among immigration researchers—the focus became the structural conditions that gave rise to observed differences in circumstances and behavior.

Attempts to establish these modes of adaptation or incorporation focused attention primarily on class alignments—above all, the restructuring of the working class. Considerable care was taken, however, not to de-emphasize the clear importance of ethnic and community rules of affiliation in determining the unique social combinations found in specific locations in the U.S. economy. Analytic attention was focused on how class and ethnicity interacted, including the nature of the regional economy, the social composition of the community, the degree of job segregation, the housing market, and institutional discrimination.

Perhaps most important, sources of change were uncovered within the com-

13. Among working-class immigrant women, conditions were doubly difficult. Monica Boyd has observed, for example, that the lower occupational status of immigrant women in Canada seems to be due not only to their being women, but to their being foreign-born as well. Monica Boyd, "At a Disadvantage: The Occupational Attainments of Foreign Born Women in Canada," *International Migration Review,* 18(4):1113 (1985).

14. Wilson, "Black Community in the 1980's."
15. Alejandro Portes, "Modes of Structural Incorporation and Present Theories of Labor Immigration," in *Global Trends in Migration: Theory and Research on International Population Movements,* ed. Mary M. Kritz, Charles B. Keely, and Silvano M. Tomasi (New York: Center for Migration Studies, 1981), pp. 279-97.

munity itself that had little to do with presumed group motivations. Instead, they were found to be structurally rooted in the availability of material resources. Within structural constraints, segments of immigrant communities have been able to mobilize resources through a variety of means. Some bring resources with them or create a critical mass through pooling dispersed resources from familial or kinship networks. Others gain access to political and economic power by serving as clients to established groups or the government. And still others, who have only their own ability to work, attempt to trade that ability for a sufficient personal and household income. This last, the largest group, has few resources for advancement, since it lacks both access to capital resources and political leverage. In fact, until immigrants become a regularized political constituency by gaining citizenship, they have virtually no political influence with which to attract economic benefits.

### The wage labor force

Based on this intertwining of class and ethnic resources, the incorporation of immigrants usually falls into three interrelated modes or patterns. The most prevalent, as previously noted, involves integration into the wage labor force. Facing the generalized pressures of the labor market, immigrant workers are subject to a variety of constraints and sources of competition. As predicted by dual-labor-market theories, these wage workers are disproportionately located in the sector of secondary jobs. A significant share, however, succeeds in gaining access to the primary sector and, as anticipated, acquires considerable monetary benefits. Portes and Bach have

shown, for example, that among both Mexican immigrants and Cuban refugees access to the primary sector increases both occupational prestige and earnings.[16] The primary mechanism for advancement, however, appears to be simply gaining access to the primary sector. Only in a limited sense are immigrants able to translate their skills or training into greater rewards once they are located in either sector of the labor market.

For these working-class immigrants, ethnicity is an important factor in differentiating their labor market outcomes. The secondary sector is characterized by antagonistic ethnic relations, in which the newcomers are segregated with members of their own group and native-born ethnic minorities. The primary sector exposes these immigrants to an Anglo labor force comprised almost totally of native-born workers. Without access to alternative resources, these wage workers must rely on networks within the community to locate jobs. Ethnically segregated job structures are reproduced through these organized social networks. Problems may arise when immigrants attempt to utilize existing working-class organizations to help secure better jobs.[17] With few exceptions, the unions and working-class organizations in most cities are dominated by older, more settled groups outside the new groups' ethnic networks.

Working-class immigrants also face the full consequences of structural shifts in the U.S. economy. Unable to garner sufficient resources through training or access to primary-sector jobs to create alternatives, they succumb to the vaga-

16. Portes and Bach, *Latin Journey.*
17. Stephen Castles, "The Social Time-bomb: Education of an Underclass in West Germany," *Race and Class*, 4 (1980).

ries of an economy under rapid transformation. The original premise of the dual-labor-market thesis fairly accurately identifies the nature of this shift in the structural changes in the job structure. In the 1960s and 1970s, working-class immigrants were incorporated into the economy on the basis of mass production. As O'Connor argued in the early 1970s, monopoly firms engaged in standardized production encouraged the proliferation of peripheral firms whose dependence on low wages required highly competitive labor conditions.[18] As Piore and Sabel have argued recently, later in the 1970s and in the 1980s the rise in new technologies—which are based more on small batch production and on customized instead of standardized goods and which are more sensitive to fluctuations in market demand—has created a more dynamic job structure.[19] But this reorganization of productive relations has had only a limited effect on the immigrant wage workers. In fact, as Bach and Tienda have shown, the more pervasive tendency among working-class immigrants has been an increased segregation in operative and laborer jobs within the manufacturing sector at a time when other major groups in the working class are moving out.[20]

⋇Another important feature of the structural constraints facing the immigrant wage worker is the match between changes in regional economies and un-evenly distributed geographical patterns of resettlement. The incorporation of many new Asian immigrants into the electronics industry in Southern California provides an example.[21] Although working-class immigrants and refugees are consigned to lower positions in this industry, in many cases the strength of economic growth in the region has provided employment opportunities and sufficient stability to establish a good household income.

But incorporation into the electronics industry has been uneven. The industry has had several recessions in the last ten years, and each time the immigrants or refugees have been among those who lost their jobs. The electronics industry has also spawned a network of underground assembly operations, located primarily in garages and employing significant numbers of women. With few exceptions, this type of work offers only the best of a bad situation for wage workers.

### Entrepreneurs

Exceptions to the limited progress in the electronics industry are important, however, for they highlight a second mode of incorporation. The opportunities made available for immigrant workers by industrial transformation have allowed for an apparent proliferation of entrepreneurial activities. Immigrant Asian entrepreneurs, for example, are frequently glamorized by the press and applauded by public officials. But they are relatively rare, fail at nearly as high rates as they succeed, and, more impor-

18. James O'Connor, *The Fiscal Crisis of the State* (New York: St. Martin's Press, 1973).

19. Michael J. Piore and Charles F. Sabel, *The Second Industrial Divide: Possibilities for Prosperity* (New York: Basic Books, 1984).

20. Robert L. Bach and Marta Tienda, "Contemporary Immigration and Refugee Movements and Employment Adjustment Policies," in *Immigration: Issues and Policies,* ed. Vernon M. Briggs, Jr., and Marta Tienda (Salt Lake City, UT: Olympus, 1985).

21. See, for example, Robert L. Bach, "Labor Force Participation and Employment among Southeast Asian Refugees in the United States" (Report, Office of Refugee Resettlement, U.S. Department of Health and Human Services, 1984.)

tant, require the labor of an ethnic or immigrant working class to both build and maintain their operations. This mode of incorporation, which Bonacich, Light, and others have analyzed so well,[22] involves the growth of a middleman entrepreneurial class. It emerges in the interstices of economic networks, often providing services to the larger economy while offering employment to fellow immigrants or other, native-born, ethnic workers. Those who have capitalized beyond small restaurants or food markets generally employ workers at low wages and offer few opportunities for advancement. In terms of the entire immigrant group, however, they constitute a significant segment of the community that provides examples for those searching for immigrant success.

### Ethnic enclaves

Another mode of incorporation has been identified as an ethnic enclave. This form is based specifically on the experiences of the Cuban community in Miami and the historical experiences of Jewish and Japanese immigrants.[23] It requires a highly differentiated class structure, concentration in a relatively small geographical area, and a commitment by members of the capitalist class to hire fellow immigrants as workers in their firms. Unlike the middleman minority pattern, however, an important exchange occurs. The capitalist class offers employment to each wave of

22. Edna Bonacich and John Modell, *The Economic Basis of Ethnic Solidarity: Small Business in the Japanese-American Community* (Berkeley: University of California Press, 1980); Ivan Light, "Asian Entreprise in America: Chinese, Japanese, and Koreans in Small Business," in *Self-Help in Urban America,* ed. Scott Cummings (New York: Kennikat, 1980), pp. 33-57.

23. Portes and Bach, *Latin Journey.*

newcomers and, primarily through a subcontracting, self-employment mechanism, offers them opportunities for economic mobility. In exchange, these workers refrain from labor militancy and, in general, support the ethnically defined boundaries of the community. Although this enclave pattern can be observed in only a few historical instances, there are many situations in which similar principles of class and ethnic relations work on a more limited scale.

### Southeast Asian refugees

A final structural pattern may be developing in the context of the resettlement of nearly 800,000 Southeast Asian refugees. Although each of the three patterns described earlier can be observed in this group, the resettlement of these refugees has involved the state and, especially, public assistance programs more than in the other cases. The relationship of the Cuban community to a succession of governments has been a very important instrument of their collective advancement, but the principles of this kind of relationship are much different for Southeast Asians. Unlike any other group of immigrants, these newcomers have been resettled in direct contact with the Anglo community through the mechanism of refugee sponsorship. The outcomes of this pattern are still unclear, but it is already evident that the sponsorship relationship serves at least as a primary source of social and economic differentiation within the refugee community. Whether it promotes economic progress or not relative to other immigrant groups is still an open question.

The general point is that the progress of immigrant and refugee groups is greatly influenced by various sources of differentiation. In most accounts of the process, however, only a few attributes of the immigrant group are offered as explanatory factors. Assumptions of differential motivations, skills, and abilities are then substituted for a thorough examination and explanation. Instead, the multiple modes of incorporation described previously, which may coexist within one community and, on occasion, may overlap, explain the progress or lack of progress among immigrants.

## THE IMMIGRANT IDEOLOGY AND PUBLIC POLICY

Profound and rapid transformations of the economy tend to be associated with major shifts in political alignments. Groups and individuals once constituting the mainstream of political and intellectual thought switch their positions as they confront new problems and search for new solutions. Given such shifts of viewpoints, it would be remarkable if the issues of immigration reform and the economic progress of immigrants in the United States were not also associated with such intellectual realignments. The emergence of a common base for understanding problems facing the largest minorities in the United States requires a reconceptualization of the role of discrimination in determining social inequality.

The recognition of the centrality of diverse but shared structural positions suggests, perhaps surprisingly, certain political strategies. For example, Wilson quotes Bayard Rustin's astute observation on the dilemma facing black progress: "What is the value of winning access to public accommodations for those who lack money to use them?"[24]

24. Wilson, "Black Community in the 1980's."

Echoing this theme, women ask themselves of what value equal rights are if they mean simply being allowed to work in low-wage, gender-segregated jobs. The need to expand the notion of equal rights to include comparable levels of involvement in all spheres, including political power and employment, is evident. To achieve that, it is necessary to restructure the U.S. economy, in order to gain control over the determination of not only the distribution of economic wealth but the conditions under which it is produced.

These issues underly the arguments about social inequality and highlight the significance of ideology and the support it provides for particular public policies. As many observers have noted, immigrants not only provide an additional, flexible work force and lessen the demand for social expenditures; they also undermine the political logic of the welfare state.[25] It focuses attention on invidious comparisons between highly unequal groups rather than pointing out the real sources of inequality and subordination. For example, the highly touted comparative success of Asian-Americans can be explained largely by their differential incorporation into job and industrial sectors and by the region of their concentration. In fact, to the extent that research on migration accepts as the critical contrast the contrast between immigrants and the native born, it reinforces the tendency of migration to reduce the power of organized labor by dividing working-class interests into competitive camps. It also adds to the tendency of migration to join with other factors in making visible the association

25. For example, see Gary P. Freeman, "Migration and the Political Economy of the Welfare State," this issue of *The Annals* of the American Academy of Political and Social Science.

between public assistance and race or ethnicity.

This is the importance of the immigrant ideology—it takes vastly different groups and, by comparing them, makes a negative statement about those who are worse off. For example, it is simply not true—as William Raspberry writes—that Southeast Asian refugees with large families are not worse off than others. Even in the study he cites, that was not the case. And certainly in other studies, household size creates economic problems in several predictable ways.

Ironically, however, Raspberry has hit upon an important point. Ideology and group myths are important, as Raspberry has pointed out, but not in the way that he uses them. Given the structural divisions that separate large groups of workers within the black community, among working women,

and amid the diverse groups of immigrants, there is a basis for a common understanding of the problem these people encounter. It is the articulation of these common problems and concerns that, if it is used as a new theoretical perspective, can provide a basis for political action and advancement. This newer perspective, rather than the myths of group attributes favored by those who are clearly in power or who fail to examine critically the nature of systemic constraints, will provide the common values for a critical mythology. Interestingly, one possible direction for this mythology is to replicate the experiences of working-class immigrants at the turn of the century: they found labor organization, political agitation, and shared values with others from the working class as the conditions for their collective economic progress.

ANNALS, *AAPSS*, **485**, May 1986

# Transnational Migration as a
# Small Window on the Diminished Autonomy
# of the Modern Democratic State

*By* MARTIN O. HEISLER

ABSTRACT: The presence of large semi-settled foreign populations in Western societies is at once a symptom of and an exacerbating factor in the problematic governance of these states. Domestic and international constraints preclude the reversal of most of the unforeseen and undesirable social, economic, and political consequences that have flowed from the narrowly conceived, short-sighted policies that gave rise to the migrants' presence. The nature of the state in the host societies and the political structures and policy processes that characterize their governments account for the miasma in most of them. The nature of the less modern, less democratic state that typifies the countries of origin contributes to their present and even greater prospective policy binds and the problematic life conditions of many of the migrants. While it is expedient for each of the three classes of actors—receiving states, sending states, and migrants—to nurture the myth of return, learning to live with the resulting indeterminacy presents great challenges to all and may require, in particular, rethinking what modern democratic states are about.

---

*Martin O. Heisler received his undergraduate and graduate education at the University of California at Los Angeles (Ph.D., 1969). He is a member of the faculty of government and politics at the University of Maryland and has also taught at Aarhus University in Denmark and at the University of Illinois. His publications include* Politics in Europe *(1974),* International Energy Policy *(coeditor, 1980), and numerous shorter works on social policy, European politics, and security policy. He was special editor of an earlier issue of* The Annals *devoted to ethnic conflict. His current research focuses on transformations of the modern state in general and the ramifications of security dependence for the governability of democracies in particular.*

T HE study of migration from less developed countries to the democratic welfare states of Western Europe provides several important insights into the nature of modern states and the travails of their governments.[1] First, 20 or 25 years ago, governments in the receiving states set in motion processes that most of them believed to be only marginally important and reversible, but that no one understood, and these led to profound, multifarious, and widespread long-term consequences no one foresaw. Soon after large-scale immigration began it assumed a life—more precisely, several different lives—of its own, and it took on distinct but invariably crucial forms and meanings for the migrants and the countries of their provenance, as well as for the countries of their destination. Neither the policymakers nor most of the citizens in the latter had imagined, intended, or desired what has come to pass.

These elements of the historical backdrop for the current situation crystallized in two short decades. They are much better understood now. What is less understood—because the massive

1. For explicit bases for comparing the American case with Western Europe, see Michael J. Piore, "The Shifting Grounds for Immigration," this issue of *The Annals* of the American Academy of Political and Social Science; Robert L. Bach, "Immigration: Issues of Ethnicity, Class, and Public Policy in the United States," ibid.; B. Guy Peters and Patricia Davis, "Migration to the United Kingdom and the Emergence of a New Politics," ibid. Several important distinctions between the European receiving countries and the United States, however, militate against subsuming the latter under the theoretical framework used here in more than a superficial way. Some of these are identified in Barbara Schmitter Heisler and Martin O. Heisler, "Transnational Migration and the Modern Democratic State: Familiar Problems in New Form or a New Problem?" ibid., nn. 1, 8.

social, cultural, political, economic, legal, and institutional forces that constitute it are very recent on the time scale of human and societal transformations and are still in progress—is that this wave of migration is fostering profound structural changes in the receiving and sending states and in the relationships between them.

On the surface, these changes have already confirmed and contributed to a diminution of the governing capabilities of modern democracies. They have constrained governments in their efforts to respond effectively and in politically acceptable ways to a multitude of challenges, not only those directly associated with migration. When such constraints are added to other domestic and external limitations, the cumulated loads on governments in some of the receiving states approach the unmanageable.

These problems are exacerbated by the effects of the continuing presence of large immigrant populations on job markets, on social programs and their budgets, and on the social trends that stimulated the importation of foreign labor in the first place. Social and political conflicts are also increased by these developments, and in some countries the political and material resources available to deal with those burdens and conflicts are diminished by the same phenomena.

Even more important in the long run, the ways in which the receiving countries deal with these unforeseen and unintended consequences of their initially modest, ad hoc labor-importation policies may alter fundamental social, political, and economic relationships and deeply rooted structures for managing conflicts and for allocating resources and responsibilities in their societies. At this level the concern is with less visible but more lasting and significant effects on states, rather than only on governments of the day. This distinction will be explicated shortly.

The present circumstances may be more favorable to many of the migrants and the states from which they came because their freedom of action and the resources available to them are increased by migration—at least in the short term. In fact, these considerations account for the unwillingness of most migrants to return to the countries of their origin in the near future and for the policies of the sending countries that encourage prolonged sojourns but not assimilation. However, almost any denouement we can envision for what is a protracted—but surely neither a permanent nor a stable—condition is likely, eventually, to pose grave problems for the sending countries and perhaps for some of their nationals abroad.

These additional, important insights can be distilled from recent studies of cross-national migration. Unlike the first, they are only implicitly treated in most of the articles in this volume—or, for that matter, in most of the literature on the current manifestations of migration.[2] The primary aim of this essay is to make explicit and coherent the main implications of current, large-scale migration for increasingly problematic governance in advanced industrial democracies and for dislocations in their state structures. The ramifications for the sending states are a secondary concern,

2. A notable exception is Gary P. Freeman, "Migration and the Political Economy of the Welfare State," this issue of *The Annals* of the American Academy of Political and Social Science. Significant explicit discussion of some aspects of these concerns are provided in Rosemarie Rogers, "The Transnational Nexus of Migration," ibid.; James F. Hollifield, "Immigration Policy in France and Germany: Outputs versus Outcomes," ibid.; some articles in Rosemarie Rogers, ed., *Guests Come to Stay: The Effects of European*

but only their adumbration is possible here.[3]

## CONSTRAINTS ON THE GOVERNMENTS OF RECEIVING STATES

The import of the presence of large, culturally generally distant semi-settled populations in Western Europe is best assessed in the context of two sets of structural realities. First, the governments of most of the receiving states must seek to manage a wide array of policy problems—not only those related to the foreigners within their borders—while operating within narrow constraints. Some of these constraints consist of internal or domestic historical, political, economic, and social limitations on freedom of governmental action.[4] Others are external in origin and, thus, generally even less tractable. Accounting in part for such external constraints is the divergence of interests between the countries of origin and the receiving states in many instances. This divergence of interests and the positions of most sending states in the triangular relationships between them, the host countries, and the migrant populations constitute an important part of the

*Labor Migration on Sending and Receiving Countries* (Boulder, CO: Westview Press, 1985).

3. Three limitations preclude a balanced and comprehensive treatment here of the import for sending countries of the extended sojourn of large numbers of their nationals: the relative dearth of empirical and analytic scholarships on these nations; the great variety of social, economic, and political conditions and processes that makes useful generalizations across them elusive; and the volatility of politics in several sending countries— both in terms of comprehensive regime changes and governmental and policy flux—during the past 10 to 15 years.

4. These are, if what may appear to some to be involuted language can be overlooked for the moment, constraints on government emanating from the state.

second set of structural realities that form the context for the concerns at hand.

Taken together, such domestic and external limits on the freedom of action of governments constitute the relatively more superficial of two manifestations of the diminishing autonomy of the state: authorities responsible and accountable for operating the mechanisms creating the society's public policies are constrained in their attempts to cope with the problems in their charge. The constraint is more limiting when it entails incompatibility between the normative templates of the society—ingrained values, beliefs, and notions of legitimate modes of governance—on the one hand, and societal expectations of governmental effectiveness or performance, on the other.

In order to distinguish this set of concerns from the more profound structural aspects of the state, I shall term this level governmental.[5] But even such constraints on governments may reflect a diminution of the autonomy of the state, as it is conceptualized here; for, where they are extensive and enduring, no simple change in the incumbents, parties, or coalitions exercising authority is likely

to enhance appreciably a society's ability to govern itself.

Some of the concomitants of large-scale migration affect the political and social structures of societies in more profound ways, in both receiving and sending countries. These circumscribe the capabilities of society to govern itself in ways consistent with fundamental, established norms and legitimate practices. For the purposes of this article, such capabilities are what I mean by the autonomy of the state. The impact of large numbers of semi-settled migrants may diminish those capabilities.

### Problems of governance: The welfare state in hard times

The strains on the governments of welfare states in the past decade have been described and analyzed in a voluminous literature,[6] and therefore only some apposite highlights need to be noted here. Most of these problems would have emerged even if large numbers of foreigners had not been present, but a focus on the consequences of that presence allows us to see clearly an interesting and ironic dynamic, discussed in several of the preceding articles in this volume.

The advent of economic hard times in most of Western Europe in 1973-74 led the governments of the host societies to terminate the recruitment of foreign labor, in order to minimize indigenous

5. This is somewhat at odds with conventional usage but it does help to distinguish between the more visible operations of the agencies and personnel of government and the deeper structures in which, in the words of Benjamin and Duvall, "the enduring structure of governance and rule in society" are embedded. See Roger Benjamin and Raymond Duvall, "The Capitalist State in Context," in *The Democratic State,* ed. Roger Benjamin and Stephen L. Elkin (Lawrence: University Press of Kansas, 1985), pp. 19-57, esp. pp. 23-27. By the governmental level I have in mind that at which, in Benjamin and Duvall's language, "the structure of the state apparatus" actually operates on a day-to-day basis, or what they might term the state as actor. See also the discussion in n. 17 of the present article.

6. The literature is too vast and diverse to permit more than representative illustrative references. A cross section of mainstream perspectives can be found in Organisation for Economic Co-operation and Development, *The Welfare State in Crisis* (Paris: Organisation for Economic Co-operation and Development, 1981). For a neo-Marxist perspective, see Ian Gough, *The Political Economy of the Welfare State* (London: Macmillan, 1979).

unemployment, the drain on public finance, and balance-of-payments problems. But the end of recruitment spurred the influx of the families of the foreign workers already in place, and this secondary wave of migration eventually contributed to the public financial—and even more to the social and political—problems of the receiving states.

The lack of effective policy control over the migrant presence was thus evident by the mid-1970s. Moreover, although the onset of the generalized recession in the highly industrialized societies of the West and the increasing loads on their treasuries merely coincided with the presence of migrants, public perceptions were frequently less objective and projected causal links. Competition for jobs and claims for social services and public assistance from migrants exacerbated the strains not only between natives and foreigners but also between governments and their citizens with the advent of greater scarcity, given the necessarily closed character of the political society of the welfare state.[7]

Thus, for instance, establishing bilingual or parent-language schools for the children of migrants when the education budget is scrutinized for savings dictated by a generalized policy of austerity or reading about possible abuses of publicly funded, generous disability retirement provisions by many foreign workers in a newspaper that carries a headline regarding the fiscal crisis of pension programs is bound, in lean times, to politicize issues relating to migrant populations. Indeed, anti-immigrant political movements have crystallized in many of the receiving states—most notably in France, Belgium, and

Great Britain. Yet, as has been suggested in several of the preceding articles and is further discussed later in the present one, the ethos of the mature welfare state is not conducive to the simple exclusion of immigrants from its economic and social rights.

The expansion of such mandated obligations of welfare states as social security and publicly financed medical care is driven in large measure by the aging of populations, while education costs are determined largely by the size of school-age cohorts. In times of high unemployment, payments to those out of work increase at the same time that tax receipts and employer and worker contributions to unemployment funds decline. Most of these considerations did not figure in the initial labor-importation policies, since, as noted, at the outset most immigrants were single males in their productive years. Therefore, as Freeman has pointed out,[8] in the aggregate they paid more into retirement and other social welfare funds than they extracted; their demands for medical care were not inordinately heavy; most had no children in schools; and they were recruited for jobs already available, unfilled by native workers. Furthermore, it was generally not contemplated that they would stay in the country if they were unemployed.

As the composition of the immigrant populations changed, many of the protections of the welfare state were extended to them.[9] This development was due in part to the expansion of benefits negotiated by sending and receiving countries in the labor agreements made

7. This closed character is explicated in Gary P. Freeman, "Migration and the Political Economy."

8. See ibid.
9. Other contributors to this issue of *The Annals* have described the dynamics that brought about this development. See, for example, Rogers, "Transnational Nexus of Migration."

in the 1970s and in part to political pressure from domestic sources.

Labor unions were loath to accept a double standard that extended lesser benefits to foreign workers than to natives in the work force, since this would have entailed lower labor costs—in the form of employer contributions to social funds—and thus a comparative advantage in hiring foreign workers. Churches and other social organizations pressed for the extension of welfare state benefits on altruistic and ideological grounds, as did at least some of the electorate identified with more progressive political parties. For many, the egalitarian ethos of the welfare state militated against the creation of an underclass of foreigners excluded from the social services and distributive mechanisms that had, over time, substantially closed the gaps between rich and poor among citizens. In sum, a double standard that excluded immigrants from the welfare state was seen by many in the host societies as inconsistent with "the dominant normative order," as well as with "the enduring structure of governance and rule in society."[10]

Where universalistic criteria of eligibility have been established in law and practice over time and where they have become—together with an egalitarian ethos that values the closing of gaps in income—integral parts of the normative basis of social relations across generations, governments have no ready means for controlling the magnitude of demands for welfare state programs. The programs are seen by citizens as entitlements vested in the state; thus, according to this view, it is not within the purview of the government of the day to alter them suddenly and substantially.[11] Attempts by a government to roll back or curb expenditures for such programs are likely to be very costly politically.

In some cases, many migrants—particularly seasonal workers—were not included in social welfare programs. Switzerland is most noticeable in this regard. In most other cases, however, migrants were included. As macroeconomic woes beset the host societies, the difference between those deemed to be in the welfare state and those who, given their semi-settled status, were seen by many to be visiting was increasingly politicized.

For 20 or 25 years, until the mid-1970s, sustained economic growth provided fiscal dividends from which Western European governments could meet the rising costs of welfare state programs without commensurate tax increases or cuts in other policy areas.[12] Then, slow economic growth—in some instances, prolonged contraction—and adverse international economic conditions, often accompanied by high long-term unemployment, made general austerity policies the rule for governments of all political complexions.

A government that tries to deal with the joint occurrence of shrinking re-

---

10. The first phrase is used by Benjamin and Duvall to denote the broadest, most inclusive conception of the state—one they deem too broad for their theoretical purposes. The second is, as indicated in n. 5 of the present article, the most inclusive conception they find theoretically and empirically useful. Benjamin and Duvall, "Capitalist State in Context," esp. pp. 27-28.

11. For the rationale, see Martin O. Heisler, *Authority and Strains in the Political Economy of the Welfare State* (Aarhus: Aarhus University, Institute of Political Science, 1979), pp. 15-30. See also Daniel Bell, *The Cultural Contradictions of Capitalism* (New York: Basic Books, 1976), chap. 6.

12. Arguably, some of the economic growth that lasted until the mid-1970s derived from the productivity of foreign workers.

sources and growing demands by either raising taxes or curtailing benefits is likely to be punished at the polls.[13] Alternatively, citizens may increasingly ignore government, laws, and other norms of civic behavior and fend for themselves through tax evasion, gray market activity, and myriad other ways, all with corrosive impact on the state.[14] There is accumulating evidence—although by its nature it is not readily demonstrable in an empirical, systematic fashion—that such activity has increased since the advent of the generalized, protracted economic downturn in the mid-1970s.[15]

One manifestation is the unofficial employment of both regularized and illegal immigrants in most of the receiving countries. Employers benefit because they can thus evade high social taxes—that is, payments into pension and unemployment insurance funds, worker's compensation, and the like—and often also because they pay workers in the gray or black labor markets below established minimum wage or union contract levels. The benefits for workers are evident. Not only can they circumvent payroll taxes, but often they can also collect unemployment or income support funds while working. Labor unions have a joint interest with governments in minimizing such activity; yet, though reliable data are obviously not available, the magnitude of the practice is thought to be high in most host countries.[16]

In the long run all such activity is clearly more damaging for the society and its transcendent political order, the state, than the simple replacement of one government with another; and it is likely to lead to a downward spiral of effective governance. The significance of these phenomena transcends the routine operations and policy chores of the governments of the day and the immediate interests of those directly affected by them. This is so because the circumvention of laws, legal agreements, government agencies, and civic norms undermines what Benjamin and Duvall term "the enduring structure of governance and rule in society"—that is, the state.[17]

13. During the last 10 years all mature welfare states in Europe have had one or more significant changes of government that represented substantial departures from established patterns. Most of their successors undertook fairly stringent austerity programs, attempting to curb the growth of public expenditures and, in some cases, to roll them back. See, for instance, Robert Kuttner, "The Erosion of the Welfare State," *Transatlantic Perspectives,* 12:8-10 (Sept. 1984). But little or no progress has been made.

14. There are many scholarly treatments of this problem. One of the earliest and still most useful is in Richard Rose and Guy Peters, *Can Government Go Bankrupt?* (New York: Basic Books, 1978). The bankruptcy that concerns Rose and Peters is political rather than financial, and thus their theme relates directly to the argument here.

15. See, for instance, Bruno S. Frey and Hannelore Weck, *Estimating the Shadow Economy: A 'Naive' Approach* (Zurich: University of Zurich, Institute for Empirical and Economic Research, 1981); Bruno S. Frey, "The Underground Economy and the Welfare State" (Paper delivered at the Joint Sessions of Workshops of the European Consortium for Political Research, Aarhus, Denmark, 1982); Arnold Heertje, Margaret Allen, and Harry Cohen, *The Black Economy: How It Works, Who It Works for, and What It Costs* (London: Pan Books, 1982).

16. To be sure, gray or black market employment is not restricted to immigrants. But for many and varied reasons, the temptation is greater for both workers and employers to use them in such ways, and the proportion of foreign workers is doubtlessly greater in most such labor markets.

17. See nn. 5, 10, and 18 of the present article. For my views regarding distinctions between government and state, see Martin O. Heisler, "Corporate Pluralism Revisited: Where is the Theory?" *Scandinavian Political Studies,* n.s. 2(3):285-86 (Sept. 1979); B. Guy Peters and Martin O. Heisler, "Thinking about Public Sector Growth: Conceptual, Operational, Theoretical and Policy Consid-

*Limits on government
from the state*

Even a mere enumeration and perfunctory discussion of the most important among such structures and relationships in modern democratic states would require more space than is available here. But some aspects, with the greatest bearing on the subject at hand, can be collapsed into a few summary factors without distorting their import:

— the compact between the state and its citizens—usually the product, accumulated over generations, of the accommodations and resolutions of political conflict, sometimes partly codified in a constitution—which speaks to the bases of the former's authority, the latter's proper claims, benefits, and responsibilities, as well as to the mutual obligations that link citizens to each other and differentiate them from noncitizens;

— the institutional and legal frameworks through which the society governs itself;

— the regime norms that delineate the legitimate behavior of government and stipulate the basic criteria for evaluating its performance as the agent of the state, and that derive in part from that compact and evolve in part from the practices of governments accepted and deemed effective by their constituents over time;

— the normatively structured distribution of resources and relationships or connections between them, including social and political status, education, leisure, organizational and political skills, and many other intangibles, along with income, wealth, and other material values; and

— the domains and scope of the state's jurisdiction.[18]

---

erations," in *Why Governments Grow: Measuring Public Sector Size,* ed. Charles L. Taylor (Beverly Hills, CA: Sage, 1983), pp. 177-97. Analytical and theoretical perspectives on the state relevant for the concerns at hand will be found in J. P. Nettl, "The State as a Conceptual Variable," *World Politics,* 20(4):559-92 (July 1968); Kenneth H.F. Dyson, *The State Tradition in Western Europe: A Study of an Idea and Institution* (New York: Oxford University Press, 1980), esp. chaps. 7-9; Eric A. Nordlinger, *On the Autonomy of the Democratic State* (Cambridge, MA: Harvard University Press, 1981); Martin Carnoy, *The State and Political Theory* (Princeton, NJ: Princeton University Press, 1984); in the introductory and concluding essays in Peter B. Evans, Dietrich Rueschemeyer, and Theda Skocpol, eds., *Bringing the State Back In* (Cambridge: Cambridge University Press, 1985); Benjamin and Elkin, eds., *Democratic State.* Not all of these authors' positions accord with those reflected in this article or, for that matter, with each other.

18. A more extensive conceptual and analytic treatment, paralleling this discussion in important respects, is given in Benjamin and Duvall, "Capitalist State in Context." Although the terminology and analytic categories used in the present article are somewhat idiosyncratic and differ from Benjamin and Duvall's, I am in general accord with their notion that of the many conceptions of the state current in the literature two are useful for comparative analytic and theoretical purposes: (1) "the structure of the state apparatus" and (2) "the state . . . as the enduring structure of governance and rule in society," subsuming "the entire institutional-legal order, . . . the machinery and the means by which conflict is handled, society is ruled, and social relations are governed." Ibid., pp. 23-26 and passim. I share these authors' view that these are two distinct but, depending on one's analytic purposes, equally useful conceptions for comparative analysis. In places, however, my notions diverge from theirs in nontrivial ways, and I do not follow here their differentiation of the contexts of the modern state. The influence of this

Each of these considerations affects the obligations and the freedom of legitimate action of democratic government and conditions the expectations citizens have of that government. Each imparts substance and specific meaning to citizenship in a particular state, and, collectively, they delineate the sphere of legitimate, authoritative actions by the governments that act for states.

In any specific situation, governments can be expected to follow one of a finite number of paths within this framework. In democratic states the most important of these are

— response to the preponderance of the preferences of voters and legitimate organized interests;

— response to particular special interests, as long as these do not conflict with substantial electoral and/ or organizational interests, and if the norms of the state compact and the scope of the legitimate authority of the state permit such actions;

— inaction, when the balance of preferences and political forces and/or the constraints of legitimacy leave no room for clear-cut action; and

— the judgments or preferences of the policymaking authorities themselves, without a priori self-limitation or reliance on the existing balance of demands and support from political constellations—again, as long as such actions are consistent with the boundaries and criteria of legitimate action.[19]

Viewed in this way, governments can be said to have followed the second path when they began the large-scale importation of foreign workers. They responded to employers' demands for particular types of labor not readily available on the domestic market. The initial labor-importation policies did not conflict with the parameters of legitimate governance, nor did they affect the state in the host societies in any appreciable sense. But when the pattern of immigration changed from single men to extended families and when the economies of the receiving countries entered a period of prolonged downturn, such freedom of action evaporated and consequences for the states ensued.

In seeking explanations for this diminished autonomy of the state in most host societies,[20] we must look to both domestic and external factors. Several

essay of Benjamin and Duvall's will be more apparent in my future work than it is here.

19. This last path lies close to and parallels some of the salient notions of autonomous action or policymaking developed in the recent literature on the state. Cf. Nordlinger, *On the Autonomy of the Democratic State;* Benjamin and Duvall, "Capitalist State in Context," pp. 45-50.

20. Switzerland is an exception to this generalization and Sweden may be partly so. More detailed and satisfactory explanations for these two cases can be found in the preceding articles in this issue of *The Annals.* From the perspective of this article, it is important to note that the Swiss state is far less extensively developed at the federal level— particularly as a welfare state—than are its counterparts in the other host countries. From the outset of labor in-migration, Swiss laws and agreements with sending countries provided foreign workers with less extensive privileges that might encourage them to remain, and men alone continued to constitute a larger proportion of migrants in Switzerland than elsewhere. Sweden, of course, has one of the most comprehensive and mature welfare states; but, as Rosemarie Rogers has stressed, its policies of encouraging integration and naturalization and its more liberal practice of extending social services, job tenure, and asylum— and the fact that a fairly large proportion of migrants are Finns who either have settled or are willing to settle—set it apart to some degree. See Rogers, "Transnational Nexus of Migration."

of the former have already been noted, and these as well as others can be summarized more cogently in terms of the preceding discussion of the state.

Thus, while sweeping generalization is risky and certainly not rigorously testable, it seems warranted to say that in the mid-1980s in none of the receiving countries is there a strong and clear balance of political forces either in favor of extending to migrants rights and privileges equivalent to those of citizens or in favor of pressing the limits of intergovernmental agreements by striving to expel as many migrants as possible. And, while some organizational actors—employers' organizations, labor unions, and churches, in particular— may have distinct and strong preferences with regard to public policies toward migrants, there is no longer a political vacuum for any of the major issues relating to migrants to permit them to prevail with the ease evident in the launching of worker immigration a generation ago. Nor, given the extensive— and in many of the receiving states, strong—politicization of the issue, can national policymakers simply translate their preferences into authoritative government action without engaging considerable political risks.

Thus, three of the four paths noted earlier seem at present at least inopportune and possibly blocked in the domestic arenas of the receiving states. In addition to the consequences of the politicization of the foreign presence just reviewed, the governments of the host societies are also constrained, albeit in varying degrees and forms in different countries, by the parameters of legitimate action and the structures and ethos that characterize the contemporary democratic welfare state.

While the lack of political consensus might seem to dictate following the fourth path—that of inaction—in fact the contradictory pressures focused on governments do not neutralize each other. Rather, pressures are exerted in several directions by different actors. Some favor the accommodation and integration of migrants; others—more noticeably in France and Belgium, perhaps, than in Germany, Scandinavia, or Britain—militate in favor of limiting their presence or increasing efforts to repatriate them; and still others, particularly employers in Germany, France, and Switzerland—the countries with the highest proportions of foreign workers— would prefer the continuation of both seasonal and long-term, year-round availability of at least some classes of workers. These cross pressures make a course of inaction difficult to justify politically.

## Unsettled relationships and the state

Muddling along, rather than inaction per se, might be the most appropriate characterization of both the policy postures of the governments of the receiving countries and the connections between their state structures and migrants. Governments do respond to cross pressures, often with considerable motion, since democratic governments must present at least the appearance of responsiveness to their constituents. But, for the reasons noted previously, there has been little movement in terms of inroads into the problems attending the foreign presence.

Many of the distinctions between citizens and noncitizens in their relationships with the states in which they live can be traced to the indeterminate status of the latter. Noncitizens are not parties to the compact that defines the state, either by birth or by the choice represented by naturalization. They do lay claim to many or most of the tangible benefits of that compact, including social services, basic elements of legal protection, income structures that reflect decades of conflict and bargaining, and so forth. In addition, they are called upon to meet such responsibilities as obedience to the host society's laws, the payment of taxes, and the like. But they are not responsive to calls for loyalty, including the tangible form of military service, nor, with rare and partial exceptions,[21] do they participate in such fundamental political processes as voting. In most cases their children—the second generation—show similar lack of response.

Many of their contacts with the state are through agencies or officials specifically charged with dealing with foreigners. In addition, because their connections with the sending countries remain extensive, they are outside their host states' jurisdiction in some nontrivial ways.

The migrants' noncitizen status, ties to their home countries—both formal and informal—and the often noted semisettled condition of most are, thus, important distinguishing factors in their relationships to the states of the host societies. Those ties and that condition hinge on the international and transnational dimensions of the subject of our concerns.

### EXTERNAL CONSTRAINTS ON THE STATE

The tasks of the governments of the receiving countries are made more difficult and state autonomy is more problematic than the overview of domestic constraints previously presented indicates, for the presence of migrants in Western Europe is of great interest to governments and in some cases to nongovernmental actors in the countries of origin.[22] Formal agreements and a wide array of public and quasi-public policies limit the freedom of action of the governments of the host societies vis-à-vis long-term, quasi-permanent residents, and they impinge on the autonomy of the states involved.

Not only do such agreements preclude involuntary repatriation—except, as Rogers has noted, in instances of serious violations of law or immigration status—but they also reach into the host societies and delve into the status and treatment of migrants abroad.[23] Furthermore, as we have noted, the policies of the sending countries work not only against large-scale repatriation in any specifiable time period but also against the naturalization or assimilation of migrants in the receiving countries.

### Circumscribed states

While these problems are far-ranging and profound, they are only one—probably the least important—of three sets of external or international constraints that converge on most of the receiving states and make their tasks of governing much more difficult than they were one or two generations ago, when the boundaries of Western states were less permeable and their autonomy less circumscribed. The substantial openness of most modern economies to internation-

21. See Rogers, "Transnational Nexus of Migration."

22. This interest is shown in detail in ibid.; Barbara Schmitter Heisler, "Immigrant Settlement and the Structure of Emergent Immigrant Communities in Western Europe," this issue of *The Annals* of the American Academy of Political and Social Science; Sabri Sayari, "Migration Policies of Sending Countries: Perspectives on the Turkish Experience," ibid.

23. See Rogers, "Transnational Nexus of Migration."

al and transnational forces and the inability of most states to provide military security for their population and territory independently probably entail more important constraints.[24]

Like economies open to international and transnational forces and like security policies dependent on alliance guarantees, large foreign populations present governments with circumstances they cannot control in practice but for which their populations hold them accountable nonetheless. Such accountability, in the context of the severely constrained freedom of action associated with thoroughly institutionalized democratic regime norms and political practice, often puts governments into a double bind, a no-win position.

*Toward diminished autonomy in receiving states?*

Attempts to respond to the challenges associated with transnational migra-

24. Among these external influences on the structure and operation of the modern state, only transnational and international economic factors have received sustained attention in the literature on the state. Early, seminal work appeared in some of the articles in *International Organization,* vol. 25, no. 3, *Transnational Relations and World Politics,* ed. Robert O. Keohane and Joseph S. Nye, Jr. (Summer 1971). For the most recent work, see the essays in part 2 of Evans, Rueschemeyer, and Skocpol, eds., *Bringing the State Back In.* See also David Cameron, "The Expansion of the Public Economy: A Comparative Analysis," *American Political Science Review,* 72(4):1243-61 (Dec. 1978). This issue of *The Annals* contains some of the few attempts to treat the transnational and international dimensions of migration from this perspective; a book in progress by James F. Hollifield promises more sustained treatment. Work in progress by the present writer addresses the consequences of security dependence for states and their governments in particular and for the convergence of domestic and external constraints in general.

tion[25] are likely to generate political conflict on the issues themselves or on procedural, essentially legitimacy grounds or both. All major classes of actors now have political voice. Citizens have the multifarious channels available in democracies. Foreigners, at least those with regular or legal status, have either indigenous champions or an agency of their home country—or, ultimately, the high law of intergovernmental labor agreements.

But this is a strange sort of conflict for most Western societies. It introduces international legal and political considerations into processes that had been, until very recently, based in the state structures, that had gained legitimacy as they evolved, and that conditioned the expectations of citizens as they were socialized. In all of the receiving countries discussed in this issue of *The Annals* save Britain, large numbers of foreign residents now have access to resources not available to the indigenous population.

Some of us, from our own normative perspectives, may see this development as a small step toward balancing scales heavily tipped toward the citizens of the host societies in socioeconomic, educational, structural support, political, and many other terms. But from the point of view of both the integrity and autonomy of the state, the extrajurisdictional resources of most migrants at least potentially circumscribe such autonomy. While the magnitude of this effect on the domain of the state's jurisdiction is small and its consequences are far less serious and widespread than the influence of international economic factors

25. Examples include coping with competition between indigenous and foreign workers for scarce jobs, social discrimination against immigrants, or zealous efforts to repatriate foreigners.

or the loss of autonomy entailed in dependence on another state for protection for population and territory, such effects and consequences are not negligible. Minimally, they suggest that the unforeseen and unintended consequences of the initially sharply limited importation of foreign workers may alter the autonomy, comprehensiveness, and exclusivity of the state in providing—again, in Benjamin and Duvall's terms—"the enduring structure of governance and rule in" host societies.

## A NOTE ON SENDING STATES

There is no more systematic evidence on the effects of the prolonged sojourns abroad of many of the nationals of sending states than there is space available here to speculate about such effects. The generalization that follows is essentially untestable at this time, but speculation along such lines may be useful if it stimulates systematic research.

A commonplace in the study of migration is that emigrants are generally not the least well endowed in many resources and skills among their co-citizens. As suggested elsewhere, relatively young, resourceful segments of the populations of the sending countries are emigrating, and such emigration may serve as a social and political, as well as economic, safety valve.[26] Few of the countries of emigration have stable, substantially legitimate states and mature regimes. Their state structures are evolving under conditions that are substantially less stressful than those that might obtain if so many of their citizens were not abroad. Remittances from migrants and the savings and pensions migrants bring with them when—if—they return pro-

vide significant capital and important, if partial, relief for generally serious balance-of-payments deficits.

Ethnic or ideological dissonance—or both—often characterize the relationships between migrants and their home societies' regimes.[27] Freedom of political expression, association, and action is greater in most receiving states than in most of the sending countries. It is thus much easier to voice discontent when the political order of one's home country is at great remove. Interestingly and probably not by coincidence, the political orientations of emigrants tend to differ markedly from the prevailing political postures of their home regimes.[28] Finally, the social mobilization of women and young people abroad augurs considerable social change, demands, or unrest were these migrants to return in large numbers to more traditional, less liberated cultural settings.

Further, while from a macroeconomic standpoint all sending countries welcome and wish to maximize the remittance of funds by foreign workers—who are generally far better off in Western Europe than in the countries that they left and to which they send money—such transfers may have distributive consequences inconsistent with those sought by the governments of countries of emigration or with the type of distributive structure they seek to institutional-

26. See Heisler and Heisler, "Transnational Migration and the Modern Democratic State."

27. For a brief and necessarily impressionistic discussion of this point for one country, see Stephen Adler, "Emigration and Development in Algeria: Doubts and Dilemmas," in *Guests Come to Stay,* ed. Rogers, pp. 271-73.

28. Thus, for instance, Moroccans and Turks in Europe are likely to be quite radical in comparison with the conservative regimes of their countries of origin, while Algerians, Spaniards, and Greeks are probably more conservative in the aggregate than the Socialist governments in power in their homelands.

ize in their state.[29] More troubling for some sending states is the permanent return of relatively affluent emigrants. They often bring their savings or pensions, not trivial amounts in the poorer sending countries, into economic activity that is inconsistent with policy goals.[30]

These are a few of the ways, neither

---

29. Adler, "Emigration and Development in Algeria."

30. It is largely to gain some measure of control over such economic activity that some sending countries have begun to work with the governments of host societies to direct the investments and economic activity of migrants into particular channels. The Netherlands and Germany have such arrangements with Turkey, for instance. Some of the most important sending countries, such as Turkey, Yugoslavia, and Algeria, expected foreign workers to obtain training abroad and, once home, to use their skills and savings to engage in economic activity to create jobs and spur particular types of development. While early returnees met these expectations, most recent returnees have not.

systematic nor representative, in which the governments and, perhaps over time, the state structures of the sending countries may lose a measure of control to the migration process. Ultimately, the critical test will be whether emigrants in large numbers can be reintegrated into the societies and states of their origin without substantially dislocating the structures of those societies and states.

This test will not occur, however, as long as living conditions and economic opportunities remain more attractive in Western Europe, the host countries continue to be limited in their potential for repatriating large numbers of migrants, and the sending countries continue to encourage the extension of sojourns. Instead, all three classes of actors—receiving states, sending states, and migrants—will have to continue to live with the indeterminacy of semi-settlement, and especially the first will continue to pay a high price for that condition.

# Book Department

## INTERNATIONAL RELATIONS AND POLITICS

ALTHEIDE, DAVID L. *Media Power*. Pp. 288. Beverly Hills, CA: Sage, 1985. $28.00. Paperbound, $14.00.

QUALTER, TERENCE H. *Opinion Control in the Democracies*. Pp. xii, 317. New York: St. Martin's Press, 1985. $29.95.

David L. Altheide and Terence H. Qualter are established experts in communication studies but their books are substantially dissimilar. In a sense, Qualter's book is a bibliographic essay that traces changing intellectual assessments of liberal democracy, focusing on the presumed role of the public within that governing framework. He ranges from the philosophic viewpoint of Graham Wallas to contemporary political sociologists. As he goes, he points to the strengths and flaws in their works.

As would be expected from one with his acknowledged stature on the topic, a sizable section of the book is devoted to propaganda and its derivatives, such as advertising. Qualter emphasizes that, despite extravagant claims for it, the actual impact of propaganda remains to be demonstrated.

The book is a mix of explicating narrow-range studies, as is found in the three chapters on attitudes, and setting forth a treatise on political philosophy. Despite its incongruence with the classical model, Qualter finds liberal democracy to be the most admired system in the world and more responsive to human desires than any other.

Altheide's book is broader in scope and more abstract in execution. For him, media subsume not only "information media" but such phenomena as "architecture, calendars, dance, conversation" and "automobiles." A key concept is format, which provides "for the transitional arrangement of symbols that define the time, place, and manner of social occasion" and "refers to the internal organization or logic of any shared symbolic activity." One format is the keyboard, which is "any device that includes parts to be purposively pressed in a social situation according to a logical scheme in order to create, interpret or receive symbolically meaningful information"—for example, "telephone dialing equipment; typewriters; electronic tuning equipment on radios and televisions; video game controls; and computer consoles." Altheide concludes with an examination of the prospects of a "mediated" society.

Some readers will not be attracted by the phraseology and intellectual perspective employed by Altheide. Nearly everyone concerned with the behavioral impact of technology, however, will be rewarded by reading his extensive reports of his empirical examples, including television coverage of the Iranian hostage crisis, content analysis of evening network newscasts, television's impact on the relations between sports reporters and sports figures, and social consequences of technology in the criminal justice system.

Although there is some overlap between these two books, they are markedly different in their methodology. Each is a solid synthesis, with Altheide going beyond that, but neither is likely to be a landmark in communication studies. Their lengthy bibliographies alone may warrant purchasing them.

T. PHILLIP WOLF

Indiana University Southeast
New Albany

CALDWELL, DAN, ed. *Soviet International Behavior and U.S. Policy Options.* Pp. xii, 292. Lexington, MA: D. C. Heath, 1985. $30.00. Paperbound, $14.95.

The inability of U.S. policymakers to understand Soviet perspectives of the international arena has been one of the contributing factors frustrating the effort to form a more productive U.S. policy toward the USSR. The result of failing to anticipate Soviet views, and, therefore, likely Soviet international behavior, yields Soviet reactions that often are not in accord with U.S. interests.

*Soviet International Behavior and U.S. Policy Options* contributes to our understanding of Soviet perceptions through its examination of the priorities of Soviet foreign policy. It stresses the impact of the international environment on Soviet policy by examining the consequences of various U.S. policy options on it, helping to fill a gap in a literature that mostly discusses the influence of Soviet domestic factors. There can be little doubt after reading this book that confrontationist American policies likely will produce Soviet hostility rather than accommodation.

Emanating from a project at Brown University's Center for Foreign Policy Development, this edited book contains nine chapters that address Soviet policy and U.S. responses regionally and functionally. The authors of each chapter generally follow the guidance of the editor, giving the book a thematic clarity that is exceptionally strong for an edited work.

Soviet priorities are discussed in each section, but they are explicated particularly well in George W. Breslauer's chapter on the Arab-Israeli conflict. Breslauer lists the Soviet concept of its roles in the international system in the following rank order: as a superpower, continental power, competitive global power, and leader of the world Communist movement. While none of these roles is expendable, it is clear that Soviet maintenance of its role of superpower is by far its most important in the international system, a view confirmed in other chapters.

The inability of the United States to influence Soviet policy to meld with U.S. interests is aptly demonstrated when the United States tries to place regional military pressure on the Soviet Union. B. Thomas Trout, for instance, concludes that Soviet resistance stiffens, rather than softens, in response to U.S.-Chinese military ties.

What of the future of Soviety policy? This book stops with the ascent of the Chernenko government, but its analysis points to the likelihood that Soviet priorities will remain largely unchanged for the near term. The international environment—especially the exigencies of the nuclear arms competition—combined with domestic policies and politics, will continue to place the Soviet Union in the position of formulating a mostly U.S.-centered foreign policy. The ability of the United States to influence Soviet policy will be limited, although the book strongly recommends that the United States should respond to Soviet efforts to expand militarily, such as in Afghanistan. Yet it should also "attempt to negotiate a cap to the competition in nuclear arms while competing in areas that do not threaten the future of civilization." One hopes that the new Gorbachev administration would respond to such an initiative in a mutually beneficial way.

GEORGE E. HUDSON
Wittenberg University
Springfield
Ohio

JAY, MARTIN. *Marxism and Totality: The Adventures of a Concept from Lukacs to Habermas.* Pp. xi, 576. Berkeley: University of California Press, 1984. $29.50.

Martin Jay, professor of history at the University of California at Berkeley, has undertaken for himself an unconventional and difficult task in this study of Western Marxism. It is his intention to analyze Western Marxist theory from the period of Lukács, the 1920s, to the period of Habermas, the 1970s. The focal point of Jay's analysis is the hegemony of the concept of the category of totality, "the all-pervasive supremacy of the whole over the parts," in twentieth-century Western Marxist social thought. Jay has largely succeeded in delineating this labyrinthian perspective in Western Marxism.

Jay's thesis is that more than any other dogma, inclination, or intellectual bias, holism—or the category of totality—is the central intellectual concern in twentieth-century Western Marxism. From the post-World War I era of Lukács, Korsch, Bloch, Gramsci, the Frankfurt school's theorists, Marcuse, Adorno, Lefebvre, Goldman, the existentialist Marxists, Sartre, and Merleau-Ponty, to the current second-generation Frankfurt school of Habermas and Alfred Schmidt, holism not only dominated but also reconstructed Western Marxist social theory. This central tenet of Western Marxist social thought has, however, a veritable multiplicity of nuances and adaptations. Expressive, decentered, longitudinal, latitudinal, and normative varieties of holistic social theory coexisted simultaneously in the Western Marxist tradition. Although no one social theorist has successfully reconstructed Marxist holism on entirely non-Lukácsian grounds, the contemporary Jurgen Habermas is given the best chance to succeed by Jay.

Jay's carefully reasoned and tightly organized text will become a seminal work in a field so exhaustively researched by legions of earlier scholars. This will be due in large part to the novelty of Jay's central thesis on holism and the intellectual mastery he has displayed. To have seen the forest through the trees in a tradition so diverse and so labyrinthian as Western Marxism is the essence of Martin Jay's achievement.

JOHN S. WOZNIAK
Fredonia
New York

LARSON, DEBORAH WELCH. *Origins of Containment: A Psychological Explanation.* Pp. xvi, 380. Princeton, NJ: Princeton University Press, 1985. $35.00.

Deborah W. Larson's cogent and lucid analysis of the historical origins of containment is presented three-dimensionally. Larson invokes the theoretical tools of the political scientist, historian, and psychologist to demonstrate that no single disciplinary model has sufficient explanatory value. Instead, she offers us a "composite multidimensional strategy" to explain why the United States embraced cold-war policies in the period following World War II. Importantly, the additional insights offered by social-psychological theories of attitude change suggest that Soviet-American relations are not permanently frozen.

Larson begins her analysis with an examination of current, mostly historical interpretations of the cold war that she discredits as being too narrowly construed. Then five major psychological theories of attitude change are presented and discussed: the Hovland approach, cognitive dissonance theory, attribution theory, self-perception theory, and schema theory. Throughout the body of the book, each theory is invoked at different times as having some explanatory value. In addition to the individual or cognitive factors suggested by psychological theory, Larson uses international systemic and societal or domestic politics variables to explain the origins of American cold-war policies and to demonstrate that containment was adopted by human beings, acting upon personality needs, influenced by political goals, operating within the constraints of both a treatening international and political domestic environment.

More precisely, Larson argues that the policy of containment was developed by W. Averell Harriman, Harry S Truman, James F. Byrnes, and Dean Acheson, in the period between 1944 and 1947; that these men acted on the basis of their perceptions of the Soviet Union; that these perceptions were the result of the way in which each actor responded to environmental and situational factors such as the economic situation in Western Europe, the emergence of a power vacuum in central Europe and the eastern Mediterranean, the vulnerability of American public opinion to emotional symbols and metaphors, and so on; and that each individual's response was influenced by personal qualities such as ideological perspective, foreign policy expertise, and political experience, to name a few. As an illustration, Harriman was the first of the quartet to adopt cold-war beliefs about the Soviet Union, which he did following the collapse in March of 1945 of the negotiations to carry out the Yalta agreements on Poland, which he interpreted as evidence of Soviet expansionist desires.

The book complements and expands upon, rather than replaces, existing analyses of this critical period and thus provides a convincing argument for political scientists to cast off their attachment to single models that are narrowly circumscribed. We are still left, however, with a retrospective analysis, and a series of frameworks that, while having explanatory value, are not capable of being used to anticipate and predict foreign policy behavior. Furthermore, there is no integrated theoretical framework, only multiple levels of analysis. In addition, Larson's selection of only four policymakers is a discretionary decision further limiting her analysis. Finally, because of the use of psychological models that employ variables such as belief and perception, the study is vulnerable to accusations concerning control and definition.

In the end, though, the book is a fascinating description and brilliant analysis of the most important period in American foreign policy. Critically, by confronting and successfully challenging the belief that Stalinist Russia posed so great a threat to the United States as to justify a policy of containment with the alternative view that the interpretations given Soviet actions by key American policymakers caused them to embrace containment, Deborah Larson leaves us with the hope that future foreign policymakers will be able to reconcile their differences and put the Soviet Union and the United States on a course of true friendship and cooperation.

LAUREN H. HOLLAND
University of Utah
Salt Lake City

PARK, CHOON-HO. *East Asia and the Law of the Sea.* Pp. 445. Seoul: Seoul National University Press; Honolulu: University of Hawaii Press, 1983. $25.00.

This is a compilation of articles published by Choon-ho Park between 1973 and 1982. There is overlap and repetition between chapters, and there is no index. Nevertheless, postscripts, numerous clear maps, a bibliography, and the attractive editorial format draw the collection together to produce a favorable impression overall.

The theme is maritime disputes between Asian littoral states. Demarcation controversies between North and South Korea and Japan in the East China Sea; claims by China, Taiwan, and Japan to the Senkaku-

Tiaoyut'ai Islands west of Okinawa; and the four-way rivalry between China, Vietnam, the Philippines, and Indonesia over the Paracel, Spratly, and other islands and shoals in the South China Sea are summarized historically, analyzed legally, and documented copiously, with useful commentaries by Park.

Choon-ho Park amply illustrates that political problems cannot be solved by appeal to legal first principles. The Asian claimants cannot even agree on whether the median principle or the extension-of-land-area—that is, continental shelf—principle prevails, or on the weight to be given to discovery or sporadic administration or nationality of fishermen or settlers of outlying islands, in spite of precedents set by North Atlantic and Mediterranean states.

Curiosities abound: China claims the Macclesfield Bank, the highest point of which is 32 feet below sea level; Japan claims Danjo Gunto, which lies on Korea's side of the Okinawa Trough; and North Korea arbitrarily asserts a 50-mile so-called military boundary zone.

Semisubmerged reefs and sea-bottom convolutions have not always attracted such attention. France, on behalf of Vietnam, claimed the Paracels and Spratlys only desultorily in the 1930s and seems to have forgotten them entirely in post-World War II peace negotiations. The claim was revived by the Republic of Vietnam in 1956 for nationalistic reasons and strengthened in the 1960s for oil reasons. The successor state, the Socialist Republic of Vietnam, continues the claims, but against odds, as China seized the Paracels by force in 1974 and shows no signs of negotiating. A new claimant, Malaysia, entered the race by occupying militarily one of the Spratly group in 1983.

It is ironic that international conventions to codify the law of the sea accelerated and made more extravagant the national maritime claims, as each Asian state rushed to guard traditional interests—such as customary fishing grounds near Korea, in Japan's case—or preempt rights to potentially valuable oil reserves. No claim has been submitted to international tribunals for adjudication as the parties continue to maneuver unilaterally for advantage or play for time, depending on whether they hope to gain or just to avoid losing.

But oil companies will not commit themselves to disputed zones, so Japan and South Korea put their conflict in abeyance in 1974 and negotiated an ad hoc joint development zone in which oil exploration has subsequently taken place in a stable, if not legally settled, environment. Thus, bilateral pragmatism may prove more effective than international law.

Choon-ho Park has taught and conducted research on international law at Edinburgh, Harvard, Hawaii, and Seoul National universities. This book is a worthy repository of a decade of his work.

STEVE HOADLEY

University of Auckland
New Zealand

ROZMAN, GILBERT. *A Mirror for Socialism: Soviet Criticisms of China.* Pp. xiv, 292. Princeton, NJ: Princeton University Press, 1985. $26.50.

This volume—a methodical exposition and interpretative analysis of a significant body of Soviet literature on modern China—is a *tour de force* concerning a most critical topic as it represents an unequivocal indictment of the two socialist systems.

Rozman's adroit presentation and skillfully arranged rendition of Soviet scholarship and research findings on social relations in modern China are organized into seven chapters. A long and absorbing introduction sets the stage. The subsequent five substantive chapters, entitled "Peasants," "Workers," "Intelligentsia," "Officials," and "National Minorities," cover critical phases in the unfolding development of modern China's most important social forces. The engaging final chapter embodies a successful mix of incisive analysis, political criticism, and well-conceived policy prescriptions.

Rozman's presentation of selected Soviet material and research findings attests a high level of sophistication in the understanding of China's political, economic, and social scene in the Soviet Union. Furthermore, Rozman credibly demonstrates the existence of divergent Soviet academic views on China, one condemning the contemporary situation in China as "Maoism without Mao" as opposed to a more optimistic view of the vicissitudes of socialism in China.

A seasoned comparative sociologist familiar with both China and the Soviet Union, Rozman has rendered a great service to Sinologists and all those with a professional interest in comparative communism and Sino-Soviet relations. Rozman has scanned, interpreted, and evaluated over 200 representative pieces of Soviet scholarship on modern China's social relations and has rendered them into a most comprehensive account. He must be commended for introducing this previously neglected and untapped body of literature on China to a wider Western scholarly community. For the uninitiated and the predisposed, Rozman's revelations may be perplexing as many Soviet specialists on China are depicted as highly competent and professional and come across as far less ideologically predisposed than one might expect. Rozman's work clearly evinces that Soviet experts on China have added substantially to the broader understanding of a socialist China by drawing on their own socialist perspective. It appears that many Soviet analysts have directed their analytical focus to issues and problems that have been largely neglected by their Western counterparts, and thus Soviet scholars have made important contributions to the study of modern China. Rozman's presentation in chapter 3 of Soviet work on the political role and socioeconomic position of workers in Chinese society illustrates this rather well; to date, there is simply no Western work offering incisive and penetrating interpretative analysis of a caliber similar to that of Soviet scholars.

On a final note, I will mention that I find less convincing Rozman's assertion that much of the work by Soviet Sinologists is of an allegorical nature and represents a great deal of subtle criticism of the Soviet system itself. This should, however, not distract from this fascinating collection of Soviet scholarship on China. The range and diversity of this volume and the insights it provides cannot be ignored by anyone having a professional interest in China.

WALTER ARNOLD
Miami University
Oxford
Ohio

## AFRICA, ASIA, AND LATIN AMERICA

BUNKER, STEPHEN G. *Underdeveloping the Amazon: Extraction, Unequal Exchange, and the Failure of the Modern State.* Pp. xiii, 280. Champaign: University of Illinois, 1985. $24.50.

*Underdeveloping the Amazon* is a detailed and graphic presentation of the impact of the exploitation of the Amazon basin by the Brazilian state and corporate interests. Stephen Bunker argues that "each human intervention in the environment transforms it in ways which limit the possibilities of subsequent interventions." Both the "natural or ecological" and the "human or social" systems interact in the exploitation process, but Bunker points out that the history of intervention in the Amazon is one of "subordination of both [man and nature] to progressively wider and more complex economic and political systems." In the context of development theory, Bunker shows that what is at issue is not whether internal forces or dependency on outsiders explains the past and current situation, but rather that the subject is better understood through an analysis of "the relations between world systems of exchange and the social, economic and political organizations of particular regions as an evolutionary series of ecosystemic transformations from the time of colonial contact until the present." He suggests that understanding the development process in a regional economy based on extraction can be best accomplished by looking at the use and depletion of energy values in natural resources.

Bunker's analysis provides extensive documentation of the mismanagement, waste, and destruction caused by various efforts to extract natural resources from the Amazon basin. He argues, finally, that the only way to stop this process is for local systems in the peripheral regions that are being exploited to develop "self-sustaining, symbiotic economies," which can maintain the ecosystem and pursue long-term conservation plans. But, as he points out, "the problem, then, is how local groups can achieve adequate power within their own environment to protect it against outside predation." Unfortunately, he has no optimistic prognosis for this occurring in the Amazon basin.

Bunker's conclusions are not surprising or original, but the manner of presentation of this analysis is outstanding. This is a very scholarly book. Bunker, a sociologist, knows the area and its history and the relevant literature intimately, and he understands thoroughly what has occurred. He writes well and clearly. His discussions of development theories are thoughtful, and his approach is a useful one for graduate students in related disciplines. This book is a major contribution to literature on Brazil and to the development field generally.

LUCY CREEVEY
University of Pennsylvania
Philadelphia

CARTER, JIMMY. *The Blood of Abraham: Insights into the Middle East.* Pp. xxvii, 257. Boston: Houghton Mifflin, 1985. $15.95.

"Looking back on the four years of my Presidency," wrote Jimmy Carter in his memoirs *Keeping Faith: Memories of a President*, "I realize that I spent more of my time working for possible solutions to the riddle of the Middle East than on any other international problem." Nearly one-fourth of his memoirs is devoted to the Camp David meetings of 1978 and their aftermath. Since he left the White House he has made a more intensive study of the history of the Middle East, and of "the complex interrelationships that have so long frustrated those who seek peace in the region."

In *The Blood of Abraham*—blood that "still flows in the veins of Arab, Jew, and Christian"—Carter seeks to provide some "insights into the Middle East," to borrow the subtitle of the book. It is a small, well-written volume, prepared in collaboration with Professor Kenneth Stein of Emory University, now director of the Carter Center at Emory. It is based mainly on his own brief but intensive involvement in the affairs of the Middle East, on talks with many Middle East political leaders and area specialists, on a post-presidential trip to the region in 1983, and on Emory University's November 1983 Consultation on the Middle East, with Presidents Carter and Ford as cochairpersons.

After a brief introduction to the "multiplicity of factors in the Middle East," the book presents brief essays on major Middle Eastern countries: Israel, Syria, Lebanon, Jordan, Egypt, and Saudi Arabia—listed in order of discussion—and on the Palestinians. There is much in these readable essays of interest and value for the general reader, if not for the Middle East specialist. The major contribution is probably Carter's pen portraits and assessments of four leaders of the Middle East with whom he had personal contacts: Anwar el-Sadat, Menachem Begin, Hafez al-Assad, and King Hussein. He does not hesitate to express personal opinions on leaders and issues, but he also tries to identify and explain different perspectives and views. The value of the book is enhanced by a 10-page chronology, listing events in the Middle East from about 9000 B.C. to January 1985, six maps, and six appendixes, including the texts of U.N. Resolutions 242 and 338 and the Camp David accords.

In his concluding chapter, "The Future," Carter voices both his hopes and his apprehensions. He describes the situation in the Middle East as neither "hopeful" nor "hopeless." In any event, he believes, "it is impossible to abandon the search for peace in spite of the almost unsurmountable obstacles." A more insightful observation was made in his memoirs when he wrote that at the time of the signing of the Camp David accords "we had no idea . . . how far we still had to go."

Jimmy Carter has done his homework on the Middle East. Let us hope that other Americans, especially those in seats of power, will do the same.

NORMAN D. PALMER
University of Pennsylvania
Philadelphia


ETCHESON, CRAIG. *The Rise and Demise of Democratic Kampuchea.* Pp. xvi, 284. Boulder, CO: Westview Press, 1984. $29.50.

KIERNAN, BEN. *How Pol Pot Came to Power.* Pp. xvii, 360. London: Verso, 1985. $29.00. Paperbound, $10.95.

I have now lived long enough to have observed the innumerable revolutions that have characterized this century and to have participated in a minor capacity in several of them. The impending end of the century bears very little resemblance to its early, pre-World War I days, which assumably is what revolution is all about. And yet it would be hard to think of a single revolution that has achieved the goals and aspirations it set out for itself. To put it as an oversimplified question, Why are revolutionaries so much more attractive when they are struggling for power than they are when they have achieved it? Why once in power do they then almost invariably behave just about as badly as did those whom they displaced?

By far the most persuasive answer I have yet come across, as the question has increasingly troubled me with the failure of each

revolution, is in *The Rise and Demise of Democratic Kampuchea* by Craig Etcheson. Kampuchea is really a classic case of revolution in that just about every internal and external element was present, including total world ignorance of what was going on and had been for a long time until the unprintable atrocities of the Pol Pot regime catapulted that lovely and benighted land into world headlines.

I was among the guilty. As chief of the State-Defense Military Mission to Southeast Asia in 1950, I was to recommend implementation of President Truman's decision to assist the French in Indochina. The focus was Vietnam, where our recommendations became the first American involvement in Southeast Asia, much against my better judgment based on a three-year stint in China during its civil war. The French also concealed the internal problems of Cambodia, as it was then known, beneath the legend of happy peasant life and spectacular temple dances by torchlight at Angkor Wat, but even so I sensed a sullenness in the people that made me uneasy. Without knowing what it was, I sensed that somehow there was something more to the Cambodian problem than just French colonialism, which in any event was infinitely worse in Vietnam. Even the American invasion of Cambodia more than two decades later, disastrous and ill conceived as it was, was not at the core of the problem.

The Chinese have known for a long time that the dynamics of any revolution are internal; that is, it must be fought and won or lost by those most directly involved. Foreign aid can be helpful, but in the end it is no more than marginal. Foreign events can be crucial, but they are not decisive unless they succeed in total destruction of the revolution, which, of course, has happened more than once throughout history. For the successful revolutionaries, it seems to be their sad fate that they are the ones who destroy those very ideals that originally inspired them.

Admittedly, Kampuchea is an extreme case in terms of the ghastly price its 7 million people paid for its horror story. Just how this happened is the subject of *How Pol Pot Came to Power* by Ben Kiernan, a history of the Kampuchean Communist Party, of how Pol Pot took it over, and of how he implemented his vision that, we would do well to remember, a number of us thought was pretty exciting stuff until the moment he unleashed his hoodlum teenage troops on the 2 to 3 million people of Phnom Penh to do with as they pleased. Pol Pot in power was not a deviation; he was only the gross intensification of what had been going on in Kampuchea for a century. Anyone who doubts this should read Etcheson and Kiernan. If the reader wants some very convincing insights into some of the major and still unresolved problems of the twentieth century, he or she should read them anyway.

JOHN F. MELBY

University of Guelph
Ontario
Canada

FLEET, MICHAEL. *The Rise and Fall of Chilean Christian Democracy.* Pp. xv, 274. Princeton, NJ: Princeton University Press, 1985. $35.00. Paperbound $14.50.

Originating as a street-brawling *falangista* organization in the 1930s, Christian Democracy in Chile became a mass-based developmentalist reform party barely 20 years later. In 1964, the party's major leader, Eduardo Frei, was elected president on a platform calling for a "revolution in liberty." In the autumn of 1973, the party joined rightists in openly calling for a military coup against the socialist government of Dr. Salvador Allende and then urged, in Frei's words, "patriotic" collaboration with Augusto Pinochet's murderous military regime. What, then, was the complex character of Christian Democracy? What interests, ideas, and objectives characterized it, and how did they affect its trajectory?

Interpreting politics from a "modified class perspective," sociologist and "progressive Catholic" Michael Fleet draws both on his own expriences and personal contacts in Chile and on survey data to provide the answers to these questions. Rejecting both liberal and Marxist "leading claims and presumptions" about the Christian Democrats, he argues that they were neither the bearers of a new popular commitment to structural change nor mere representatives of "the bourgeoisie." Rather, "bourgeois forces" defined them as their "primary antagonists," and, indeed, under Frei's presidency "the bourgeoisie [was] the principal victim of a distributive pattern favoring white and blue collar workers." If the Christian Democrats vacillated politically, compromised programatically, and ultimately sided with "bourgeois forces" against the Left, this simultaneously reflected, Fleet suggests, both the social roots of the party and the "logic of partisan political competition." Thus, for instance, to strengthen its parliamentary and electoral position vis-à-vis the Left, the Christian Democratic Party tried to wound, and eventually succeeded in briging down, a government that was carrying out or deepening reforms that the Christian Democratic Party favored in principle or—as with agrarian reform—actually had initiated.

This is an appealing argument, buttressed by Fleet's sensitive interpretations of concrete political events. But his presentation of quantitative findings, based on his secondary analysis of data from several surveys taken between 1958 and 1973 in Greater Santiago, too often confuses, rather than clarifies, that argument.

A central question in the book is the political relevance of the "class situation" of the constituencies of the various parties. As a proxy for class, Fleet uses occupational status. But his tables actually are based either on data on employment in different economic sectors—for example, industry, finance, transportation—that he somehow converted into occupational categories or on precoded categories in which, as he says, "people in very different productive roles and relationships are being lumped together." In some tables, for instance, "independent workers" appear in his "petite bourgeoisie," while in others they show up among "blue collar workers." Using such data to indicate the class bases of the parties is, to say the least, hazardous. In addition, although he recognizes that Frei drew most of his votes—63 percent in 1964—from women, none of his tables separates the responses and occupational statuses of men from those of women. His findings on the way different classes responded to the country's sharpening political crisis may thus be misleading. He asserts, for instance, that "far more workers"—meaning both white and blue collar—who had voted for Frei in 1964 switched to rightist Jorge Alessandri in 1970 than to Allende, and he concludes that "class polarization" was thus decreasing rather than growing. But if, as I would guess, the workers who switched to the Right were mainly women and those who switched to the Left were mainly men, how would this affect Fleet's conclusion?

I am also unsure about how Fleet arrives at his characterization of Christian Democracy's "dominant elements" as "petit bourgeois." There is only one table, numbered 2.3, that distinguishes, as of 1958, the core of former *falangista* activists, party supporters, and "unaffiliated freistas"; it is based on numbers in these categories, respectively, of 8, 16, and 6 persons. Finding that none of the party supporters was "petit bourgeois" compared with half of each of the other two categories is a weak reed, indeed, on which to rest such a crucial characterization. None of the other tables shows that Christian Democratic voters were outstandingly "petit bourgeois," although they were, as Fleet suggests, "multiclass." Table 2.7 shows that in 1964, for instance, about two-thirds of Frei's votes came from white-collar workers—32 percent—and blue-collar workers—32 percent—whom Fleet defines as strata of the working class. At the same time, the 31 percent of Frei's voters that came from "professionals, technicians, and small businessmen"—Fleet's "petite bourgeoisie"—was more than matched by Allende's 33 percent.

Would that Fleet, who is an astute observer of Chilean politics, had taken greater care

with both his quantitative analysis and his interpretation of his findings.

MAURICE ZEITLIN
University of California
Los Angeles

ISMAEL, TAREQ Y. and JACQUELINE S. ISMAEL. *Government and Politics in Islam.* Pp. viii, 177. New York: St. Martin's Press, 1985. $27.50

MOMEN, MOOJAN. *An Introduction to Shi'i Islam: The History and Doctrines of Twelver Shi'ism.* Pp. xxii, 397. New Haven, CT: Yale University Press, 1985. $25.00.

*Government and Politics in Islam* is a survey of Islamic political thought and Islamic reform followed by chapters on the Muslim Brotherhood, contemporary activism in Iran, contemporary activism in Egypt, and a survey of Islamic politics today. Despite the title, the book in fact covers only that one-sixth of the world's Muslim population that is resident in the Middle East, thus excluding the important communities of South and Southeast Asia, Central Asia, and Africa. While there are some useful summaries, the categories of analysis are not compelling and the method precludes contextual analysis.

Moojan Momen's book offers far more. It is a detailed survey of the history of the majority of Shii community, the Twelver, which is dominant in Iran, particularly important in certain regions of the Indian subcontinent, and evident today in parts of Lebanon. Historical sections are presented chronologically with a thorough attention to personalities, sects, regimes, and intellectual developments. Following the chronological section, the book continues with thematic chapters on issues of doctrine, the place of the imam, jurisprudence, Sufism, and popular religion. Chapters of interest, given current political developments, include intelligent treatments of political theory, the religious hierarchy, and a survey of contemporary political activism, particularly strong on Iran. Momen avoids easy clichés about any inherent tendency in Shiism to revolution, and presents a balanced and informed tone throughout.

The work is clearly written, carefully organized, and overflowing with detail. There are 11 tables, four maps, and appendixes offering a chronology of political and religious events, a list of Shii dynasties, and biographies of prominent ulama. No less than 68 plates of black-and-white photographs illustrate everything from miniature paintings and important shrines, to pious flagellants observing the festival of Muharram in Karachi.

While some of the survey is familiar, much here is new and usefully assembled. The book is, as the title says, an introduction and is not conceptually innovative, but it is solid and useful throughout. Yet fascinating developments are alluded to: for example, that the number of religious scholars exploded in the course of the nineteenth century, and that the concept of a single central leader—the *marja at-taqlid,* or focus of emulation—probably goes back no further than the eighteenth century.

The publisher is to be particularly commended for the care with which names and terms are presented with full diacritics.

BARBARA D. METCALF

*Journal of Asian Studies*
Berkeley
California

McNAUGHER, THOMAS L. *Arms and Oil: U.S. Military Strategy and the Persian Gulf.* Pp. xiii, 226. Washington, DC: Brookings Institution, 1985. $26.95. Paperbound, $9.95.

Oil shortages and escalating prices have adversely affected the economies of importing nations. These developments have been associated with worrying, politically destabilizing events such as the Arab-Israeli conflict, the Iranian revolution, the Soviet invasion of Afghanistan, and the Iraqi-Iranian war.

In this context, Thomas McNaugher has undertaken a detailed and dispassionate assessment of what precisely the American stakes are and the appropriateness of military measures to deter or to defeat future inaccessibility of Persian Gulf oil.

McNaugher naturally considers the consequences of Soviet military action in the region, but he is equally concerned with the combinations of other unsettling circumstances that could block the production or shipment of regional oil. These include political dislocations within producing nations and intraregional conflicts and rivalries for which considerable precedent exists.

McNaugher's analysis considers the range of probabilities of various scenarios when oil supplies would be placed at risk. While he foresees little prospect of a full-scale or even a partial Soviet intrusion without extreme deterioration of great power relations, he does not back away from calculating what U.S. military responses would be feasible and what they could accomplish. He in fact is more concerned with scenarios entailing severe instability on the Arabian peninsula and its environs, and its potential for inducing great power responses.

A large part of the book is devoted to appraising regional state, Soviet, American, and other Western power military capabilities. On the American side, McNaugher considers basing, prepositioning, interdictive action access, air- and sea-lift capabilities, and, of course, the nature, size, and armament of forces charged with protecting or retaking oil fields. He is especially concerned with the need for systematic American planning, to cover a very wide spectrum of contingencies.

While his conclusions are not overly sanguine, there is no counsel of despair. McNaugher construes intraregional security efforts, including those under the auspices of the Gulf Cooperation Council, as helpful and to be further encouraged. He in fact feels that, for a number of contingencies, the United States is presently not far from having the military capabilities to support a policy based on arms and other assistance leading to a multilateral security framework. But he insists on the need to be circumspect, both because of the volatility of the region and because military preparation simply cannot stand without the additional leg of sensitive diplomacy.

This is a book rich in detail and sensible in its advice. It is a serious contribution to a critical subject about which debate is too often uninformed or reflexively conducted.

HENRY S. ALBINSKI
Pennsylvania State University
University Park

METCALFE, ALAN. *In Their Own Right: The Rise to Power of Joh's Nationals.* Pp. xvi, 268. St. Lucia: University of Queensland Press, 1984. $A20.00.

In Australian politics the Texas-sized state of Queensland is the deep north. Its premier, Johannes Bjelke-Petersen, has maintained control for 17 years with a highly successful mixture of reactionary social policies, aggressive promotion of economic development, and a high-profile defense of Queensland's state's rights against successive central governments in Canberra. It is clearly a mixture that many Queenslanders support. Joh came to power as the leader of a shaky coalition of his own Country Party and the slightly less conservative Liberal Party. The rural-based Country Party later changed its name to "National Party" and went into competition with its coalition allies for city voters. When the coalition collapsed spectacularly in 1983 all conventional wisdom of Australian politics indicated that the government would lose office in the consequent elections. Instead, a stunning electoral victory saw the Liberal Party—elsewhere in Australia the dominant conservative alternative to the Labor Party—virtually annihilated, and Joh's party installed on its own in power. Bjelke-Petersen has no challenger as

the most successful politician in contemporary Australian politics.

A book analyzing the reasons for Bjelke-Petersen's success could well be of general interest to political scientists. Unfortunately, this book is not. Its author is a senior official in the National Party, and the account is an unabashed eulogy of the premier and his machine organizer, Sir Robert Sparkes. As a chronicle of events, an insider's account is useful for students of Queensland politics. However, there is no analysis of the sociology of the Queensland electorate, which is the key to understanding Joh's success. Ultimately, the book is party political propaganda, arguing in defense of an electoral gerrymander and a patronage style of government that are survivors of a long-gone period of Australian politics. Joh does not need such defense; he has always had the numbers.

MICHAEL HOGAN
University of Sydney
New South Wales
Australia

MOSHER, STEVEN W. *Journey to the Forbidden China.* Pp. ix, 180. New York: Free Press, 1985. $17.95.

MABBETT, I. W. *Modern China: The Mirage of Modernity.* Pp. 231. New York: St. Martin's Press, 1985. $29.95.

Both books claim to be breaking new paths—Mosher has discovered poverty in rural China; Mabbett, historical continuity—and both promise more than they deliver. An anthropologist who had just finished a year's fieldwork in Kwangtung, Mosher bases *Journey to the Forbidden China* on a brief trip by private van he made to Kwangsi and Kweichow provinces in 1980. In his personal observations of this backward area, Mosher himself, and not the peasants, is often the main focus. He writes, for example, "I was about to become the first foreigner in thirty years to journey unescorted to the rural heartland of China and I was going to find out the truth about the revolution and the peasants." Though his trip was terminated by security officials after only nine days, Mosher indicates he found that truth. But though there is little doubt that his observations of incredible isolation, ignorance, and poverty are valid, his narrative is unrelievedly bleak and occasionally petulant. He finds not a single positive aspect of life in the region, not a single positive accomplishment on the part of the Communist regime since 1949. Just as Chinese Communist political and economic policies have swung from one extreme to the other, so have American observations of China. In the early 1970s reports out of China were rather starry-eyed; Mosher's book represents the recent extreme of disillusionment. Nevertheless, Mosher's account of the grinding poverty of southwest China should act as an antidote to the idea that the new economic policy in the People's Republic of China of allowing freer rein to private enterprise should end all rural poverty; the natural resources for successful entrepreneurial activity seem to be quite absent in the region Mosher visited.

Early chapters of *Modern China* contain some interesting, if disjointed, observations on China's geography, customs, and history, though not without error. Footbinding, for instance, is attributed to the Manchus. The proclaimed heart of the book is Mabbett's belief that Buddhism has had a great role in shaping China, even since the Communist takeover. Mabbett finds a precedent for Mao's personality cult in the Matreiya cults; Mao's Great Leap Forward mentality makes him a "quintessentially Ch'an figure"; current Chinese ideology is linked to the Shao Lin monastery of old. But his arguments in support of this Buddhist continuity are impressionistic and far weaker than those usually advanced in favor of Confucian continuity, which Mabbett rejects. What is actually most valuable is Mabbett's final discussion of the problems of frustrated young intellectuals, whose second-rate educations were not likely to lead to worthwhile careers. It is their resentment of a system that favored the better-educated offspring of those with con-

nections to the Communist regime that Mabbett postulates did much to fuel the Cultural Revolution, though it ultimately betrayed them.

CHARLOTTE L. BEAHAN
Murray State University
Kentucky

SHAW, TIMOTHY M. *Towards a Political Economy for Africa: The Dialectics of Dependence.* Pp. xiii, 134. New York: St. Martin's Press, 1985. No price.

Shaw's book presents a critical insight into and penetrating overview of Africa in the post-Bretton Woods era. Shaw provides a comparative analysis of the continent's political economies as it progresses from its first 20 years of independence into the final two decades of the twentieth century.

Africa is endowed with abundant resources and is the most centrally located of all the continents but most marginal politically, hence economically. The lack of economic use of its resources engendered by political instabilities in the continent has led to the massive starvation and undernourishment of a disproportionate number of its peoples.

The continent is faced with a development crisis of great proportions. The growing awareness of this unenviable situation has produced a realistic reevaluation of policies at the grass-roots and national levels from both inside and outside Africa. Students of Africa have set aside their naive expectations of the independence decade to reexamine their analytical frameworks regarding assumptions, prescriptions, and projections.

The reevaluation of alternative strategies and scenarios has led to two modernization perspectives: the traditionalist exogenous orientation toward international incorporation as a means to development, and the radical endogenous orientation toward self-reliance and the satisfaction of basic human needs first as the prerequisites for development.

*Towards a Political Economy for Africa* reinforces Newton's—as well as Hooke's—law in mathematics that displacement equals force. For autonomous and meaningful development to occur at personal, national, and continental levels, substantial shifts will have to take place in the class character of Africa's political economies.

Shaw provides analysis of new data and proposes a novel framework for analysis that takes into account the contemporary crises and class coalitions. He advances an understanding through comparisons of different social coalitions and contradictions, as well as an understanding of the oversimplifications that characterize Africa as a homogeneous dependent continent. The richness of African political economies is revealed in the commonalities and contrasts of its cultures.

This book is a timely enterprise and a great contribution to intellectual debate as well as to developmental design.

JOHN B. ADESALU
Bureau of Labor Statistics
Washington, D.C.

STOLER, ANN LAURA. *Capitalism and Confrontation in Sumatra's Plantation Belt, 1870-1979.* Pp. xii, 244. New Haven, CT: Yale University Press, 1985. $22.50.

This probing ethnographic history of plantation policies and worker resistance challenges many widely held assumptions about the nature and effectiveness of labor unions and protest movements in North Sumatra and, by extrapolation, worldwide. It paints a clear picture of the survival strategies utilized over time by Javanese villagers living on the periphery of North Sumatran rubber, tobacco, and palm oil plantations. The insights provided on the priorities, organizations, and actions of international business, on the one hand, and of the Javanese laborer, on the other, have a much broader application than this volume's title would suggest; the book should be widely read and used in general courses on development, history, and economics.

Central to Stoler's thesis is the primacy of class conflict; she seeks to tear away other elements that might obscure this elemental conflict, such as ethnic, racial, and gender considerations. But her concept of capitalist penetration is not determinist; on the contrary, she argues that it is "a process activated through, not simply imposed on, class relations." Viewed from this perspective, and bolstered by numerous references to documents in Dutch state and ministry archives and to local newspapers as well as to interviews of Asian and European scholars, politicians, workers, and employees, Stoler analyzes critical events during the last hundred years that caused shifts in how plantation labor was recruited and treated, and how these Javanese men and women responded.

Of particular significance is the presentation of the "paradox" of a putatively radical labor force occupying plantation land in order to organize a traditional Javanese farming village. Far from providing the base for the creation of an independent peasantry, Stoler argues that the effect of these villages over the long run has been to subsidize the reproduction of a labor force for the plantations. Instead of freeing the villager from dependency on plantation work, the existence of surplus labor has fostered the increased use of temporary workers whose lower pay and absence of benefits reduces the cost of labor while acting as a damper on efforts to organize the regularly employed work force.

The clarity with which Stoler presents a view of history from the perspective of the laborer is due to her training as an anthropologist. Much of her research in Sumatra was conducted while living in a worker's village. Her observations of the impact that limited economic alternatives have had on the villagers' attitudes toward theft, corruption, and prostitution or toward the primacy of the household are illuminating. Nonetheless, these workers still see themselves as Javanese in an alien society; while the villagers still explain unusual events as the working of spirits, they attribute the most evil black magic to Bataks or Malays.

There are many more insights in this tightly argued book than there is space to discuss: the exploitation of the workers by both the Communist Party and the new nationalist government; the alienation from Sumatran revolutionary leaders felt by the Javanese workers; and the impact of the depression on wages and labor recruitment. More unusual is Stoler's documentation of the differential treatment and wages received by female workers from their early coercion into prostitution to their later firing in order to avoid the expense of mandated maternity and menstruation leave. This varied and colorful history does not prove to me, however, that class is the overwhelming consideration throughout. I urge others to read this powerful book and draw their own conclusions.

IRENE TINKER

Equity Policy Center
Washington, D.C.

WOOD, JOHN R., ed. *State Politics in Contemporary India: Crisis or Continuity?* Pp. xiii, 257. Boulder, CO: Westview Press, 1984. Paperbound, $20.00

It is surprising that there has not been a major study of state politics in India since 1967. Two separate volumes, one edited by Myron Weiner and the other by Iqbal Narain, were published that year shortly after Indira Gandhi assumed the leadership, if not yet control, of a weakening Congress Party. The volume under review neatly encompasses the Indira Gandhi era in a somewhat more definitive manner than intended. Its "addendum to the preface" notes Prime Minister Indira Gandhi's assassination in October 1984 as the book went to press.

Crisis rather than continuity is the contemporary reality of Indian politics as a consequence of the assassination, asserts John R. Wood. That does not seem to be the case. Rajiv Gandhi inherited his mother's preeminent position, but has chosen to follow a conciliatory rather than a confrontational style. Nonetheless, the basic concerns of the volume and the richness of analysis remain valid.

Of India's 22 states, 7 are analyzed in separate chapters, most of them from a political-economy perspective. These are India's major states, including Uttar Pradesh and Bihar in the north Hindi heartland, West Bengal in the east, Karnataka and Kerala in the south, and Maharashtra and Gujarat in the west.

Changes do occur in Congress policies as well as in the party's social composition. Roderick Church identifies some of these trends in a carefully crafted concluding chapter. In particular, he attempts a largel successful effort to construct a coherent taxonomy of major caste clusters. His fourfold classification is not simply the old *varna* system. Upper castes, for example, include all the twice-born groups, while the middle castes are the principle land-owning groups. Lower castes are almost a residual category including all others with the exception of the scheduled castes and tribes who as usual are at the bottom of the scale. Nonetheless, this scheme avoids the problem of forward and backward castes, which may be definable for a limited area, but provide almost insurmountable difficulties for all-India comparisons.

Indira Gandhi, as described in frank terms by John Wood in the introduction, largely abandoned compromise while centralizing power. Nonetheless, the immensity and complexity of India made absolute control from the center impossible. Jayant Lele describes the continuing nature of Maratha elite control in Maharashtra even with the introduction of the populist strategy in 1972. In particular, he cites the failure of centrally imposed chief ministers such as A. R. Antulay to maintain power as follows: "no matter how arbitrary she [Indira Gandhi] may appear, an apex arbitrator in the Congress system can never call all the shots."

This argument is taken several steps further by James Manor in his chapter on Karnataka. Mrs. Gandhi's "over-centralization," he argues, "has caused understanding of and influence over those [state] units to diminish." Gundu Rao, as was true of Antulay, could not maintain power even with Indira's support. But Gundu Rao's and Mrs. Gandhi's efforts did succeed in blurring the lines between parties and social support bases in Karnataka.

Atul Kohli's and Ouseph Varkey's chapters on West Bengal and Kerala, respectively, deal with the two states of India where the Communist parties have been most successful in electoral terms. There the similarity tends to cease. West Bengal, for all its tumultuous politics, is a paragon of party coherence compared to Kerala. The Communist Party Marxist, Kohli successfully documents, has been at least partially transformed from a militant, radical party into a governing, reformist party within a relatively stable party system. Kerala, as ably described by Varkey, witnesses the alternate decline and rise of the Left amid shifting political coalitions that are as complex as Kerala's social mosaic.

Neither Uttar Pradesh nor Bihar have experienced the degree of social change manifested in the other states studied in this volume. Thus, it is especially interesting and perhaps revealing that the authors of these chapters focused on agrarian interests and politics. There may be a time lag rather than more basic differences involved. Paul Brass, for example, points out that as non-Congress parties became increasingly important after 1967 more attention has been paid to the interests of rich and middle peasants. Charan Singh and his Jat support base provide one focus. Congress strategy has responded by "squeezing the middle peasantry" in appealing to the top and bottom of the social and economic scale.

India's most backward state, according to Harry Blair, Bihar, also is undergoing structural change. Slowly, "a rising class of middle caste progressive farmers is spearheading the transformation." Politics have become more crude, venal, and unstructured as it no longer is restricted to the aristocratic few.

It has to be reemphasized that all of the seven state studies in this volume were written prior to Prime Minister Indira Gandhi's death. Her highly centralist and person-

alistic style essentially remained unchallenged within the Congress Party, although the studies reveal significant weaknesses as regards the larger public. Nonetheless, one generalization that emerges clearly is the continued vitality of politics and social change at the state level. These federalist tendencies, so much a part of India's social structure as well as of its politics, appear to be in the process of being enhanced under Rajiv Gandhi. But, unlike the zero-sum political framework during the Indira Gandhi era, stronger states and a more vital center now seem to be possible.

PAUL WALLACE
University of Missouri
Columbia

*EUROPE*

BRUCE-GARDYNE, JOCK. *Mrs. Thatcher's First Administration: The Prophets Confounded.* Pp. xi, 199. New York: St. Martin's Press, 1984. $27.50.

SKED, ALAN and CHRIS COOK. *Post-War Britain: A Political History.* 2nd ed. Pp. 478. New York: Penguin Books, 1985. Paperbound, $7.95.

JOHNSON, PETER. *Neutrality: A Policy for Britain.* Pp. 133. New York: St. Martin's Press, 1985. No price.

About all that these three books have in common is that they deal with aspects of contemporary Britain. *Mrs. Thatcher's First Administration* is the special pleading of a former treasury minister, at times critical to be sure, but essentially concerned to make the best possible case for the controversial economic and financial policies pursued between 1979 and 1983. *Neutrality* is a reasoned argument, given its assumptions, that Britain should pull out of the Western alliance and the North Atlantic Treaty Organization (NATO) and become a neutral power like Switzerland or Sweden. And *Post-War*

*Britain* is the new edition of a general survey, deservedly well received when it first appeared in 1979, the last hundred pages of which are a tentative assessment of Thatcherism's first term.

Jock Bruce-Gardyne acknowledges that when the Tories went to the electorate in June 1983 they had, by any yardstick of vote-winning potential, a wretched tale to tell. For every 10 men and women unemployed in 1979 there were now 26. The economy had shrunk; in the case of manufacturing output it had shrunk dramatically. Even taxes, which the Tories in 1979 had promised to cut, had been increased for all but the well-to-do. Yet Mrs. Thatcher secured the largest parliamentary majority since 1945. Understandably for a former conservative minister of state and economic secretary to the treasury, Bruce-Gardyne minimizes the Falkland factor as being too remote from daily life to provide an adequate explanation of the Tory landslide. Denying that the Thatcher government was blindly obsessive in the stringency of its monetary control and over-zealous in pursuit of shrinking budget deficits, but admitting the serious errors committed particularly during the first year in office, he gives the voters high marks for recognizing that Britain's future depends on improved economic performance. The voters also receive praise for judging that on balance the Thatcher program offered some hope of achieving it.

Almost certainly Bruce-Gardyne overstresses general approbation of little-understood economic policies and underestimates the explosion of pride and patriotism over the Falklands achievement, just as he depreciates public reaction to the demoralization and divisiveness of the Labour Party. Much more balanced are Alan Sked and Chris Cook. Like Bruce-Gardyne, they point out the elements of continuity as well as new departures in Conservative policy. But where he treats the failure to reverse Britain's relative economic decline defensively, they simply outline the record—a 4.2 percent fall in the gross domestic product between 1979 and 1982, a falling-off in industrial production of

10.2 percent and in manufacturing of 17.3 percent from 1979 to 1983, and a 141 percent increase in unemployment. They, too, are especially critical of the government's mistakes in its early years, but give it rather good marks for its toughness and determination not only on domestic issues, but over the Falklands as well. Their conclusion that the voters in 1983 were prepared to give Mrs. Thatcher and her colleagues the benefit of the doubt appears closer to the realities of contemporary Britain than the more politically engaged evaluations of Bruce-Gardyne.

Peter Johnson's argument for a dramatic change in Britain's defense policy is the work of a much-decorated Royal Air Force officer who served as postwar director of civil aviation in occupied Germany and then as civil air attaché at the British embassy in Bonn. Describing how neutrality works in such cases as those of Switzerland and Sweden, he argues that the interests of Britain—and its vulnerability—are now quite different from those of the two superpowers. Those interests can no longer be served by commitments to the Western alliance and to NATO, however vital those commitments were a generation ago. The position of Britain in the world, he insists—maybe a bit hyperbolically—has changed in the last half-century perhaps more rapidly and drastically than that of any other nation in history over a comparable period. Britain is now of the second rank, and, whether that fact is palatable or not, the United Kingdom is in itself neither a target nor a factor of any real consequence in the calculations of the greatest powers. As a result, the risk in a stance of neutrality, backed by a strong home defense is less than that in alliance—and the degree of real protection, greater. Johnson is aware, of course, that should Britain move toward neutrality, friends will be lost and relationships disturbed. But, he points out, rearrangements of national attitudes following great disturbances have occurred again and again in history. In the long run, a neutral Britain might have more to contribute to tackling the world's most urgent problems than a Britain aligned with one antagonist in an

East-West conflict. It is tempting to dismiss this discussion of British neutrality as unrealistic and, to use the customary cliché, naive. But the argument is nevertheless a legitimate and responsible one that needs to be examined, whatever conclusions one may reach.

Two of these books, then, are tracts for the times and will, I am sure, be read as such. As for *Post-War Britain,* the additional materials in the new edition are a sensible and convincing first evaluation of what has already become the most controversial government in the history of post-war Britain.

HENRY R. WINKLER

University of Cincinnati
Ohio

BUTLER, DAVID and PAUL JOWETT. *Party Strategies in Britain: A Study of the 1984 European Elections.* Pp. ix, 171. New York: St. Martin's Press, 1985. $25.00.

This book describes what was almost a political nonevent in Britain, the 1984 election to the European Parliament. Only 32 percent of the electorate voted in the 78 constituencies. Two well-known columnists advised readers not to vote. A survey of eight leading newspapers over the three weeks before election day, 14 June, shows that only in the *Times* of 22 May was the election a lead story. Butler and Jowett conclude that in normal general election terms this election was a "fiasco." The parties inevitably saw it as a test of the Conservative government's popularity. Consequently, it fought on national issues and the European Economic Community (EEC) seldom became an issue in the campaign.

The work has useful introductory chapters containing a brief history of Britain's relationship with the EEC; a survey of the parties' electoral fortunes between 1979 and 1984; and an account of the activities of members of the European Parliament elected for the first time by popular vote in 1979. It is clear that Britain's 78-member delega-

tion was the most idiosyncratic though, oddly, it had the reputation of having the best attendance. Most of the 60 Conservatives were a good deal more pro-European than their party. On the other hand, the 17 Labour members contained an anti-European majority.

By comparison, the account of the actual campaign is very brief. This is partly the result of the voters' lack of interest and activity, but also of the large constituencies and the centralization of the campaign. Feeling that the European elections "were too important to be left to the Euro-politicians," the cabinet decided to write the manifesto and to entrust the running of the campaign to the Tory Central Office. Much of the three parties' public effort was put into press conferences and the grabbing of national headlines. Butler and Jowett followed these happenings, but failed to do the necessary footslogging among the constituencies. Hence the title is a fair reflection of the book's content. There is a good analysis of the parties' campaign funds and of the way the headquarters' staffs spent the money. Relationships with the media, primarily a London affair, are also spelled out in some detail. The parties blamed the media for the lack of interest. The popular newspapers told their readers the election was a bore and the television companies relegated it to the less popular news slots. Basically, however, as Butler and Jowett argue, the real reason for the lack of interest was the small impact of the European Parliament on people's lives.

FRANK BEALEY

University of Aberdeen
Scotland

DYKER, DAVID A. *The Future of the Soviet Planning System.* Pp. 172. Armonk, NY: M.E. Sharpe, 1985. $25.00.

David Dyker's book is an excellent analysis of Soviet economic planning—its strengths, weaknesses, and prospects. Dyker is a well-informed and thoughtful British economist whose 1983 book, *The Process of Investment in the Soviet Union,* shed new light on this basic topic. Here he offers an incisive analysis of the actual operating procedures followed in Soviet planning for industry, agriculture, and construction. Instead of repeating the usual formal description, he gives a pungent evaluation of key features of current practice.

Dyker was briefly a student in the USSR in the late 1960s and has taught courses on the Soviet economy for 15 years. Readers will enjoy his colloquial British style, as, for example, in the following: "After all the talk about primitive socialistic accumulation and pumping-over, it never happened, because Stalin made such a bloody mess of collectivization." Dyker draws appropriately on contemporary microeconomic theroy while laying bare the anomalies of Soviet plan administration.

The compact text begins with a chapter on historical origins, stressing the command principle and "the theory and practice of resource mobilization." Chapter 2 offers a shrewd analysis of how the "ratchet principle" and the "Micawber principle" have shaped interaction between planners and enterprise managers. The third chapter explains the ineffectiveness of the 1965 reforms, the 1975 "mini-reform," and some 1983 developments. Two substantial chapters discuss the special problems of agriculture and the construction sector. A final chapter discusses the implications of developments in Eastern European planning as they bear on the future of the Soviet ecnomic planning system.

This book is less discursive than Nove's *Soviet Economic System* and less formal than the Gregory and Stuart text, *Soviet Economic Structure and Performance.* While serving as an accessible undergraduate text, Dyker's analysis will also stimulate the thinking of all fellow students of the Soviet economy. His numerous references guide the reader to well-selected Western studies and a wide range of relevant Soviet

commentary by critical observers. Reliable reference books are not usually this lively; this volume deserves a paperback edition.

HOLLAND HUNTER
Haverford College
Pennsylvania

HOLMES, MARTIN. *The Labour Government, 1974-79: Political Aims and Economic Reality.* Pp. vii, 206. New York: St. Martin's Press, 1985. $27.50.

The democratic socialist parties of Europe, however much pressed by doctrinaire socialist factions within them, have without exception adopted the mixed economy when they have come into office. The lead was given by the Swedish Social Democratic Party when it adopted Keynesian policies in the late 1930s. Since the war, the German and Austrian parties have followed Sweden in successfully managing their economies with varying degrees of public ownership, but nothing that would be recognized as a socialist transformation of their societies. Britain has managed less well in spite of some success in the first postwar years, while the French Socialist Party is now struggling to deal by traditional methods with its economic problems. What are the reasons for the difference?

Clues to the answer will be found in this book, which describes in some detail the economic problems and the policies used to deal with them of the British Labour government of 1974-79. It is not very well written and is based almost entirely on interviews with ex-ministers and senior civil servants; the economic analysis tends to be unsophisticated. Nevertheless, it gives a fairly clear picture of what happened.

All British governments since the war have had to deal with inflation and a fragile balance of payments. The habit of governments of both parties of introducing inflationary preelection budgets has left their successors the task of retrieval. The nature of the British Labour Party, heavily dependent on the trade unions and increasingly infiltrated by militant ideologues, has made the task of facing reality difficult.

Under left-wing influence the Labour government produced for the 1974 election a policy of industrial intervention that was unreal and irrelevant and dealt with inflation using a succession of income policies that led in the end to the Winter of Discontent: a series of damaging and unpopular strikes in the public services. Millions of pounds were provided to shore up declining industries. As Holmes perceptively points out, there appeared to be no recognition that these industries were not only overmanned but uncompetitive both in the design of their products and the technology of manufacture. These facts are basic to understanding the cause of Britain's economic decline, which is exacerbated by the attempts of British workers to achieve the standard of living of their more successful foreign competitors. Even if they had recognized these facts the Left had no policy to deal with them.

Faced with inflation, which appeared a greater electoral handicap than more than a million unemployed, and under pressure from the International Monetary Fund the Labour government did introduce a radical change in economic policy: it gave up Keynesianism and adopted monetarist ideas. The Left was defeated but carried the fight on in the party outside Parliament; but so also were the Center and Right, which followed the revisionist views of the Keynesian Anthony Crosland. The results in reducing inflation were good until the preelection budget of 1978 set the cycle off again; but the election was lost and another, more ruthless government came into power to deal with problems for which no economic theory could provide the answer.

AUSTEN ALBU

Sussex
England

PAUWELS, JACQUES R. *Women, Nazis, and Universities: Female University Students in the Third Reich: 1933-1945.* Pp. xv, 200. Westport, CT: Greenwood Press, 1984. $29.95.

FLEMING, GERALD. *Hitler and the Final Solution.* Pp. xxxvi, 219. Berkeley: University of California Press, 1984. $15.95.

Jacques R. Pauwels, the author of *Women, Nazis, and Universities,* states that relatively little is known about the average German in National Socialist society in spite of the fact that more than 50,000 studies have been published on subjects dealing with the Third Reich and its main actors. He asserts that one of the topics that has been almost entirely ignored by historians until rather recently is the part women played in the Nazi state. Pauwels states that he does not intend, with his study, to supersede existing works on women students in Nazi society but to complement them and to include also Nazi policies dealing with female academic aspirations.

Considering that the so-called Nazi revolution was considered a male achievement and the Nazi Party a "bastion of male chauvinism," it is not surprising that the official attitude toward female academic aspirations was entirely negative. According to the Nazi male-supremacist notion, women were intellectually unfit for higher education. It was also thought that university studies tended to "defeminize" them, thus making them "spiritually and physically unfit for motherhood."

In addition to the male exclusionist attitude and the eugenic argument, a third reason for the Nazi opposition to women at the institutions of higher learning was the current academic unemployment.

All the efforts, such as a *numerus clausus* of 28 December 1933, to curtail women's academic aspirations were never followed through and thus proved to be ineffective. The ambitious Four-Year Plan and the elimination from the professions of so-called non-Aryans brought about shortages of university-trained professionals. The practice of limiting the number of female students was soon abandoned, and, in fact, women were actually encouraged to pursue university studies in practically any field in order to supply needed university-trained specialists.

During the first years of the Third Reich, statistics show, the number of female students declined. However, Pauwels emphasizes that this decline was not the result of Nazi antifeminism but was part of an overall decline of the German student population caused by the small size of the age groups born during World War I and the Great Depression. Nazi anti-intellectualism also contributed to the decline of university enrollment.

World War II became the catalyst of an unprecedented academic emancipation of German women. Between the summer of 1939 and 1941, the number of male students at all German universities dropped by nearly 50 percent, from 50,325 to 27,327. Toward the end of the war, in mid-1944, there were only 14,285 male students. The number of women enrolled increased from 6342 in 1939 to 41,210 five years later. University studies provided many women with a welcome opportunity to evade compulsory labor service, an opportunity described as "the flight to the universities." However, the attendance at universities did not release them from obligatory "war services," such as soldiering and "hospital, agricultural, and factory services," although most women students failed to respond to the efforts of the Nazi student organization to indoctrinate them in national socialism and to fulfill wholeheartedly their "war services."

Even worse, Pauwels found evidence that many female students pursued a "decadent life style," according to Nazi standards of morality, which included the taking of sexual liberties and not only those restricted to racial comrades. Reports even indicated that they monitored enemy radio stations, a particularly grave offense. There was widespread indifference to national socialism on the part of many female students, marked by mass apathy, skepticism, and even hostility.

The military reverses, such as the catastrophe at Stalingrad, which forced the Nazi leadership to replenish the armed forces by withdrawing 1.5 million men from the labor force, made the need for university-trained women even more pronounced. Thus Pauwels concludes that "the instrinsically misogynic Nazi regime deserves no credit for the impressive advances of German women in the field of higher education during the Second World War" and he believes that the situation would have been terminated as soon as victory was achieved.

*Women, Nazis, and Universities* is a well-documented and readable study, although there is some distracting repetition of several findings and arguments.

Pauwels's evaluation of the changing Nazi policies makes a strong case for the functionalist school of interpreting national socialism in sharp contrast to the traditional school, which is also referred to as intentionalist because its proponents believe that there is a direct relation between Hitler's ideology and actual Nazi policies and practices. The intentionalist approach is very much in evidence in Gerald Fleming's book, *Hitler and the Final Solution*. Fleming sets out to prove that Hitler was involved directly in the Final Solution, the physical extermination of the Jews. He attempts to demonstrate that there is a direct line from Hitler's pathological hatred of the Jews to the Nazi persecution of the Jews and to the Final Solution, in spite of the fact that there is no written evidence of Hitler's giving the order. Saul Friedländer confirms in his introduction that Fleming's book occupies an essential place in the current debate over the Final Solution between the intentionalists and the functionalists, who maintain that the policies that culminated in the killing of millions of Jews were not following a master plan but were the product of "cumulative radicalization."

The nonexistence of a written liquidation order for the Jews is explained as the result of Hitler's effort not to be personally linked with this policy. He was aware that a majority of the German population did not share his hatred and certainly would have condemned his far-reaching actions. Therefore, a kind of code language or euphemism was used within the leadership, as was done earlier when the euthanasia program was implemented. Thus "evacuation," "special treatment," and "elimination" meant extermination. "Elimination" was a term used by Hitler himself on several occasions and can be found in written documents.

Fleming attempts to prove his main assertion by citing Heinrich Himmler, who on several occasions referred to the "führer's wish" as the origin of the liquidation order. Examples of Himmler's placing the responsibility for the Final Solution directly on Hitler are his secret address before an audience of generals on 26 January 1944 in Posen as well as speeches delivered by him on 5 and 24 May and 21 June of the same year. Fleming gives ample evidence that "führer's wish" was regarded by his lieutenants as a direct order of Hitler. Fleming provides only one instance of an apparent direct line from Hitler to the mass killings of Jews. It is contained in a radio communication, transmitted in late July 1942, and signed "Adolf Hitler, Führer's Headquarters." It was addressed to Reichkommissar Erich Koch, in Rovno, Ukraine, instructing him to liquidate within a specific period of time all of the Jews that were still alive within the general region of Rovno.

Fleming's study, presented in a broad chronological framework, probably succeeds in proving the assertion of Hitler's direct involvement in the Final Solution. There are, however, those who will not accept his intentionalist position either because they are determined to pursue their revisionist interpretation of the Nazi period or because they must obtain confirmation for any event by unrefutable documentation.

Even though there have been numerous accounts published dealing with the monstrous bureaucratic machinery created for the mass execution of Jews—even before the Wannsee Conference of 20 January 1942, when the procedural guidelines for the liqui-

dation through labor were formulated—and dealing with the callous murder of millions of human beings, Fleming's study makes a deep psychological impression. Again the unanswerable question is raised of how all this could have happened.

ERIC WALDMAN
University of Calgary
Alberta
Canada

SHANOR, DONALD R. *Behind the Lines: The Private War against Soviet Censorship*. Pp. xii, 179. New York: St. Martin's Press, 1985. $13.95.

KNEEN, PETER. *Soviet Scientists and the State: An Examination of the Social and Political Aspects of Science in the USSR*. Pp. x, 138. Albany: State University of New York Press, 1984. $34.50. Paperbound, $12.95.

The access to a variety of independent and objective information sources is requisite for the proper function of any democratic society. But according to Soviet ideologists, objectivity in class society is a sham, and, therefore, information and public opinion should be controlled and the people protected from anti-Soviet propaganda and the flood of foreign information, considered harmful to the interests of the state and the party.

Donald Shanor discusses in his book the system of information delivery and control, and the mechanism charged with creating public opinion in the Soviet Union; he emphasizes the political propaganda aspects of the Soviet press, radio, television literature, theater, and other arts. He examines also the impact of the immense volume of letters written daily to the Central Party Committee and to the editors of various central and local newspapers.

Shanor contends that because the information produced by the official Soviet media is one-sided and biased, the public turns to unofficial sources in order to satisfy its craving for objective information. The unofficial information network includes foreign radio and television programs, video cassettes, letters from abroad, foreign travel reports, as well as *samizdat* and *tamizdat* literature. *Samizdat* literature is unofficially published and clandestinely circulated in the Soviet Union; *tamizdat* literature most commonly refers to works by Soviet authors not approved for publication in the Soviet Union and published abroad. In conclusion, Shanor speculates on the impact of new computer technology on the dissemination of propaganda and the dangers it poses to the state's control of information.

The book deals with many important issues, and a number of relevant observations are made, but this is not an academic book. Most facts cited are probably correct, but the information is without reference to any particular source and those interviewed and quoted are anonymous and in most cases biased.

There is no question that there is in the Soviet Union a burning thirst for objective information, free from distortions and propaganda, but it is also evident from this book that the craving is limited to certain segments of the population. Shanor admits that villagers and blue-collar workers have little interest in unofficial news and that the impact of unofficial information on the daily operations of the Soviet state is difficult to assess. Yet one gets the impression from the book that the influence of the unofficial information network on Soviet life is overwhelming and that it is an important rival of the official media.

Shanor suggests that separating truth from wishful thinking is one of the main tasks of the Soviet individual who tries to become better informed. It is a task that applies in equal measure to those residing in the West.

One aspect of Soviet society affected by restrictions on information exchange, and other government control, is scientific research. In his book, Kneen gives a general outline and analysis of the demographic and social composition of the Soviet community of natural scientists and of the organizational framework within which they function. He discusses also the political and social relationships of the scientists with the state, the Party, and society in general.

There is an inherent distinction between the objectives and essence of Soviet humanities and social sciences and those of the natural sciences. The former are a vehicle of a particular ideology, while the latter appear to have universal value. Kneen suggests that one of the main attractions of a career in the Soviet natural sciences is the relative insulation it affords from direct political involvement, yet he claims that central planning and political control, administered through the Communist Party, as well as the character of training and the working conditions of Soviet scientists, may impede their development and reduce their effectiveness.

According to this study one of the most important drawbacks in the development of Soviet sciences is the lack of opportunity for Soviet scientists to travel abroad and to communicate freely with foreign scientists. Kneen alleges that as "the scientific worth of fundamental research can only be judged initially in terms of the recognition it receives in the international scientific community," the isolation of the Soviet sciences has a detrimental effect on the level of its development. He corroborates this allegation by pointing to the small number of Soviet scholarly papers cited in international scientific publications.

Kneen's inferences are plausible, but the reliability of his methods of investigation are questionable and his conclusions require further substantiation. Scientific findings, as opposed to ideological and philosophical notions, have independent and universal value, regardless of the international recognition they receive. In fact, much of the research in the natural sciences conducted in the Soviet Union is classified because of its importance for the development of industrial and defense technology. Kneen's attempt to determine the qualitative value of the Soviet natural sciences with the help of quantitative, statistical, and sociological means is only partially successful because the real value of scientific discovery and the level of scientific research can be established correctly only with the help of a scientific scale of values.

N. N. SHNEIDMAN
University of Toronto
Ontario
Canada

## UNITED STATES

BERGAN, FRANCIS. *The History of the New York Court of Appeals, 1847-1932.* Pp. viii, 342. New York: Columbia University Press, 1985. $35.00.

The United States Supreme Court not surprisingly captures the attention of the media and the public, resulting in the overshadowing of the highest court in each state. Francis Bergan's three-part historical analysis of the New York Court of Appeals is a welcome addition to the literature and poignantly illustrates the influence of the Court of Appeals exercised upon its counterparts in the other states.

The court dates only to voter ratification of a new constitution in 1846 changing completely the state's judicial system, including abolishing the chancellor and the court of chancery and vesting equity jurisdiction in the state supreme court. The new court, however, accumulated a backlog of cases that led to demands for additional changes in the judicial system.

Relative to the question of election or appointment of judges, the constitutional convention of 1867-68 inserted in the new judiciary article, ratified by the voters, a requirement that the issue be submitted to the electorate as a separate question in 1873; appointment of judges was rejected by the electorate. The article also provided that the reestablished Court of Appeals would not be responsible for the appeals pending in the old court. As a consequence, the new Court of Appeals commenced its work without a backlog of cases, which was transferred to the temporary commission of appeals.

The Court of Appeals, effective 1 January 1870, continued to be plagued by a backlog of cases and the commission of appeals, scheduled to be terminated in 1873, had its life extended for an additional two years by the state legislature. The constitutional convention of 1894 devised a solution for the work load problem of the court by creating the appellate division of the state supreme court, a general trial court. The division functions as an intermediate appeals court. Specifically, the Court of Appeals was deprived of jurisdiction over appeals from an original court determination of facts, as such appeals were lodged in the appellate division, the decisions of which were final. The unique advantage of this approach is the reservation of "truly significant legal policy questions for final settlement by the Court of Appeals."

In Bergan's view, "the arrival of Cardozo at the Court of Appeals was an event so significant that it opened a judicial era. In perspective, Cardozo stands with James Kent at the pinnacle of the New York judiciary." Bergan added that "the general professional adulation of his judicial style was so great that after more than half a century it remains difficult to view him objectively."

Throughout his discussion of the three periods—1847-70, 1870-94, and 1894-1932—Bergan intersperses pertinent cases to illustrate the cases' changing nature and increasing complexity. Particular emphasis is placed upon the growing work load of the court and the various proposals considered or implemented to reduce its case load to a manageable level.

There is little to criticize in this book other than the failure to include a summation chapter highlighting major trends in the Court of Appeals, including persistent issues and problems, and an assessment of the quality of the court's decisions over the era reviewed.

JOSEPH F. ZIMMERMAN
State University of New York
Albany

KAMIENIECKI, SHELDON. *Party Identification, Political Behavior and the American Electorate*. Pp. xiv, 228. Westport, CT: Greenwood Press, 1985. $35.00.

Sheldon Kamieniecki updates—and offers revision of—electoral behavior theory. His primary concern is the evolving role of party identification, a concept that has assumed a central position in voting literature since its generation by Converse, Conway, Miller, and Stokes in *The American Voter*. His systematic review includes the topics of party identification and social background, orientation to the political system, views on groups and issues, candidate evaluations, and electoral behavior. He accomplishes this feat while still managing to pitch his work to the advanced undergraduate level, and he thus produces a book suitable for college or university library collections.

Kamieniecki has five major findings. First, Republican and Democratic identifiers are distinct in terms of their social, attitudinal, and behavioral characteristics. These distinguishing characteristics have changed only modestly over the past 30 years. Second, the isolation of strong party identifiers has the potential of better explaining primary turnout and outcomes.

Third, Kamieniecki finds that the number of independents is growing in its proportion to the electorate and that its growth comes disproportionately from the upper socioeconomic range. This finding, of course, is not new, as can be seen from Nie, Verba, and Petrocik's *The Changing American Voter*. Kamieniecki further asserts that certain attitudes characterize the emerging independent activists and partially explain independent voting patterns.

Fourth, in his view, his "findings challenge the prevailing assumption in the literature that strength of identification is inverse to independence, and they strongly suggest that partisan strength and independence are two separate components of party orientation." It is increasingly clear that the placement of "independent" in the neutral position on a seven-point party identification scale is inappropriate and dilutes the predictive capacity of the measure.

Finally, in predicting electoral behavior, the party difference index is found to be a better predictor than either the seven-point or four-point strength-of-identification measures.

The primary shortcomings of Kamieniecki's work are stylistic, methodological, and theoretical. His writing style, though clear, is flat and appears redundant because he uses the same form to discuss each set of hypotheses. His major methodological problem is excessive use of zero-order correlation coefficients. Although this statistic is readily comprehensible to advanced undergraduates, it simply will not support the multiple variable model that Kamieniecki is proposing and presumes to test. Finally, I must join the voices that decry the separation of voter choice from the issue of voter turnout. Although Kamieniecki begins to explore turnout phenomena in the context of his description of Republican, Democratic, and independent voters, he fails to integrate the issue meaningfully into his modification of dominant theoretical models. In spite of these reservations, I recommend *Party Identification and the American Electorate*. It belongs in most college or university libraries and on the shelves of all serious students of electoral behavior.

DAVID G. BAKER

Hartwick College
Oneonta
New York

LEVY, DAVID W. *Herbert Croly of "The New Republic": The Life and Thought of an American Progressive*. Pp. xvii, 335. Princeton, NJ: Princeton University Press, 1985. $32.50.

This is a thoughtful and well-written addition to the literature on the intellectual side of the Progressive Era. Useful primarily as an introduction to Croly and his circle, *Herbert Croly* rests on exhaustive research in archival and printed sources. A fascinating opening chapter introduces the reader to Herbert's gifted and prolific parents. Jane Cunningham Croly was a journalist and an author of books for women and children, a woman torn between the traditional views of woman's place that she purveyed in her writing and the facts of her extraordinary achievements. David G. Croly launched many editorial and intellectual enterprises, all of them promoting his version of the social philosophy of Auguste Comte. Levy's stress on Herbert's continuing debt to his father's Comtianism disagrees with the views of other students of Croly's life, who emphasize the influence of the Harvard pragmatists.

The heart of the book lies in Levy's discussion of Croly's career in the decade beginning in 1909. Publication of *The Promise of American Life* that year led to acquaintance with progressive activists and thinkers, notably Theodore Roosevelt and, indirectly, Willard and Dorothy Straight. In turn, the Straights' financial backing and personal support provided Croly with the means to launch the *New Republic* in 1914.

Croly's great ambition was to foster a cohesive intellectual community whose activities would influence public policy. His delineation of the fundamental conflict in American life between Jeffersonian individualism and Hamiltonian conceptions of assertive government gained him access to Theodore Roosevelt, whose neo-Hamiltonianism embodied Croly's prescriptions of public life. Ironically, however, it was only during Mr. Wilson's war, which Croly and his circle saw as an opportunity to promote planning and governmental activism, that the *New Republic* enjoyed its only real flirtation with power. Even here, Croly and his associates remained on the margins and quickly grew disillusioned. In the 1920s, still under Croly's energetic direction, the *New Republic* remained a lively journal of opinion and gained distinction in its cultural and literary departments. The brave hopes of shaping public policy, however, receded even as Croly himself became absorbed in some of the more spiritual aspects of his Comtian heritage.

*Herbert Croly* supplements, but does not supplant, Charles Forcey's *Crossroads of Liberalism* (1961), the standard study of the *New Republic* group. Written with obvious esteem for its subject, Levy's book is nonetheless frank in its acknowledgment of Croly's personal, ideological, and stylistic limitations. Levy's clear and straightforward prose is handsomely complemented by Princeton's attractive production and convenient footnote placement.

ROBERT H. ZIEGER
Wayne State University
Detroit
Michigan

MINTZ, FRANK P. *The Liberty Lobby and the American Right: Race, Conspiracy, and Culture.* Pp. 251. Westport, CT: Greenwood Press, 1985. $29.95.

This book presents the ideas, workings, and personnel of the Liberty Lobby, a relatively recent ultraconservative and nativist subculture in America. As a tribe competing with other tribes, this organization brought together a strange combination of people, including libertarians, believers in fascism, anti-Semites, atheists, secularists, states' rights advocates, Catholics, and Protestants. Immigrants and foreigns fared badly with this organization, yet the patriotism of immigrants in time of war could not be denied. And a hard-pressed Israel and a Communist-threatened Vietnam played havoc with the simplistic theory of nonintervention and Nordic supremacy. As in earlier times, Jews were accused of having strangleholds on governments and business. Extreme rightists generally regarded blacks and Asians— American Indians are not mentioned—as inferior and dangerous to the American way of life. A few racists, not content with the eugenic approach alone, favored repatriation of blacks to Africa and a lowering of the torch of the Statue of Liberty for Orientals and others.

Chapter headings indicate the basic content and direction of Mintz's account. There is no preface. Between the introduction and the conclusion are well-annotated treatments of the legacy of the interwar period, postwar precursors, anti-Zionism, holocaust revisionism, the struggle against respectability, a Lobby-Birch symbiosis, and analyses of the views of two Liberty Lobby intellectuals, Revilo Oliver and Austin J. App. Briefly, Oliver wanted Caesarism in government, while App longed for the revival of a Greater Germany.

Created by Willis Carto in 1957, the Liberty Lobby is portrayed as an umbrella organization for neo-Nazis, the John Birch Society, and other Radical Right groups. To them William Buckley's conservative *National Review* was but a mainstream periodical. Communist conspiracy lurked almost everywhere in Liberty Lobby literature. Favorite suspects and targets were the Federal Reserve System, Franklin D. Roosevelt, the New Deal, Dwight D. Eisenhower, the United Nations, Dean Rusk, Nelson Rockefeller, William Fulbright, Henry Kissinger, and Robert McNamara. Following Goldwater's defeat in 1964, the Liberty Lobby switched its support to George Wallace in 1968. Failure of Wallace's party, the American Independent Party, to gain more than a million votes in 1972 may have marked the beginning of erosion for the symbiosis.

Mintz features book titles, among them Oswald Spengler's *Decline of the West,* Francis P. Yockey's *Imperium,* Henry Ford's *International Jew,* and John O. Beaty's *Iron Curtain.* To some extent Mintz's informative volume is a critique of Liberty Lobby literature. In 1984, *Spotlight,* the official Liberty Lobby publication, claimed 200,000 subscribers. About 100 radio stations were carrying Liberty Lobby programs. Mintz is to be commended for diligent research. Whether the Liberty Lobby would concur in his selection of data, his judgments, and his interpretations, it is difficult to say.

ARLOW W. ANDERSEN

University of Wisconsin
Oshkosh

STARES, PAUL B. *The Militarization of Space: U.S. Policy, 1945-1984.* Pp. 334. Ithaca, NY: Cornell University Press, 1985. $25.00.

It is difficult to imagine a more timely or more difficult research project than the one of which this book is the invaluable product. Given the intense secrecy with which the Pentagon has wrapped all documentation of the military uses of outer space, Paul B. Stares's ingenuity in extracting detailed information from interviews—many from anonymous retired military and civil officials—from unpublished material, and from numerous hints and obscure references in congressional hearings is no less than awesome. His acknowledgments, for example, include appreciation for the help given by the staffs of three presidential libraries—Kennedy, Eisenhower, and Johnson—in the process of declassifying documents.

The work began as his doctoral dissertation at the University of Lancaster and was completed in its present form with the support of the Brookings Institution and the Rockefeller Foundation. It now appears as the twelfth in the Cornell Studies in Security Affairs, the perceptive editors of which deserve the commendation of every student of international politics.

The organization of the study is chronological: successive chapters deal with space policy in the pre-Sputnik period of 1945-57, in the Eisenhower administration with its creation of the National Aeronautics and Space Administration, under Kennedy and his expansion of the space agency for the moon mission, under Johnson and the 1967 treaty on the peaceful uses of outer space, under Nixon and Ford, in Carter's two-track policy of weapons development alongside efforts at arms control, and in Reagan's Star Wars initiative. Interpolated chapters review U.S. and Soviet antisatellite weapons research and testing and the debate over Soviet laser and directed energy beam research.

The focus throughout is on antisatellite weapons systems. Both sides now have the capability to destroy satellites, though only at relatively low orbits, low being estimated at about 5000 kilometers. It is somewhat surprising to learn that more than 2000 satellites carrying military payloads have been launched, or about two-thirds of all satellites in orbit, though it is thought that there are still no weapons deployed on them in violation of the 1967 treaty. The military satellites of the United States—some 643—and of the Soviet Union—some 1394—perform such significant military functions as photographic and electronic reconnaissance; oceanic, meteorological, and geodetic surveillance; communications; navigation; early warning; and nuclear-explosion detection.

If the extent of the military role in space is surprising, it is in turn the more surprising that neither side devoted much effort to antisatellite weapons development for so long a time. Several explanations for this delay are given: both the United States and the Soviet Union gave higher priority to missile development; interservice rivalry among the three U.S. military services diluted budgets and allocation of the scientific pool available; after some complaints about U.S. so-called spy satellites the Soviets apparently decided that their own photographic reconnaissance satellites were a valuable military asset and a tacit agreement evolved to table the issue; the Vietnam war diverted U.S. research and development resources into areas of more immediate priority; and the 1967 treaty on peaceful uses of outer space gave some limited assurance that satellites would not carry weapons—at least for the immediate future.

In his concluding chapter, Stares suggests the desirability of a U.S.-Soviet treaty limiting antisatellite weapons deployment. Conceding that such a treaty may be violated, he feels it could set useful guidelines on such points as limiting altitude to 5000 kilometers, separation of distances for launchings and orbits, inspection procedures, communication channels in event of accidental happenings, advance notice of actions subject to misinterpretation, and defined processes for resolving disputes. Similar provisions are in effect under the protocols of the U.S.-Soviet

Agreement on Incidents at Sea, which could supply a useful model for a treaty on incidents in space.

Stares's final conclusion is not optimistic. He fears that Reagan's Star Wars initiative will prevent any realistic arms control agreement on weapons in space, but still hopes that deployment of such weapons, in contrast to research and testing, can be limited by negotiation.

A useful glossary of acronyms helps the reader through the maze of some 100 government and international agencies and weapons systems, and valuable year-by-year tables are appended covering U.S. military and civilian space budgets, U.S. and Soviet military satellite launchings from 1957 to 1984, and U.S. and Soviet antisatellite tests that are identified as successes or failures.

OLIVER BENSON
University of Oklahoma
Norman

SOCIOLOGY

DEESE, JAMES. *American Freedom and the Social Sciences.* Pp. viii, 237. New York: Columbia University Press, 1985. $25.00.

A juxtaposition of American freedom and the social sciences reveals, according to James Deese, an inherent conflict, for it represents logically contradictory ideas.

The idea of American freedom is based on the belief that human beings "are capable from time to time of exercising free choice undetermined by the operation of any universal laws." The exercise of free choice is voluntary and spontaneous. It is not under the control of some eliciting stimulus, which compels or necessitates a particular response unwillingly, but is directed by reason and moral imperatives. American political philosophy is founded on this belief in rationalism and the freedom of individuals to regulate their own lives.

In contrast, the predominant view of contemporary social science—mainly social psychology, sociology, and anthropology—is, according to Deese, based on the belief that human beings "are victims of circumstances, behave mindlessly and irrationally about things that matter, and cannot arrive at decisions without being the victims of external conditions that impinge upon them." Being in the grip of this stark material and mechanical determinism, the social sciences accept as relevant causes only physical and biological variables, presumably in the expectation of achieving experimentally valid results and general causal laws akin to those in the natural sciences. By denying the operation of free will the social sciences explicitly question the responsibility of individuals for deeds that violate legal and moral rules, and they are thus negating the very principle upon which American democracy is based.

This framework is undeniable. But to what extent and in what way is American freedom actually threatened by this preoccupation of the social sciences with their unimpressive—so far, at least—results of reducing the causes of human behavior to the operation of genetic factors and experimentally manipulable conditions of the environment? Is there a real danger here? Deese does not discuss this issue, although on the first page of his book he announces that his purpose is to deal with "the collision course between two mutually contradictory ideas that are competing to determine the future of American Society."

But the specific manifestations and the concrete effects of this collision course are not the subject of his analysis. Instead, his book, in eight of its nine chapters, offers an illuminating and thorough critique of the social sciences. The chapters contain valuable discussion of the rise and the variation of scientific determinism, as well as consideration of the claims of behaviorism, social psychology, and psychohistory, all of which are committed to a vain emulation of causal explanations in the physical mode. Deese's harsh but just conclusion is that "Social Science as the objective source of knowledge about the causes of human actions is at least an intellectual embarrassment and at worst a fraud."

In consequence, Deese advocates the abandonment of the belief that no scientific study of human events is possible unless it is analyzed in the framework of material determination. He advocates instead the adoption of a framework of human determination, in which such nonmaterial and nonmechanical factors as meanings, intentions, values, beliefs, and reasons are causally relevant for the understanding of human events. Humanistic sociology and humanistic psychology have already done so.

Other social sciences might follow suit and concentrate on descriptive, structural, and motivational analysis of human affairs rather than pursue a futile goal of emulating the hard sciences. Such a development would also put an end to the collision course between American freedom and the social sciences with which Deese is rightly concerned in this book.

THEODORE ABEL

University of New Mexico
Albuquerque

EHRENREICH, JOHN H. *The Altruistic Imagination: A History of Social Work and Social Policy in the United States.* Pp. 271. Ithaca, NY: Cornell University Press, 1985. $24.50.

Ehrenreich's underlying thesis is that social work cannot be understood unless one understands the social forces that brought it into being and shaped its destiny.

Ehrenreich begins the defense of his thesis by presenting a detailed narrative of how the social organizations of American society were profoundly altered by the industrial/urban transformation that began in earnest after the Civil War and came to fruition in the two decades or so before World War I. Though this period is dubbed the "Progressive Era" by historians, Ehrenreich incisively describes it as a time of mixed blessings: the phenomenal rise of the United States to the world's leading industrial power was offset by the introduction of a host of social problems—monopolistic competition, poverty, urban blight, and the like—that have since become synonymous with industrial society. Indeed, so devastating were the cumulative effects of these problems on the country that a major social movement—progressivism—replete with programs and ideologies, arose to stave off the crisis.

It is within this context that Ehrenreich locates the genesis of modern American social policy and social work. The principal elements of social policy at this early juncture included the introduction of scientific management to increase the efficiency of labor, the expansion of trade unionism, the founding of philanthropic agencies, and the creation of a nationwide consumer-goods market. The principal players who came forward to form the nucleus of the new occupation of social work came from the ranks of the old, traditional middle class who expressed concern for the victims of a rampant industrialism.

Once having traced the origins of social policy and social work to the Progressive Era, Ehrenreich continues the same line of analysis for the decades that followed. Thus, the major social issues associated with each era—the New Deal of 1933-38, the Affluent Society of 1945-60, and the Great Society of 1961-68—are identified, along with a detailed description of the social policies that were enacted to counter them.

From this point on the book's focus turns more directly to showing how social work's fortunes rose and fell with each change in social policy. For example, we are told that at the beginning of the Great Depression, the leaders of social work had to change their traditional case approach, in which they treated individual clients on a one-to-one basis, to an approach that emphasized the amelioration of macrosocietal problems.

In the light of this changing environment, social workers increasingly came under the auspices of federal and state bureaucracies, and their practice addressed the problems of poverty and dependency. Not only did this change provide new and different employment opportunities for the old guard of the social work community, but it also necessi-

tated the recruitment of many more workers. According to Ehrenreich, this influx of new recruits into the fold, plus the shift in emphasis—from case work to social amelioration—led to a crisis within the social work community.

The professional knowledge base of social work as well as the standards of credentialing its members, which were so painstakingly delineated by the pioneers of social work, was abruptly dismantled by the exigencies of reformist social policy. Unhappily for social workers, the same scenario was to unfold in the post-World War II period when, as before, social work had to alter its mission to respond to the new social policies—this time, policies of the Kennedy-Johnson Great Society programs.

What have all these social movements, with their ever-changing social policies, meant to social workers? By and large, Ehrenreich argues that they have ultimately served the social workers' best interests even though, as a calling, social work is still trying to attain full legitimation as a profession. He further contends that social work's inability to come to closure on whether it should address individual problems or societal problems still stands as an impediment to full-fledged professional status.

*The Altruistic Imagination* is a solid piece of scholarship that is sure to command the attention of several audiences, including historians of twentieth-century America, occupational sociologists, and, of course, social workers.

ALFRED AVERSA, Jr.
Fairleigh Dickinson University
Teaneck
New Jersey

JACKSON, BRUCE. *Law and Disorder: Criminal Justice in America.* Pp. x, 324. Champaign: University of Illinois Press, 1984. $19.95.

Bruce Jackson, professor at the State University of New York at Buffalo, is also widely known as a photographer and film-maker. As the director of the Center for Studies in American Culture, he deals primarily with items concerning crime, prison life, racial problems, and black folk music. His provocative book, *Law and Disorder,* attempts to get to the roots of the widespread dissatisfaction with the criminal justice system in America and to suggest appropriate strategies for reform. The result is the product of over 20 years of intensive studies, interviews, and firsthand observations.

Jackson turns his chief attention to the question of how the criminal justice machinery works: how decisions are made and according to which criteria priorities are set. His approach is less of a theoretical nature than of a pragmatic one. The main focus is on the actual workings, though against the background of the normative decision-making program. Jackson examines the criminal jurisdiction and the laws, the indicators of crime, and the deficiencies of the official crime statistics. He also examines the daily routine of prison inmates and, in addition, the administrative run of crime control and the expenditure of the criminal justice administration.

With regard to the failures of the existing system he closes his work with an endeavor to develop approaches of reform and to propose alternatives in order to cope more effectively with the phenomenon of crime. Jackson insists for good reasons that the practices of crime control run the risk of dealing with the effects of criminality instead of starting at its causes. He pleads for flanking and preventive strategies as well as for more intensive efforts toward rehabilitation.

Jackson's book is sensitive and combative, written in a descriptive language, a language close to life. It is true that Jackson did not thoroughly try to verify his assumptions empirically. His merit consists in having identified and localized the deficiencies of the criminal justice system in America. The analysis is refreshing and illuminating, profitable even for the European reader. Over against this, however, Jackson's reform proposals are less original and less convincing.

This lack is due to the complexity of the genesis of crime and the antagonistic basic principles and politics of crime control. For those reasons, we will even in the future come to know a crisis management rather than a systematically laid-out procedure to meet with the difficulties. Nevertheless, dissatisfaction with criminal justice will at least provide for a continuing discussion and reduce us not to compound with the status quo but, with this prick in our flesh and with renewing imagination, to look for new paths.

GUNTHER KAISER

Max-Planck-Institut für ausländisches
   und internationales Strafrecht
Freiberg
Breisgau
West Germany

NOONAN, JOHN T., Jr. *Bribes.* Pp. xxiii, 839. New York: Macmillan, 1984. $29.95.

In Robert Bolt's award-winning *Man for All Seasons,* Sir Thomas More, then a privy councillor to King Henry VIII of England, encourages an ambitious young acquaintance to accept a teaching post rather than seek a place at court, in order to avoid being tempted to accept bribes. The young man, of course, ignores More's advice.

Throughout history, according to John T. Noonan's *Bribes,* few people in positions of power have been as resistant to bribery as Bolt would have us believe More was. In fact, the act of bribery is both ancient and virtually universal in world history. *Bribes* is an extended exploration of the history of the acts of offering and accepting bribes, based on detailed case studies and documented with a rich variety of source materials. If Noonan accomplished nothing more in this lengthy work, it would be an interesting but overly long scholarly curiosity. It is, fortunately, much more than that, as Noonan attempts to draw general conclusions about the social, political, legal, religious, and moral contexts of and reactions to bribery, and about changes in the reactions to bribery throughout history.

According to Noonan, "The core of the concept of a bribe is an inducement improperly influencing the performance of a public function meant to be gratuitously exercised." While bribery is a legal concept, Noonan correctly argues that it must be viewed from a far wider perspective, particularly if the changing views of bribery are to be understood. The wider context is thus more important than the narrower, legal definition, as only by viewing the context can changes in bribery laws be explained.

Noonan divides the history of the bribe into four periods. The first, encompassing the ancient, classical, and early medieval ages, sees the struggle of nonreciprocity—gifts being accepted without returning the favors—against the existing reciprocal bonds of society. The second period, the late Middle Ages and the Renaissance, is a time of strong antibribery sentiment in society, rooted in religion and finding its expression in law.

The third and fourth periods that Noonan studies, concentrating on the Anglo-American tradition, are closely related. Beginning in sixteenth-century England, antibribery sentiment was implanted into society, religion, law, and literature. In the fourth period, Noonan follows this tradition across the Atlantic, where it was expanded and refined, until this antibribery tradition today "is asserted as an American norm around the earth." In 1977, the U.S. Congress went so far as to pass the Foreign Corrupt Practices Act, which was designed to prevent American businesses from bribing foreign officials.

*Bribes* is nothing less than an interdisciplinary magnum opus. Its author has delved deeply into the realms of history, religion and theology, anthropology, sociology, literature, law, political thought and practice, and linguistics to pull together his case studies and subsequent analyses. With this book, the whole truly is greater than the sum of the parts. If it can be criticized at all—and no brief review can do this book justice—it will be criticized for being too detailed, too long, and thus sometimes confusing. The

main threads may be too easily lost amid all of the detail. But Noonan more than compensates for this by his excellent writing and rich discussion of the changing contexts of the bribe throughout history. This work will long stand as the authoritative study of this topic.

JOE PATRICK BEAN
Concordia Lutheran College
Austin
Texas

STENEK, NICHOLAS H. *The Microwave Debate.* Pp. xvii, 279. Cambridge, MA: MIT Press, 1984. $25.00.

MEEHAN, RICHARD L. *The Atom and the Fault: Experts, Earthquakes, and Nuclear Power.* Pp. xiv, 161. Cambridge, MA: MIT Press, 1984. $13.95.

These two books are important contributions to our understanding of the problems society faces in learning to use and control technology. A historian, not a scientist, Stenek diagnoses the general case by probing a live paradigm, the dispute over the dangers to the public from microwave, radio-frequency (RF) radiation. Ongoing controversies over siting television transmitters, satellite uplinks, and microwave relay towers attest to the vigor and cogency of the debate about where to draw the line to protect society from potential harm while enabling it to reap the benefits of new technology.

Meehan writes from the standpoint of a participant in "several nuclear power plant and other environmental controversies in which the disagreement over scientific and engineering facts was a central issue that had to be played out in the public arena in accordance with legal rules." By incorporating perspectives other than his own, he both validates and reinforces Stenek's broader treatment.

Among the issues Stenek examines are public skepticism, controversial media involvement, the bureaucracy, conflicting values, vested interests, and scientific uncertainty. The study is peopled by crusading heroes, international spies—remember the Soviet microwave bombardment of the U.S. embassy in Moscow—journalists, policymakers, entrepreneurs, and scientists. One could hardly wish for a more thorough and balanced investigation.

Stenek presents many reasons why the microwave debate, and similar ones, continue unabated. Scientific evidence, however massive, can never be dispositive; perhaps scientific questions to define the problem sharply are not even being asked. When experts and scientists who testify at public hearings disagree, someone has to decide whom to believe. But public officials, judges, and juries find themselves with the impossible burden of finding solutions that elude the experts. A circle of indecision results because the other institutional actors are not anxious to grasp the nettle. Congress can toss hot potatoes to the executive branch, who can drag their feet—agency rule making can be interminable. The media are free to popularize the controversy without weighing or even facing the facts. Scientists can ask for more funds and more time to produce more studies.

What needs to be changed for society to break the circle of indecision?

First, says Stenek, we must place less emphasis on science and more on values. Our faith in science's ability to provide objective information leads us to collect ever more data without stopping to wonder whether the problem is amenable to scientific conclusions. Making decisions about harnessing new technology requires much more than scientific facts; it requires information about economics, politics, law, and social implications.

Second, we should be asking how low a protective standard can be set without infringing on economic development, instead of asking how high it can be set without causing demonstrable injury.

Third, all concerned need to put more effort into first defining the problem, the better to focus on the optimum solution.

Stenek recommends that vested interests— in this instance, the military and the involved industries—should never have a controlling influence on research although they might reasonably desire or be required to support it. They have the same—but no greater— right to express their opinions and protect their interests as do consumers and anyone else in the forums where these public choices are made.

He also recommends that Congress face up to its responsibilities to represent the public in these situations. When Congress passes its decision-making authority to executive agencies or the courts, the ability of the public to influence policy decisions is effectively destroyed. One can vote against a congressman who seems to favor one interest over another, but not against a federal regulation or a court decree.

Last and least, Stenek recommends that greater public involvement be encouraged because only public pressure can break the circle of indecision. But such involvement requires good information and lots of it, which requires in turn public education about the issues, relying largely on the media, who must become somehow more evenhanded and thorough in treating the issues.

Meehan's account of the "politics of expertise" raises cogent questions about the use of experts and expert opinion in administrative processes. He is deeply concerned about the triumph of legalism over technical competence and scientific truth seeking.

He concludes that seismic faulting beneath or near nuclear power plants is indeed a potential safety problem, warranting the past controversy at some—but not all— reactor sites. However, the controversy has been exacerbated by environmentalists and other experts from the social-economic-political milieus, who typically are more concerned with the problem than with the solution.

The controversy is further exacerbated by the lack of an explicit safety standard against the faulting hazard. The existing federal regulation provides procedural guidance but begs the question of how safe is safe enough. Absent such a standard, scientists can not avoid mixing science and values. However, a decision about acceptable annual risk of core damage or radioactive release—one in a thousand, a million, a billion years?—once made through the political process, makes essential and feasible the setting of specific standards so that technicians can go about their work, free of any overtones of policy-making.

Meehan believes advocacy is inherent in scientific and engineering methods and that the existing public hearing process is sensible, discouraging domination of the process by any elite or powerful school of expertise. He believes there is a useful place for the scientist or engineer who is able to articulate the logical bases for his or her disciplinary codes and standards to act as a special master, examiner, advisor, or witness and not just as an expert on narrow technical matters.

In conclusion, Meehan points out that experts find truth by invoking a socially sanctioned process. To the lawyer, truth is what emerges from correct legal procedure; to the scientist or engineer, from certain methods of which observational verification is not always more important than peer interaction. Values are thus integral with logic and discovery.

The combined message of these two books reminds me of Peter Drucker's warning in *Management* that

if the institutions of our pluralistic society of institutions do not perform in responsible autonomy, we will not have individualism and a society in which people have a chance to fulfill themselves. . . . To make our institutions perform responsibly, autonomously, and on a high level of achievement is thus the only safeguard of freedom and dignity. [*Management* (New York: Harper & Row, 1974), pp. ix-x.]

WALTER V. CROPPER

Santa Fe
New Mexico


## ECONOMICS

AARON, HENRY J. and HARVEY GALPER. *Assesing Tax Reform.* Pp. xii, 145. Wash-

ington, DC: Brookings Institution, 1985. $22.95. Paperbound, $8.95.

This timely work is reasonably nontechnical and should prove valuable to a wide audience of those interested in the current debate over tax reform.

Aaron and Galper begin with a critique of the federal personal and corporate income tax that is a bit brief. Their six-part indictment is that it distorts investment, earnings, and saving, penalizes work, and is unfair and overly complex. They show that the effective tax rate on investment ranges from 91 percent to -22 percent and explain how the tax system can turn a money-losing investment into a winner. They also note that individual retirement accounts may change how and where we save without affecting the overall saving rate. But that is about it. Work disincentives—so central in the supply-side worldview—get about eight lines of text. Perhaps it is unfair to ask for more in so brief a book, but I suspect that no one who was not already in favor of reform will be won over by this work.

Aaron and Galper separate tax reform from the deficit problem. Reform, they believe, will take several years and the deficit will not wait. Hence, they suggest several quick fixes to raise revenue. But there may be a political problem with such a separation. If the deficit were now to go away, so might the political will to plug all those loopholes.

Chapter 2 discusses the principles of tax reform. It is argued here that using the tax system to promote worthy causes is usually unfair and inefficient, the mortgage interest deduction being a case in point. Aaron and Galper then discuss issues concerning how to measure and tax income such as whether accrued or realized income should be taxed, what the proper accounting period should be, and the role of inflation and other distortions. They conclude the chapter with a section on compliance and administration and some discussion of the problems of transition from the old to any new tax system.

Chapters 3 and 4 evaluate the Treasury tax plan, Bradley-Gephardt, Kemp-Kasten, and Aaron and Galper's own plan—a cash-flow income tax. Chapter 3 is the best short summary I have seen of the major tax reform schemes. Aaron and Galper conclude that any of them would be a vast improvement over the present mess, but they point out that all fail to solve serious problems. None adequately deals with accrued versus realized income, corporate double taxation, inflation, and the distortion of saving.

The solution to all these problems, we discover, is a cash-flow income tax—that is, a tax on current income, minus saving plus gifts and bequests. This is based on the principle that all income should be taxed once and only once. Under this scheme all depreciable assets would be immediately and fully deductible, thereby neatly doing away with problems of depreciation and capital gains. Although the corporate income tax would remain, a cash-flow tax would integrate it with the personal income tax, ending the present double taxation of dividend income. Most special deductions and credits would end, with the exceptions of charity and housing, which would retain some special privileges. A number of technical issues are discussed in an appendix to the chapter.

Chapter 5 discusses sales, value added, and energy taxes, while chapter 6 provides a critique of various short-run revenue-raising schemes. The book ends with a discussion of the politics of tax reform that says little that is new but contains some useful horse sense. The tax mess has come about, Aaron and Galper note, due to the efforts of well-meaning folks to promote worthy causes. These causes tend to have concentrated benefits—and therefore committed interest groups—and diffuse costs. Moreover, tax concessions have been politically easier to enact than spending increases because they do not increase the apparent size of the government. This implies that tax reform may increase political pressures for spending and that reform may be as hard to sustain as to implement.

MARK ALDRICH

Smith College
Northampton
Massachusetts

CALLIES, DAVID L. *Regulating Paradise: Land Use Controls in Hawaii.* Pp. viii, 245. Honolulu: University of Hawaii Press, 1984. Paperbound, $14.95.

FOSTER, CHARLES H.W. *Experiments in Bioregionalism: The New England River Basins Story.* Pp. xvi, 231. Hanover, NH: University Press of New England, 1984. $22.50.

An unresolved problem of democratic government, exacerbated in federal polities, is how to conduct long-range planning. The U.S. federal system is a marble cake of intertwined activities rather than a layer cake of functional separation. Two problems arise in the planning sphere. First, how should we allocate planning responsibilities within the marble cake? Callies's study of Hawaii, where the planning region corresponds to an isolated island state, is a detailed case study on this question. Second, governmental jurisdictions do not necessarily match land, resource, or environmental issues. The experimental solution has increasingly been creation of substate and federal-interstate regional planning bodies. Foster's study of "bioregionalism" is a detailed case study on interstate cooperation in water resources. These two books are good illustrations of the current status of U.S. regional planning.

Callies comprehensively surveys the legal framework of planning. He demonstrates how complex land-use control has become in a special situation in which 40 percent of the land is owned by the federal and state governments, multiple permit requirements are pervasive, and a wide range of legal control instruments exists. Hawaii has three separate state statutes for land use, planning, and environmental impact, together with a variety of federal statutes, which affect local—that is, county—planning. His book is an excellent, well-organized survey—with each chapter devoted to a specific planning topic—of what land-use planning now involves.

Foster reviews the post-1945 history of river basin planning in New England. Again an unusual situation is studied, because there is no dominant river system in this region. The basic cleavage is north—rural water sources—versus south—urban water uses. The evolution of federal-state cooperation is shown to be highly political in character. Between 1950 and 1956 a federally organized interagency committee led to state representation with "states' rights" the predominant issue; between 1957 and 1966 the states failed to agree on an interstate compact; between 1967 and 1981 a federal-interstate river basins commission operated under federal enabling legislation; in 1981 the Reagan administration abolished such commissions as worthless. The commission has been succeeded by an interstate water council with federal participation. Foster could produce little evidence of actual water resource achievements by any of these devices. He emphasizes rather the establishment of working relationships and the demonstrated functioning of "consensus"—unanimity—decision making and federal-state "coequality" as viable regional principles.

The strengths of both books lie in the authors' considerable expertise and in their detailed case-study approach. But as a result both books have the same analytical flaw. Each author tends, to presume implicitly that planning is a good solution. This presumption is not argued through. While Callies recognizes the choice between development and control in Hawaii, he does not commit himself on the crucial issue; the book is necessarily descriptive and not evaluative. Foster tends to attribute the various changes in organizational scheme to politics; perhaps the problem in New England is simply insoluble because no unifying river basin exists, unlike the situation in other regions. Each author needed to set the otherwise excellent case study within an analytical framework.

DUANE WINDSOR

Rice University
Houston
Texas

EADS, GEORGE C. and MICHAEL FIX. *Relief or Reform? Reagan's Regulatory Dilemma.* Washington, DC: Urban Institute Press, 1984. $19.95. Paperbound, $12.95.

George C. Eads is a professor in the School of Public Affairs at the University of Maryland and Michael Fix is a senior research associate and attorney at the Urban Institute. This book is another in a series of studies published by the Urban Institute examining changes in economic and social policy under the Reagan administration.

The primary objective of the book is to evaluate the Reagan administration's strategies for providing regulatory relief—as opposed to reform—and the success or failure of these strategies in achieving the administration's goals. The book is divided into two main parts. The first part provides the background necessary for understanding the more detailed examination of the Reagan regulatory program that appears in the second part. Chapter 2 examines the impact of regulation on the economy, specifically the claim made by many in the administration that the economy's poor performance during the 1970s was due to the burden of government regulation. Eads and Fix conclude that, although regulation has been somewhat of an economic burden, "regulation cannot be blamed . . . for more than a small fraction of the economy's poor performance."

Chapters 3 and 4 summarize regulatory reforms and innovations that took place during the Nixon, Ford, and Carter administrations and legislated deregulation that occured during the Ford and Carter years. Chapter 4 also contains short but interesting histories of the battle over deregulation of the airline and trucking industries.

Chapter 5 outlines critiques of regulation prominent at the time Reagan took office. Supporters of the critiques include libertarians who want no regulation, economists who want to substitute marketlike mechanisms whenever possible for existing command and control regulation, and those in favor of decreasing the amount of regulatory oversight while maintaining the same basic regulatory structure.

The balance of the book is devoted to a summary and critique of the Reagan regulatory relief strategy. In chapter 6, Eads and Fix examine efforts, particularly those early in the administration, to increase executive-office regulatory oversight, primarily by creating the President's Task Force on Regulatory Relief and centralizing oversight authority in the newly established Office of Information and Regulatory Affairs within the Office of Management and Budget.

Chapter 7 summarizes the administration's efforts to reduce regulatory oversight internally—through agency appointments and budget restrictions. Many early Reagan appointees were known to be hostile toward their agencies. Others came to their positions with little or no experience in the business or activity they were to oversee. These initial appointments may have had political value by pleasing certain constituency groups, but as Eads and Fix point out, public and congressional distrust of a James Watt or an Anne Burford may make regulatory reform efforts in the future more difficult.

Chapter 8 examines administration efforts to deregulate via changes in administrative rules and procedures and finds that the administration has been most successful changing regulations in older agencies with broad nonrestricting enabling statutes. Examples of deregulating through rule changes are presented in case studies of a revision of the passive-restraint standard; recession of liquor labeling requirements; redefining "stationary source" for purposes of determining air pollution control requirements; changes in the implementation of the Davis-Bacon Act, requiring prevailing wages on federally supported construction projects; and the deregulation of the radio industry. Chapter 9 examines enforcement efforts and difficulties the Reagan administration has had convincing its critics that it is serious about enforcement. Such difficulty is understandable in light of the severe cutbacks in enforcement budgets. Chapter 10 explores the administration's efforts to transfer regulatory responsibilities from the federal to the state governments, efforts that have not met with

great success, due largely to the failure of the administration to provide also the funds necessary to implement programs on the state level. The final chapter of the book assesses the Reagan regulatory reform efforts and concludes that they have been a moderate success. It appears, Eads and Fix argue, that the cost to business of regulation has been lessened and the economy benefited by business expectations of further regulatory relief. On the other hand, the administration's program did not live up to its promises of sharply reducing the regulatory burden.

*Relief or Reform?* is a well-written and well-researched book and is must reading for students of regulatory policy. It is strongest in its descriptive and historical chapters and weakest in its analysis of the impact of regulatory reform on the economy. The variables are too complex and the incentives operating on businessmen too varied for Eads and Fix to make any firm connection between Reagan's program and increases in productivity. The treatment of Reagan's record will please neither conservatives nor liberals; such dissatisfaction probably means that the treatment is fairly well balanced and objective. In the final chapter I am not sure that Eads and Fix were critical enough of the impact that administration policies will have on long-term regulatory reform. This administration, because of public and congressional distrust of its motives—well-documented in the book— will have a difficult time pursuing further regulatory relief or reforms.

ZACHARY A. SMITH

Ohio University
Athens

GINZBERG, ELI, WARREN BALINSKY, and MIRIAM OSTROW. *Home Health Care: Its Role in the Changing Health Services Market.* Pp. viii, 186. Totowa, NJ: Rowman & Allanheld, 1984. $27.50.

This book, a final report of a study by the Conservation of Human Resources, Columbia University, for the Health Services Improvement Fund, Inc., examines the nature of home health care in the 17 southern counties of New York state and more generally for the state as a whole. While only empirically representative of a given geographic area, the results yield insights and factual data that prove to be of broader significance. The content presents a review of the literature, a profile of the client population, descriptions of the services utilized, and discussions surrounding other programmatic and policy issues related to home health care.

The literature review attempts to be comprehensive. It traces the development of the formal provision of home health care in the United States from its beginnings in 1796 as simple home nursing services in Boston up to the multifaceted programs of the 1980s. The most informative aspect of the literature review is the discussion on recent research and demonstration projects that have been undertaken to examine cost-effective approaches to the provision of home services compared to the costs of institutionalization. Lacking in the review is any discussion of the literature concerning patient care or evaluating the quality of provided services.

The data collected in the research project involved a patient survey and an agency survey. The sample for the patient survey was constructed so as to be representative of home health patients in the New York metropolitan area in the early 1980s. Data collection involved uniform record reviews of closed cases. These case records were drawn from a representative sample of all certified home health providers in the 17 southern counties of New York. Responses were analyzed as bivariate relationships between demographic characteristics, clinical diagnosis, types and intensity of provided services, costs and financing sources, outcomes, and other relevant variables. This basic information, while only representative for the designated areas for the defined time period, provides administrators and service planners with valuable information. One of the more interesting findings shows that patients who need rehabilitation and are expected to im-

prove receive the most home visits and the highest intensity of care and show the greatest improvements in functional status levels at discharge. Home health care is less frequently used for home maintenance of the chronically ill elderly. Third-party payers provide most of the funding for skilled services, while personal care services are paid as out-of-pocket expenses by the patient. Clearly, part of the explanation for the care patterns lies in the policies governing the provision of home health care, which focus on acute rather than chronic conditions.

While the contingency tables on the 570 cases are informative, I wish the investigators would have gone beyond the presentation of bivariate relationships and used multivariate statistical techniques to explore more complex patterns of relationships.

In contrast to the representativeness of the patient survey, the agency survey was conducted more as a series of case studies with 8 of the 64 certified agencies in the geographic area. The 8 sites were selected to cover the range of providers in terms of sponsorship, location, size, and function.

In addition to the literature review, it is the inclusion of the survey instruments—both the patient and agency questionnaires—in the appendixes that makes this volume a valuable addition to a library collection. Administrators, planners, and students in the health and human services, faced with the need to conduct similar studies, will find these instruments of enormous value.

The basic conclusions of the book have great relevance for other geographic areas as well as the county as a whole. First, because of the aging population structure the demand for health services will grow, but home health care cannot become an effective substitute for institutional care without major changes in the incentive structures currently built into the health financing mechanisms, particularly Medicare and private health insurance. Inasmuch as personal care associated with chronic illness is the primary health care need of the elderly, the key to establishing long-term community care services requires that the funding of home health services be broadened to include personal care irrespective of the need for skilled care. Second, home health care can become an important and cost-effective aspect of long-term care only with the development of appropriate community infrastructures and coordinated, comprehensive services for the elderly.

Information presented in this study describes the home health care system before the establishment of the diagnostic-related groups (DRGs), the prospective payment plan under Medicare. Now that hospitals must discharge elderly patients more quickly under the DRG regulations, it would be interesting to compare more recent statistics from a similar patient survey to the results of the present study. Such comparisons could show the extent to which the DRGs have changed the home health patient population.

JOEL LEON

Washington University
St. Louis
Missouri

MINTZ, SIDNEY W. *Sweetness and Power: The Place of Sugar in Modern History.* Pp. xxx, 274. New York: Viking Press, 1985. $20.00.

There is no book in English that contains so much interesting, unusual, and often amusing information on the marginalia of the history of sugar consumption during the Christian Era. The numerous quotations on sugar from chronicles, belles lettres, and the recipes from cookbooks from the Renaissance to this century constitute a mine of delightful and quaint lore that should attract all who are interested in the history of food, as should the material on production culled from little-known and unexpected sources.

But economic history this is not and is not intended to be. It is erudition in the service of a grand anthropological theory, forced, in my view. Starting from the translucent premise in the second sentence that "food systems

dramatically demonstrate the infraspecific variability of humankind," the increase and expansion of sugar consumption in England—the proving ground of the theory—from a few hundred pounds a year by king and magnates to well over a million tons during the last quarter of the nineteenth century is construed as a demonstration of the quest of lower orders to emulate their betters and to proclaim their rise in status. As consumption increased, sugar "was *transformed* from a luxury of kings into the kingly luxury of commoners" (italics in original). As consumption continued to rise, "thus understood, sugar became . . . a spurious leveler of status."

What is not so clear is why, having lost its status significance, England's per capita consumption continued to rise from 30-35 kilograms during the last part of the nineteenth century to about 55 kilograms in the sixties. Sugar's status symbol must be as great or even greater in such diverse societies as the United States, where per capita consumption—including the sugar equivalent of corn alternatives—has risen to around 57 kilograms; Australia, to 50-55; Costa Rica, to approximately 60; Cuba, to 65-70; the USSR, to 47-48; Bulgaria; and Saudi Arabia. In the last four countries, as in many others, most of the rise took place within only a few decades. The status quest must be particularly mighty in various African countries, where per capita consumption has risen from a few hundred grams to 10 kilograms or more in 30 to 40 years. Eventually we are given a more prosaic explanation, namely:

If we take into account the underlying hominid predisposition toward sweetness, and add to it the astounding [why astounding ?] caloric yield of sucrose . . . together with the steady decline in the cost of sugar over the centuries, we have some reason for sugar's success in gaining new consumers.

Indeed. As to "some," quite a few years ago students of the world sugar economy found that 85 to 90 percent of consumption changes in time, and variations over four or five scores of countries are explainable by price and income alone, without resort to status or power factors. Forecasts of consumption made on the basis of the regression coefficients have proved their significance.

ALBERT VITON
McLean
Virginia

RUGGIE, MARY. *The State and Working Women: A Comparative Study of Britain and Sweden.* Pp. xiv, 361. Princeton, NJ: Princeton University Press, 1984. $35.00. Paperback, $14.50.

Ruggie's new volume is a complex and thought-provoking study of major legislation that has shaped work opportunities for women in two nations, both of which are considered "forerunners in the development of the modern welfare state." The focus is on government legislation and policies affecting female workers in Britain and Sweden. These countries have made efforts to intervene in the play of market forces so as to promote a greater measure of equality between the sexes. State-society relations are viewed through the metaphor of intervention, the state having the power to enact legislation it deems beneficial to elements in the population.

Sweden and Britain are termed "ostensibly similar nations." They differ, however, in size—Sweden's population totals about 5 million as compared with Britain's 56 million—and in industrialization, which in Sweden not only occurred later than in Britain but was also much less diverse.

In Britain particular problems for women, such as discrimination in placement, promotion, and pay, were recognized and the state has attempted to compensate women through special training and placement services. In Sweden, however, the state has been "more facilitative in aiding women's advance." As early as the 1930s, Sweden began to experiment with modest forms of planning involving increasing levels of public financing and taxation. Women began to be drawn into the labor market through "microeconomic intervention," including labor-market analysis, career guidance, and retraining. Britain has allowed conditions of employment to be determined by free market forces and has focused on the economy as a whole, distinguishing chiefly between industrial and nonindustrial jobs while Sweden has paid more attention to the micro-level dimensions of the economy.

In both countries some 75 percent of women are employed in public-sector jobs. This figure indicates a lower level of intervention in the public sector than in the private sector.

The final two chapters of Ruggie's study are devoted to a comparison of child-care programs in Britain and Sweden. Ruggie views those of Sweden as superior in part because they are designed for use by all working mothers and are more comprehensive, not being limited to children of mothers who are on welfare, as in Britain. Moreover, a special Royal Commission on Child Care Centers established in Sweden as early as 1968 provided guidelines for Sweden's program.

Ruggie's whole volume is based on a prodigious amount of research, relying on primary sources such as official government reports analyzed in tables, charts, and graphs. It is an important addition to our understanding of the position of women in the two nations. The depth of intervention, Ruggie concludes, has been greater in Sweden than in Britain. She stresses that further progress for working women in breaking down occupational segregation would be promoted by their participation in the labor movement, rather than depending on "dominant coalitions in their behalf."

CAROLYN ZELENY
Wilson College
Chambersburg
Pennsylvania

## OTHER BOOKS

ALLAND, ALEXANDER, Jr. *Human Nature: Darwin's View.* Pp. x, 242. New York: Columbia University Press, 1985. No price.

AMBROSE, STEPHEN E. *Rise to Globalism: American Foreign Policy since 1938.* Pp. xix, 376. New York: Penguin Books, 1985. Paperbound, no price.

ANDREW, CHRISTOPHER and DAVID DILKS, eds. *The Missing Dimension: Governments and Intelligence Communities in the Twentieth Century.* Pp. vi, 300. Champaign: University of Illinois Press, 1984. $27.95.

ANTONIO, ROBERT J. and RONALD M. GLASSMAN, eds. *A Weber-Marx Dialogue.* Pp. xxi, 334. Lawrence: University Press of Kansas, 1985. $29.95.

ARBLASTER, ANTHONY. *The Rise and Decline of Western Liberalism.* Pp. xi, 394. New York: Basil Blackwell, 1985. $34.95.

AVINERI, SHLOMO. *Moses Hess: Prophet of Communism and Zionism.* Pp. xii, 266. New York: New York University Press, 1985. $22.50.

AXELROD, ROBERT. *The Evolution of Cooperation.* Pp. x, 241. New York: Basic Books, 1984. $17.95.

BARTOLINI, STEFANO and PETER MAIR, eds. *Party Politics in Contemporary Western Europe.* Pp. viii, 184. Totowa, NJ: Frank Cass, 1985. $24.00.

BECKETT, IAN F.W. and JOHN PIMLOTT, eds. *Armed Forces and Modern Counter-Insurgency.* Pp. vi, 232. New York: St. Martin's Press, 1985. $27.50.

BOLL, MICHAEL M., ed. *The American Military Mission in the Allied Control Commission for Bulgaria, 1944-1947.* Pp. ix, 334. New York: Columbia University Press, 1985. $30.00.

BRADFORD, M. E. *Remembering Who We Are: Observations of a Southern Conservative.* Pp. xx, 178. Athens: University of Georgia Press, 1985. $15.95.

CALVERT, PETER. *Revolution and International Politics.* Pp. 222. New York: St. Martin's Press, 1984. $25.00.

CAVES, RICHARD E. and LAWRENCE B. KRAUSE, eds. *The Australian Economy: A View from the North.* Pp. xiv, 415. Washington, DC: Brookings Institution, 1984. $32.95. Paperbound, $12.95.

CERTEAU, MICHEL DE. *The Practice of Everyday Life.* Pp. xxiv, 229. Berkeley: University of California Press, 1985. $24.95.

CHAN, ANITA, STANLEY ROSEN, and JONATHAN UNGER, eds. *On Socialist Democracy and the Chinese Legal System: The Li Yizhe Debates.* Pp. 310. Armonk, NY: M.E. Sharpe, 1985. $35.00. Paperbound, $14.95.

CLAESSEN, HENRI J. M. et al., eds. *Development and Decline: The Evolution of Sociopolitical Organization.* Pp. xii, 369. South Hadley, MA: Bergin and Garvey, 1985. $34.95.

COOKE, WILLIAM N. *Union Organizing and Public Policy: Failure to Secure First Contracts.* Pp. xvi, 159. $16.95. Paperbound, $11.95.

COPPA, FRANK J., ed. *Dictionary of Modern Italian History.* Pp. xxvi, 496. Westport, CT: Greenwood Press, 1985. $55.00.

DAY, MARY WARD, ed. *The Socio-Cultural Dimensions of Mental Health.* Pp. xvii, 168. New York: Vantage Press, 1985. $13.95.

DEGRE, GERARD. *The Social Compulsions of Ideas: Toward a Sociological Analysis of Knowledge.* Pp. xvii, 232. New Brunswick, NJ: Transaction Books, 1985. $39.95.

DUKE, MICHAEL S., ed. *Contemporary Chinese Literature: An Anthology of Post-Mao Fiction and Poetry.* Pp. 137. Armonk, NY: M.E. Sharpe, 1985. $35.00. Paperbound, $14.95.

DUNLOP, JOHN T. *Dispute Resolution: Negotiation and Consensus Building.* Pp. xx, 296. Dover, MA: Auburn House, 1984. $24.95.

ELSTER, JON. *Making Sense of Marx*. Pp. xv, 556. New York: Cambridge University Press, 1985. $49.50. Paperbound, $15.95.

FALK, RICHARD, FREIDRICH KRATOCHWIL, and SAUL H. MENDLOVITZ, eds. *International Law: A Contemporary Perspective*. Pp. xiii, 702. Boulder, CO: Westview Press, 1985. $50.00. Paperbound, $21.00.

FARNETI, PAOLO. *The Italian Party System*. Pp. xxxi, 199. New York: St. Martin's Press, 1985. $27.50.

GOOBY, PETER TAYLOR. *Public Opinion, Ideology and State Welfare*. Pp. vii, 157. Boston: Routledge and Kegan Paul, 1985. Paperbound, $14.95.

GRAVIL, ROGER. *The Anglo-Argentine Connection, 1900-1939*. Pp. xv, 267. Boulder, CO: Westview Press, 1985. Paperbound, $22.00.

HAM, CHRISTOPHER and MICHAEL HILL. *The Policy Process in the Modern Capitalist State*. Pp. xiii, 210. New York: St. Martin's Press, 1984. $29.95.

HARRINGTON, MICHAEL. *The New American Poverty*. Pp. 271. New York: Penguin Books, 1985. Paperbound, no price.

HILL, RONALD J. *Soviet Union: Politics, Economics and Society*. Pp. xviii, 232. Boulder, CO: Lynne Rienner, 1985. $11.95. Paperbound, $23.50.

HUGGINS, NATHAN. *Afro-American Studies*. Pp. 96. New York: Ford Foundation, 1985. Paperbound, $3.50.

HUME, DAVID. *Essays: Moral, Political, and Literary*. Pp. lii, 620. Indianapolis, IN: Liberty Classics, 1985. $17.00. Paperbound, $8.50.

IGNATIEFF, MICHAEL. *The Needs of Strangers*. Pp. 156. New York: Viking, 1985. $14.95.

JASTER, ROBERT, ed. *Southern Africa: Regional Security Problems and Prospects*. Pp. xiv, 170. New York: St. Martin's Press, 1985. $27.50.

JENNINGS, J. R. *Georges Sorel: The Character and Development of His Thought*. Pp. xi, 209. New York: St. Martin's Press, 1985. $25.00.

JIMÉNEZ DE WAGENHEIM, OLGA. *Puerto Rico's Revolt for Independence: El Grito de Lares*. Pp. xvii, 127. Boulder, CO: Westview Press, 1985. Paperbound, $18.50.

JOHNSON, OWEN V. *Slovakia 1918-1938: Education and the Making of a Nation*. Pp. xvii, 516. New York: East European Mongraphs, 1985. Distributed by Columbia University Press, New York. $40.00.

KAPLAN, MARION A. *The Marriage Bargain: Women and Dowries in European History*. Pp. xi, 182. Binghamton, NY: Harrington Park Press, 1985. Paperbound, $6.95.

KOCH, H. W., ed. *Aspects of the Third Reich*. Pp. viii, 611. New York: St. Martin's Press, 1985. $29.95.

KOERNER, KIRK F. *Liberalism and Its Critics*. Pp. 396. New York: St. Martin's Press, 1985. $39.95.

KORNHABER, ARTHUR and KENNETH L. WOODWARD. *Grandparents and Grandchildren: The Vital Connection*. Pp. xxxiv, 279. New Brunswick, NJ: Transaction Books, 1985. Paperbound, $9.95.

KWAK, TAE-HWAN, CONGHAN KIM, and HONG NACK KIM. *Korean Reunification: New Perspectives and Approaches*. Pp. xix, 525. Boulder, CO: Westview Press, 1985. $32.50.

LAWSON, TONY and HASHEM PESARAN, eds. *Keynes' Economics: Methodological Issues*. Pp. 265. Armonk, NY: M.E. Sharpe, 1985. No price.

LINCOLN, BRUCE, ed. *Religion, Rebellion, Revolution*. Pp. ix, 311. New York: St. Martin's Press, 1985. $27.50.

LIND, PETER. *Marcuse and Freedom*. Pp. 305. New York: St. Martin's Press, 1985. $27.50.

LUARD, EVAN. *The United Nations: How It Works and What It Does*. Pp. viii, 187. New York: St. Martin's Press, 1985. Paperbound, $11.95.

LUNN, HUGH. *Johannes Bjelke-Petersen: A Political Biography*. Pp. xxi, 384. St.

Lucia: University of Queensland Press, 1985. $25.00.

MacKENZIE, DAVID. *Ilija Garasanin: Balkan Bismarck.* Pp. xi, 453. New York: Columbia University Press, 1985. $40.00.

MANSFIELD, HARVEY C., Jr. *The Prince: Niccolo Machiavelli.* Pp. xxvii, 124. Chicago: University of Chicago Press, 1985. $18.00. Paperbound, $5.95.

MARNHAM, PATRICK. *So Far from God: A Journey to Central America.* Pp. 253. New York: Viking, 1985. $17.95.

MATHISEN, TRYGVE. *Sharing Destiny: A Study of Global Integration.* Pp. 185. New York: Columbia University Press, 1984. $26.00.

McCOY, ALFRED W. *Priests on Trial.* Pp. xii, 259. New York: Penguin Books, 1984. Paperbound, $6.95.

MINNIS, PAUL E. *Social Adaptation to Food Stress: A Prehistoric Southwestern Example.* Pp. x, 239. Chicago: University of Chicago, 1985. $20.00. Paperbound, $8.00.

MOMMSEN, WOLFGANG J. *Max Weber and German Politics 1890-1920.* Pp. xxi, 498. Chicago: University of Chicago Press, 1985. $50.00.

OGENE, F. CHIDOZIE. *Interest Groups and the Shaping of Foreign Policy: Four Case Studies of United States African Policy.* Pp. 224. New York: St. Martin's Press, 1983. $27.50.

OSBORNE, RICHARD and ROY EDGLEY, eds. *Radical Philosophy Reader.* Pp. 360. New York: Schocken Books, 1985. $28.00. Paperbound, $8.95.

PETERSON, PAUL E. *The Politics of School Reform 1870-1940.* Pp. x, 241. Chicago: University of Chicago Press, 1985. $25.00. Paperbound, $11.95.

PILAT, JOSEPH F., ROBERT E. PENDLEY, and CHARLES K. EBINGER, eds. *Atoms for Peace: An Analysis after Thirty Years.* Pp. xvi, 299. Boulder, CO: Westview Press, 1985. Paperbound, $26.50.

POLSBY, NELSON W. *Political Innovation in America: The Politics of Policy Initiation.* Pp. xiv, 185. New Haven, CT:

Yale University Press, 1985. $22.50. Paperbound, $7.95.

RANNEY, AUSTIN and HOWARD R. PENNIMAN. *Democracy in the Islands: The Micronesian Plebiscites of 1983.* Pp. xx, 126. Washington, DC: American Enterprise Institute for Public Policy Research, 1985. Paperbound, no price.

RIGBY, T. H., ARCHIE BROWN, and PETER REDDAWAY, eds. *Authority, Power and Policy in the USSR.* Pp. xiv, 207. New York: St. Martin's Press, 1985. $10.95.

RIPLEY, RANDALL B. *Policy Analysis in Political Science.* Pp. xvi, 229. Chicago: Nelson-Hall, 1985. Paperbound, $12.95.

ROCCA, RAYMOND G. and JOHN J. DZIAK. *Bibliography on Soviet Intelligence and Security Services.* Pp. xi, 203. Boulder, CO: Westview Press, 1985. Paperbound, no price.

SCHLOZMAN, KAY LEHMAN and JOHN T. TIERNEY. *Organized Interests and American Democracy.* Pp. xiii, 448. New York: Harper & Row, 1985. Paperbound, no price.

SCHMIDT, JAMES. *Maurice Merleau-Ponty: Between Phenomenology and Structuralism.* Pp. 214. New York: St. Martin's Press, 1985. $30.00. Paperbound, $10.95.

SCHMIDT, STEFFIN W. et al. *American Government and Politics Today.* Pp. xxviii, 708. St. Paul, MN: West, 1985. No price.

SCOTT, SAMUEL F. and BARRY ROTHAUS, eds. *Historical Dictionary of the French Revolution, 1789-1799.* Pp. xvii, 532. Westport, CT: Greenwood Press, 1985. No price.

SEAVER, PAUL S. *Wallington's World: A Puritan Artisan in Seventeenth-Century London.* Pp. ix, 258. Stanford, CA: Stanford University Press, 1985. $29.50.

SHAPIRO, BARBARA J. *Probability and Certainty in Seventeenth-Century England.* Pp. x, 347. Princeton, NJ: Princeton University Press, 1983. $37.00. Paperbound, $12.50.

SIMECKA, MILAN. *The Restoration of Order: The Normalization of Czechoslovakia.* Pp. 167. New York: Schocken Books, 1985. $22.50. Paperbound, $6.95.

SIMON, JOHN Y., ed. *The Papers of Ulysses S. Grant.* Vol. 14. Pp. xxvi, 548. Carbondale: Southern Illinois University Press, 1985. No price.

SMITH, THERESA C. and INDU B. SINGH, eds. *Security vs. Survival: The Nuclear Arms Race.* Pp. ix, 194. Boulder, CO: Lynne Rienner, 1985. $25.00.

STAERCKE, ANDRE DE et al. *NATO's Anxious Birth: The Prophetic Vision of the 1940's.* Pp. xv, 192. New York: St. Martin's Press, 1985. $25.00.

SUSSMAN, MARVIN B., ed. *Personal Computers and the Family.* Pp. 202. New York: Haworth Press, 1985. $19.95. Paperbound, $9.95.

TEITELBAUM, MICHAEL S. *Latin Migration North: The Problem for U.S. Foreign Policy.* Pp. 79. New York: Council on Foreign Relations, 1985. Paperbound, $4.95.

TERRY, SARAH MEIKLEJOHN, ed. *Soviet Policy in Eastern Europe.* Pp. xv, 375. New Haven, CT: Yale University Press, 1985. $32.50. Paperbound, $13.95.

TINBERGEN, JAN. *Production, Income and Welfare: The Search for an Optimal Social Order.* Pp. xiii, 210. Lincoln: University of Nebraska Press, 1985. $21.95.

TURNER, HENRY ASHBY, ed. *Hitler: Memoirs of a Confidant.* Pp. xxvi, 333. New Haven, CT: Yale University Press, 1985. $29.95.

VAN ALSTYNE, WILLIAM W. *Interpretations of the First Amendment.* Pp. x, 136. Durham, NC: Duke University Press, 1984. $24.75.

Turkish labor migration, 22, 47-48, 73-74, 87-97
homeland organizations abroad for migrants, 85, 86
motives, 89-91
Turkish migration policy, 91-93
*see also* Muslim immigrants in Western Europe

Underclass, 10
Undocumented immigrants, *see* Immigration, illegal
Unemployment
in immigrant-receiving countries, 123, 132-33
of immigrants, 132-33
in Turkey, 93
United Kingdom
foreign workers in, 129-38
housing in, 137-38
immigration to, 22
United States
immigrants in, 22, 139-52
immigration policy, 142-44
Urbanization, 92, 94

Welfare state, 11, 19-20, 51-63, 106, 151, 156-58

Yugoslav labor migrants, homeland organizations abroad for, 85-86

# Of Special Interest

## MENTAL HEALTH SERVICES
### The Cross-Cultural Context

**edited by PAUL B. PEDERSEN,** *Syracuse University,*
**NORMAN SARTORIUS,** *Division of Mental Health,*
*World Health Organization*
**& ANTHONY J. MARSELLA,** *Department of Psychology,*
*University of Hawaii*

When mental health professionals work in a culture different from their own, they are faced with a fundamental question: Should they adapt the methods of their own culture—or substitute the unique approaches of the indigenous culture?

In addressing this question, the authors challenge potential ethnocentrism in the assessment, diagnosis, and therapy of clients. They seek to increase the visibility of indigenous mental health traditions, stressing that the constructs of "healthy" and "normal" are not the same for all cultures. Discussions are organized according to culture-general and culture-specific approaches. The "general" chapters focus on technique, method, or treatment *across* cultures, while "specific" chapters emphasize the cultural context of mental health services in *particular* populations.

Throughout the international community of mental health professionals, there is a growing need for cultural alternatives to the delivery of mental health services. The authors speak to this need, offering invaluable guidelines for matching appropriate services to culturally different clients.

Sage Series on Cross-Cultural Research and Methodology, Volume 7
1984 / 296 pages / $29.95 (h)

**SAGE PUBLICATIONS, INC.**
275 South Beverly Drive
Beverly Hills, California 90212

**SAGE PUBLICATIONS LTD**
28 Banner Street
London EC1Y 8QE, England

# NEW! from Sage

## FIELD METHODS IN CROSS-CULTURAL RESEARCH

edited by **WALTER J. LONNER**,
*Western Washington University,*
& **JOHN W. BERRY,** *Queen's University, Canada*

This book is designed to meet the needs of the field-worker faced with a research question and the teacher who is talking about research problems and issues in the classroom. The intent, therefore, is to provide field-workers—both those actually in the field and those preparing to go into the field—with a handy, comprehensive, practical, and up-to-date book containing helpful guidelines, background material, and even some specific "how to's." It is directed to behavioral scientists who are sophisticated in many research areas. To determine the topics to be covered, the editors carried out a survey of over 100 experienced researchers in cross-cultural psychology; the chapters in the book parallel the results of the survey.

The book provides the relatively sophisticated and thoughtful field-worker a reasonably comprehensive statement of epistomological and methodological issues, a review of what has succeeded for many and failed for others, and in general an overview of common concerns and questions that will be asked and that need to be answered during various phases of any cross-cultural research project. The chapters are arranged so that broader, more methodological issues are considered first, including theoretical issues involved in cross-cultural comparison. Following are more concrete methods, including chapters on sampling, carrying out fieldwork, problems of translation, and problems of using observations in the field.

**CONTENTS:** Introduction / 1. Making Inferences from Cross-Cultural Data Y.H. POORTINGA & R.S. MALPASS / 2. Strategies for Design and Analysis R.S. MALPASS & Y.H. POORTINGA / 3. Sampling and Surveying W.J. LONNER & J.W. BERRY / 4. Fieldwork in Cross-Cultural Psychology R.L. MUNROE & R.H. MUNROE / 5. The Wording and Translation of Research Instruments R.W. BRISLIN / 6. Observational Methods S. BOCHNER / 7. Cross-Cultural Assessment: From Practice to Theory S.H. IRVINE / 8. Assessment of Personality and Psychopathology G.M. GUTHRIE & W.J. LONNER / 9. Assessment of Social Behavior M. SEGALL / 10. Assessment of Acculturation J.W. BERRY, J.E. TRIMBLE, & E.L. OLMEDO / Index

**Cross-Cultural Research and Methodology Series, Volume 8**
**1986 (March) / 356 pages / $27.50 (flex.)**

**SAGE PUBLICATIONS, INC.**
275 South Beverly Drive,
Beverly Hills, California 90212

**SAGE PUBLICATIONS LTD**
28 Banner Street,
London EC1Y 8QE, England

**SAGE PUBLICATIONS INDIA PVT LTD**
M-32 Market, Greater Kailash I, New Delhi 110 048, India